I0125577

Nancy R. E. M. Bell

**Columbus**

And Other Heroes of American Discovery

Nancy R. E. M. Bell

**Columbus**
*And Other Heroes of American Discovery*

ISBN/EAN: 9783337196196

Printed in Europe, USA, Canada, Australia, Japan

Cover: Foto ©Andreas Hilbeck / pixelio.de

More available books at **www.hansebooks.com**

CHRISTOPHER COLUMBUS.

AND OTHER HEROES OF

# AMERICAN DISCOVERY

BY

## N. D'ANVERS

*COPIOUSLY ILLUSTRATED*

GEORGE ROUTLEDGE AND SONS, Limited

NEW YORK: 9 LAFAYETTE PLACE

London and Manchester

**The Caxton Press**
171, 173 Macdougal Street, New York

# AUTHOR'S NOTE.

The present volume is intended to give a general idea of the progress of exploration in the districts now forming Canada and the United States, with the general advance of the white man westwards. The chief authorities consulted in the preparation of the "Heroes of the Exodus to the West" were the reports to their superiors of the early Jesuit missionaries; George Bancroft's "History of the United States; Bryant's "Popular History of the United States;" and Bancroft's "Native Races of the Pacific." But reference has also been made to the original works of all the great travelers in the districts under notice; while much valuable geographical information has been culled from the Journals of the learned Societies both of England and America, and from Réclus's "Geógraphie Universelle."

N. D'ANVERS.

Hampstead, 1884.

# CONTENTS.

## CHAPTER I.

America known to the Ancients—The Island of Atlantis—Scandinavian Emigration—Eric the Red and Gunnbiorn—Bjarni Herjulfson and Leif the Lucky—Discovery of Vinland—Thorvald and the Skrællings—A terrible Struggle—An heroic Amazon—Retreat of the Danes—Return of Freydis to Vinland—Massacre of Colonists by her Orders—Total Disappearance of Scandinavian Settlement—Madoc of Wales—The Brothers Zeni—Marco Polo—Early Life of Columbus—The Astrolabe applied to Navigation—A Hearing at last—Duplicity of John II.—Columbus in Poverty and Exile—A generous Prior—Hope and Despair—Isabella is won over—Full Powers granted to Columbus—The Start from Saltos—Discontent of Sailors—Variation of Compass—Mutiny—Land Ahead!—Discovery of the West Indian Islands—Return to Spain—Second and Third Voyages—Death in Poverty and Disgrace—Amerigo Vespucci—The Cabots—First Landing in North America—The Cortereals—Breton Fishermen.   .   7

## CHAPTER II.

The Spanish in the Gulf of Mexico—Vasco Nuñez de Balboa concealed in a Cask—His Pardon—Shipwreck and Rescue of Explorers by Balboa—His Discovery of the Pacific—His Murder by Anias—Expedition of Ponce de Leon—The Discovery of Florida and Search for the Fountain of Youth—Leon's Death from poisoned Arrows—Discovery of the Mouths of the Pacific by Francis Garay—Lucas Vasquez de Ayllon in Florida—His Cruelty to the Natives—Their Retaliation—Verrazano on the Atlantic coast of North America—The Invasion of Florida by Pamphilo de Narvaez—His Disappointment, Retreat, and Death—The Captivity and Escape of four of his Followers—The Expedition of Hernando de Soto—Meeting with Juan Ortiz—His romantic Story—An Indian burned alive—A native Princess—At the foot of the Apalachian Mountains—Southward to Mavilla—Struggle with Indians—Westward ho ! and Discovery of the Mississippi—De Soto in a new Character—His Death and Burial in the Mississippi—Escape of his Men under his Successor, Luis Muscoso de Alvarado—Murder of Louis Cancello, the Missionary—Expedition of De Luna.   .   30

## CHAPTER III.

Verrazano sent out by Francis I.—Discovery of the Hudson—Jacques Cartier in Canada, and his Discovery of the St. Lawrence—Touching Scene at Hochelaga—Foundation of Fort Charles on the Site of Quebec—Kidnapping of Donnacona and other Natives, and return to Europe—Death of Indian Captives, and cold Reception at Hochelaga on the Return of Cartier without them—Break-up of the Colony and Flight of Cartier—Arrival of Roberval—Sad Fate of his People—Ribault and the French Refugees on the River of May—Return home of Ribault—Assassination of Pierria—Escape of Colonists in a crazy Pinnace—Their Murder of a Comrade for Food—Their Rescue by an English Vessel—Laudonnière's Colony on the May—Mutiny, and Troubles with the Indians—Famine, and Arrival of Ribault—Disgrace of Laudonniére—Arrival of Menendez—Massacre of French Huguenots by Spaniards—Escape of a little Remnant to Anastasia—Second and third Massacres—Gallant Bearing of Ribault—Foundation of St. Augustine—Vengeance of De Gourgues on the Spanish—Murder of Missionaries in Florida—St. Augustine burned by Drake.    .    . 49

## CHAPTER IV.

Sir Humphrey Gilbert's unsuccessful Voyages, and Death by Drowning—Sir Walter Raleigh's Renewal of his Brother's Patent—Grenville and others sent out to Virginia by Raleigh—First Settlement at Roanoake—Its Abandonment by White—Birth of Virginia Dare—Search for the lost Colony—Death of Bartholomew Gilbert—Gosnold's Expedition—Formation of the Southern and Northern Companies—Failure of the Latter to gain a Footing in Maine—Arrival in Chesapeake Bay of Colonists sent out by the Southern Company—Foundation of Jamestown—Smith's Visit to the Potomac—His Captivity among the Indians and Rescue from Death by Pocahontas—Smith chosen President—The Coronation of Powhatan—A new Charter obtained—Emigrants shipwreck—Smith wounded, and compelled to leave Virginia—Subsequent Troubles—Arrival of Sir Thomas Gates—The Colony reduced to sixty starving Men and Women—Jamestown abandoned—Arrival of Lord De La Warre—Return to Jamestown—Marriage and Death of Pocahontas—Gradual Growth of Virginia—Terrible Massacre of 1622, and the Results of that Massacre—Arrival of Lord Baltimore in Jamestown—First Settlement of Maryland—Father White.    . 64

## CHAPTER V.

The French in Maine, and their Settlement at Port Royal—Jesuit Missionaries at Grand Manan—Destruction of French Colonies by Argall—John Smith and Thomas Hunt on the Coasts of Maine—Vines on the Saco River, and Dermer on Long Island—Early History of the Pilgrim Fathers—Arrival of the *Mayflower* off Cape Cod—Preliminary Exploration by Miles Standish—Discovery of Plymouth Harbor, and first Landing on Plymouth Rock—An Indian Visitor—Arrival of fresh Emigrants—Complications with them and with the Indians—An Indian Chief saved by Englishmen—Indian Plot revealed—Ringleaders slain by Standish—Puritan Refugees at Cape Ann—Standish sent out against them—Peace made by Conant—Conant's Settlement at Salem—The Dorchester Company—Endicott sent out by it to Massachusetts—Arrival of Winthrop with 800 Emigrants—Foundation of Boston and other Towns—Roger Williams expelled from Salem—His Settlement in Rhode Island, and Foundation of Providence—Visit of Indian Chief from Connecticut to Boston—Emigration to Connecticut—John Winthrop appointed Governor—Tearing down of Dutch Arms, and Foundation of Saybrook Fort—Hooker's Emigration to Connecticut, and Foundation of Bradford—Troubles ahead—Discovery of the Hudson—Fight with Indians—Discovery of Hudson's Bay and Death of Hudson—Foundation of New Netherland Company—Dutch Explorations in Delaware, etc.—West India Company founded—Settlement of Walloons at Albany—Foundation of New York—The Swedes on the Delaware—Disputes between them and the Dutch, and between the Dutch and the English. . 82

## CHAPTER VI.

Champlain in Maine—Foundation of Quebec—Discovery of Lakes Peter and Champlain—Foundation of Montreal—First Navigation of the Ottawa—Discovery of Lakes Huron and Nipissing—An Iroquois Execution—Canada taken by the English, and restored to the French—Death of Champlain—Fathers Brébœuf and Daniel on Lake Huron—Raymbault and Pigart on Lake Nipissing—Jogues among the Iroquois—His Murder—Capture, Conversion, and Execution of one of his Murderers—Terrible Iroquois War—Father Dreuillette among the Sioux—His Death in the Forest—Allouez on Lake Superior—Rumors of a great River on the West—Marquette discovers the Mississippi—Descent of the River in native Canoes—Arrival in Arkansas—Saved by the Pipe of Peace—Up the Mississippi to the Illinois—Across North-eastern Illinois—Death of Marquette on the shores of Lake Michigan—Expedition of La Salle—Loss of the *Griffin*—Building of a new Vessel—Discovery of Lake Peoria—Down the Mississippi to the Sea—Second Expedition of La Salle—Fruitless Search for the Mouth of the Mississippi—Wanderings in Texas and New Mexico—Despair—Attempt to walk back to Canada—Murder in the Jungle—Murder of the Murderers—The *Coureurs de bois* in the North-west—Baron La Hontan's Trip down the Mississippi—Rumors of the Sea on the West—Journey of Father Charlevoix. . . . . . . . . . 112

CHAPTER VII.

Expedition of Diego de Hurtado—Ulloa's Trip up the Gulf of California—Da Nizza in Arizona—The Cities of the Plain—Murder of Dorantes and his Companions—Da Nizza visits Cibola in Disguise—Expedition of Alarchon and Coronado—Discovery of the Mouth of the Colorado—Cibola taken by Coronado—Discovery of the Town of Quivira—Discovery of Cape Mendocino by Cabrillo—Viscaino's Trip up the North-west Coast—Numerous Deaths from Scurvy—Discovery of the Mouth of the Columbia—Death of Viscaino—Expedition of Juan de Fuca—Supposed Discovery of Queen Charlotte's Sound—De Fonte and Barnardo in the North-western Archipelago—Father Kino among the Picture-Writers and Sun Worshipers—Discovery of the Mimbres—Establishment of a Mission on the Gila—Descent of the Apaches on the Settlements of the Whites—Expulsion of the Jesuits, and Murder of Natives—Pearl-fishers on the Californian Coast—The Jesuits expelled from Lower California—Exodus of Jesuits from Lower to Northern California—First Colony founded at San Diego—Discovery of the Bay of San Francisco—Decline of the Power of the Jesuits, and their gradual Withdrawal from California. . . . . . . . 140

CHAPTER VIII.

Murder of Captains Stone and Oldham—Massacre on Block Island—Intervention of Roger Williams—The Last Stand of the Pequods—Emigration of Eaton and Davenport to Connecticut—Foundation of New Haven—First Settlement of Refugees in Carolina—Their Lands given to eight Noblemen—Arrival of Cavaliers and Planters—Misery of the Colonists—Relief at last—Oglethorpe's first Settlement in Georgia—His Meeting with the Indian Chiefs—Pennsylvania granted to Penn—His Reception in Delaware—His Voyage up the River—Treaty with the Indians—Foundation of Philadelphia—Rapid Growth of Pennsylvania—Foundation of Harrisburg—The French and Indian War—Foundation of Pittsburg—The War of Independence—Freedom won for the Thirteen Original States of the Union—Declaration of Independence on the 4th July, 1776. . . . . . . . . 153

# Contents.

## CHAPTER IX.

D'Iberville's Arrival at the Mouth of the Mississippi—Foundation of the first French Fort on the Bay of Biloxi—English Expedition to the Mississippi—The Mississippi Scheme—Foundation of New Orleans—Bursting of the Bubble—Louisiana ceded to England—Boone's first Trip to Kentucky—Taken Prisoner by the Indians—Escape—Meeting with his Brother—Murder of Squire Boone's Servant—A White Man's Skeleton found in the Woods—Hunters on the Ohio and in Tennessee—First Settlers start for Kentucky—An Indian Ambush—Retreat—Boone in Despair—Fresh Hope—Boone's Third Trip at the Head of a Surveying Party—Purchase of Lands from the Cherokees—Foundation of Boonesborough—Influx of Emigrants across the Alleghanies—First Settlement of Tennessee, Ohio, Illinois, and the South of Michigan—The English supplant the French in Louisiana—Restriction of the Name of Louisiana to a small Tract—First English Settlements in Mississippi and Alabama—Acquisition of Florida—First Spanish and English Settlements in Texas—Acquisition of California, Arizona, and New Mexico—Gradual Retreat of the Red Men before the White Settlers.   .      .      .      .      .   164

## CHAPTER X.

The new-born Republic—Pike's Embarkation on the Mississippi at Fort Louis—Sledge Journey along the Banks of the Mississippi—A Chippeway Encampment—A Native Pictorial Record—A Member of the North-west Company—On Snow-shoes to Leech and Red Cedar Lakes—A Council of Chippeway Warriors—Back to St. Louis—New Expedition organized—The Osage Captives—Along the Arkansas—Arrival at the Head-waters of the Mississippi—Search for the Red River of the South—The Rio del Norte mistaken for it—The Explorers taken Prisoners by the Spaniards—Journey across Texas to Natchitoches—Lewis and Clarke embark on the Missouri at St. Louis—The Mouth of the Platte, or Nebraska—Among the Sioux—Difficulty with Indians at the Great Bend—The Mouth of the Yellowstone River—Encounters with White and Brown Bears—The two Forks of the Missouri—Long Hesitation as to which to follow—Lewis solves the Problem by the Discovery of the Great Falls—Terrible Storm, and Narrow Escape of Clarke—The Gates of the Rocky Mountains—Across the Mountains and Discovery of the Source of the Missouri—Search for Shoshones—Three Indian Women surprised—In the Shoshone Camp—Vain Attempt to reach the Source of the Columbia—On the Summit of the Rocky Mountain Range—Down the Pacific Slope to the lower Course of the Columbia—

Construction of Canoes—Down the Columbia to the Great Falls—Successful Navigation of them—In the Great Narrows—The Sea at last—Winter among the Flatheads—Home again. . . . . . . 175

## CHAPTER XI.

Discovery of Behring Straits—Cook and Meares—Rescue from Starvation—Encounter with Natives—Vancouver on the Western Coast—Gray's supposed Discovery of the Columbia—Coxe's Survey of Hudson's Bay—James in Distress in Hudson's Bay—Foundation of the Hudson's Bay Company—Discovery of Rupert's River—Disputes with the French—Knight's Voyage and his terrible Fate—Discovery of Relics of Knight and his Comrades—Moore and Smith in Hudson's Bay—Cession of Canada to England, and its Results—Heroes of the Transition Time—Hearne's Discovery of Athabasca Lake and the Coppermine River—Massacre of Esquimaux—Discovery of the Arctic Ocean—Result to Geographical Science of that Discovery—Hearne's Return to Hudson's Bay—The Indian Exile wrestled for—Enthusiasm of the Company—The Rise of the North west Company—Mackenzie's Journey to the Slave Lake, and Discovery of the Slave, Athabasca, or Mackenzie River—His Voyage to Great Bear Lake—Return to Fort Chippewyan—Journey across Country to the North Pacific—The Work of all Explorers united by his last Trip. . . . . . 200

## CHAPTER XII.

The Pacific Fur Company—Voyage of the *Tonquin*—Foundation of Astoria—Massacre on the *Tonquin*—Terrible Revenge—The great Small-pox Chief—Start of the Land Expedition—An Ambush—Unexpected Rescue—Treachery of an Interpreter—Among the Crow Indians—The Black Mountains—The invisible Lords of the Mountain—Arrival on the Banks of the Mad River—Across Country to the Henry River—Construction of Canoes—Embarkation on the Henry—A Canadian drowned—The Lion Caldron—Across Country again—Among the Akai-chies—News of the Astorians—Threatened Attack of the Natives—Arrival on the Banks of the Columbia—Along the River to Indian Encampment—News of Tragedy on the *Tonquin*—Down the Columbia to Astoria. . 220

## CHAPTER XIII.

Cass's Voyage up the Mississippi—Long and James on the Platte, or Nebraska—Discovery of the two Sources of the Platte—Among the Mountain Passes—Eating of poisonous Berries—Meeting with a Bear—Ascent of Pike's Peak—Search for Head-waters of the Arkansas—The Canadian taken for the Arkansas, and followed to its Junction with the latter River—Start of new Expedition

from the Ohio—Cannibalism among the Natives—The Apostle of the Indians—
Across the Prairies to Lake Michigan—Through Illinois to the Mississippi—
Up the Mississippi to the Minnesota—The Head-waters of the Minnesota—
The primal Home of the Red River of the North, the St. Lawrence, etc.—
Up the Red River to Lake Winnipeg—From Lake Winnipeg to the Lake of
the Woods, and thence across Country to Lake Superior—Schoolcraft's Ascent
of the Mississippi, and Discovery of its actual Source.      .    .      . 233

CHAPTER XIV.

Wilkes' Survey of the Western Coast—Fremont's Ascent of the Kansas—Encounter
with Arapaho Warriors—Arrival at Fort Laramie—A threatening Letter—
Fremont's Reply—On the Sweet Water River—Discovery of Mountain Lake
and Fremont's Peak—A winged Messenger—Back to Fort Laramie—To the
Rocky Mountains again—On the Banks of the Bear River—Discovery of the
Great Salt Lake—Embarkation on the Lake—Sudden Change in the Character
of its Waters—From the Salt Lake through the Great Basin to Fort Hall and
thence to the Columbia River—Attempt to return Home by a New Route—
Lost in the Wilderness—Discovery of Lake Tlamath—Search for an Opening in
the Mountains—Discovery of Pyramid Lake—Meeting with Snake Indians—
Hunger—Salmon discovered in a River flowing into the Lake—News of White
Men on the South—All Hope of reaching United States abandoned—Fremont
resolves to cross the Sierra Nevada—First Peak scaled—Meeting with Indians—
A Gap in the Mountains discovered at last—Ascent of the Californian
Mountain—Opening a Path through the Snow—A terrible Prophecy—Flight of
Guide—First Sight of Seaboard Range of Mountains--Intense Excitement—
Down the Eastern Slopes of the Californian Mountain to the Banks of the
Sacramento—Arrival at Sutter's Fort—Back to St. Louis by way of the South
Pass—Fremont's third and last Journey.      .      .      .      .      . 240

CHAPTER XV.

Early History of the Mormons—Murder of Smith—Expulsion from Illinois—Across
the frozen Mississippi—Through the Wilderness—Summons to the War—
Young Men sent to the Aid of the Republic—Arrival on the Shores of the
Great Salt Lake—Building of Salt Lake City—Expedition of Stansbury—
California ceded to the States—Discovery of Gold near Sutter's Fort—World-
wide Excitement—Rush of 30,000 Emigrants Westward—Terror of Indians at

Approach of the White Men—Sufferings in the Mountains—Jealousy of Settlers—
Prairies set on Fire—Survivors of the 30,000 rescued by White Men from
California. . . . . . . . . . . 255

## CHAPTER XVI.

Cozens' Start from Merilla—First Encounter with Apaches, and Murder of Laws—A
Bear Hunt—To the Ruins of Le Gran Quivara—Two Mules stolen—Back again
to Merilla—Cozens and Cochise, an Apache Chief—Cochise offers to act as
Guide to the Encampment of his Warriors—The great Mirage known as
Greenhorn's Lake—A Chaos of Rocks and Precipices—Following an Indian
Trail—Down the Ravine to the Apache Valley—First Sight of Apache Village
with Huts built on truncated Mounds—Excitement among the Apaches—
Cochise explains Cozens' Presence—Eager Welcome—Arrival of Magnus
Colorado, the great Scalper—Trying Interview between Magnus and Cozens—
Eternal Friendship sworn—A blood-stained Baby's Frock—Scalp Dance and
its attendant Horrors—Back again to Mexico—Second and third Trips to the
North—With Jim Davis the Emigrant's Friend, to the Navajoe Country—
Ascent of the Sierra Madre—Encounter with a Panther—In the Zuni Valley
among the blue-eyed Indians—Ruins of Zuni—Encounter with Navajoes—Jim
Davis's Story—Re-capture of stolen Cattle—A fall of Three Hundred Feet—
Marvelous Preservation of Cozens—Nursed by the Zunis—Murder of Stewart's
Family by Apaches—Escape of Stewart to Zuni—His Death of a broken Heart—
Return of Cozens to Mexico. . . . . . . . . 258

## CHAPTER XVII.

Crisis in British America—Consolidation of its various Parts into one great Colony—
Decay of the Hudson's Bay Company—Establishment of an International
Boundary Line—Journey of Palliser—Admission of British Columbia to the
Dominion, and Conditions of that Admission—Surveys for Railway—Fleming's
Expeditions—Dispute between the British Government and the United States—
Joint-Commission sent out to determine the Boundary Line—Results obtained
by it. . . . . . . . . . . . 269

# HEROES OF AMERICAN DISCOVERY.

## CHAPTER I.

COLUMBUS, HIS PREDECESSORS AND HIS IMMEDIATE SUCCESSORS.

ALTHOUGH the discovery of America used to be dated from the voyage of Columbus to the West Indies in 1492, there can be little doubt that this great hero was by no means the first explorer of our era to visit the

New World. The existence of land to the west of the Pillars of Hercules was even known to the ancients. Frequent mention is made by Greek and Roman authors of islands on the West, especially of the fair Atlantis, concerning which Plato gives many details, declaring it to have been of vast extent and great beauty, but to have been swallowed up by the sea in pre-historic times. Some modern authors are of opinion that the Canaries are the only existing remains of this Atlantis; others that the so-called island was in reality the mainland of America. Leaving this question to those now studying it with the aid of the recent discoveries in the New World, we pass on to find trustworthy accounts in the old sagas—of which the principal, recently discovered in an Icelandic monastery, are preserved in the Royal Library at Copenhagen—of the presence of Danish settlers in Greenland as early as 982 A. D. These were led thither by the great Eric the Red, who is supposed, however, merely to have acted on information left behind by an early settler of Iceland, named Gunnbiorn, a century before. Gunnbiorn was the true discoverer of Greenland, which he had sighted—though not visited—naming it Hvidsaerk, or the "White Shirt," because of the perpetual covering of snow worn by its highlands.

THE GLACIERS OF GREENLAND.

In a voyage from Iceland to Greenland, four years after the visit of Eric the Red to the latter country, a Danish navigator named Bjarni Herjulfson was driven far out of his course to the South, and saw land stretching away on the West; but he returned home without making any exploration of the new territories, for which, says tradition, "he was greatly blamed." His reports, however, of what he had seen, led to the fitting out and heading of a far more important expedition by Leif the Lucky, who, making direct for the most southerly point gained by his predecessors, reached the modern Newfoundland, which he called Helluland, and, landing, found it to be "a country without grass, and covered with snow and ice."

From Helluland, Leif sailed to the present Nova Scotia, which he named "Markland," or woodland, because of its extensive forests; and thence he is said to have been driven by a contrary wind on to the coast of New England, but on what part of that coast there is no evidence to show, although it is generally agreed to have been in about N. lat. 41° 24', a little to the north of Rhode Island. Excursions inland revealed the newly-discovered district to be rich in vines and timber; and loading his vessel with grapes and wood, Leif made haste to return home with his trophies, giving such glowing accounts of his adventures on his arrival, that a short time later his brother Thorvald started with a crew of thirty men for the land of promise.

Thorvald is supposed on this trip to have coasted along the shores of Connecticut, Rhode Island, and Long Island, and in the ensuing year, 1004, to have sailed as far north as Cape Cod (N. lat. 42° 5', W. long. 70° 10'), where he was wrecked in a violent storm. His vessel was not, however, materially damaged, and having repaired it, he coasted along the present Massachusetts till he came to what is now the harbor of Boston. There he landed, and wandering to and fro in the beautiful scenery with his men, he for the first, time came upon some natives, probably Esquimaux, who were resting peaceably beneath their quaint skin-boats.

With the cruelty characteristic of the wild sea-kings of the North, Thorvald at once gave the signal for attack. The poor Skrællings, as he dubbed the natives, were quickly overpowered. One only escaped, and the others were foully murdered. No wonder that this was the beginning of the end of Thorvald's enterprise. That very night, as he and his followers were sleeping peacefully, untroubled by any remorse for their evil deeds, they were roused by the war-whoop of the Skrællings, come at the bidding of the one survivor to avenge his comrades.

The white men took refuge in their ship, and all escaped unhurt except Thorvald himself, who received a wound in the side, from which he shortly afterward died. He was buried within sight of the Atlantic, on what is now Massachusetts Bay, and his sorrowing followers returned home with the terrible tidings in the ensuing spring.

Undaunted by the fate of his brother, another son of Eric, Thorstein by name, set out for Vinland in 1005, but he failed to find it, and returned home, stricken with mortal sickness, in the same year. On his deathbed, however, he prophesied that his widow, Gudrid, would marry again, and hinted that a great career of discovery and conquest was before her future children. He was right in the first part at least of his speech, for two years later we find Gudrid, as the wife of a sturdy Icelander named Karlsefne, forming part of the largest expedition yet sent out from Greenland to Vinland—an expedition consisting of no less than three ships, and one hundred and forty men and women.

That an important colony was founded by the new adventurers there appears no reason to doubt, although it is impossible to fix its exact locality. Booths were erected, stores were laid in for the winter, and amicable relations were opened with the Skrællings, who came in great numbers, first to stare at the intruders, and then to trade with them, exchanging valuable furs for red cloth, etc.

A slight and almost ludicrous incident was the first thing to break up what had appeared to be the beginning of a long course of successful colonization. A bull belonging to one of the leaders of the expedition rushed suddenly among the buyers and sellers, so terrifying the natives, who had never before seen an animal of that description, that they fled to their kayaks, or skin-boats, in the greatest confusion, returning some weeks later in greatly increased numbers, and armed with bows and arrows, to revenge themselves for what they took to be an intentional insult.

Fierce indeed was the struggle in which they were now involved, and, overwhelmed by superior numbers, the colonists seemed likely to be exterminated, when the tide was turned by the courage of Freydis, a daughter of Eric the Red, who, imbued with the brave spirit of her father, suddenly faced the savages, and brandishing a sword which she had taken from a dead warrior of her own race, she invited the enemy to come and slay her if they would, even tearing open her dress to make clear her meaning.

The Skrællings, perhaps taking these strange gestures for the signs of superhuman agency, gazed for a moment in awe-struck silence at the lonely figure standing thus unprotected among the slain, and then, with cries as wild and weird in the ears of the Northmen as those of their champions to the natives, they one and all turned and fled.

The terrible slaughter among their men had, however, so disgusted the leaders of the colony, that they soon afterwards returned to Greenland ; and, but for the ambition of Freydis, the history of the Scandinavian colonies in North America would have ended then and there. Unable to forget her triumph, and eager for yet further distinction, this remarkable woman did not rest until she had organized a new expedition, which, under the leadership of two brothers named Helgi and Finnbogi, set sail in 1011, and, landing in Vinland without molestation from the natives, took possession of the booths erected by their predecessors. All seemed likely to go well, when the overbearing conduct of Freydis, who was not one to shine in the peaceful work of colonization, led to dissensions among the explorers. By a crafty artifice she managed to pick a quarrel with the two brothers, and, with the co-operation of her husband, Thorvard—who, though naturally a mild and inoffensive man, appears to have been entirely under the control of his stronger-minded wife—she succeeded in effecting their massacre, and that of all who were inimical to her supremacy. The survivors, terror-struck by the fate of their companions, yielded without a struggle to the rule of Freydis, who, first binding them all by an oath never to tell of her conduct at home, set them at work to cut timber and collect the curiosities and valuables of the country. Then, when she had acquired enough to insure her wealth for the remainder of her life, she embarked for Greenland with the little remnant of the original party. The Icelandic sagas, already referred to, tell how the iniquity of Freydis gradually leaked out, and how, though she herself escaped unpunished, her sins were visited upon her children.

With her return home the attempts at American colonization by the Northmen appear to have ceased, but tradition tells of many a trip by contemporary adventurers of other nationalities ; for, between the fitful excursions from Greenland—which, as we have seen, left no real or permanent impress on the people or districts visited—and the well-organized expedition of modern times, we hear of Arab sailors of the 12th century having sighted land in the unknown Western Ocean, graphically called, from its real and imaginary horrors, the Sea of Darkness ; and of a voyage made in 1170 by Madoc, son of the Prince of North Wales, who, after sailing for many weeks away from his native land, came to a country, supposed to have been the modern Virginia, differing in every respect from any European land.

Certain travelers of the 17th century tell of white men speaking the Welsh tongue having been met with among the Indians far away in the West, lending some slight semblance of veracity to the tradition that a colony was indeed founded by the Welsh; but in the absence of all confirmatory documents, we are compelled to reserve judgment on the subject, passing on to the better authenticated story of the voyage of the brothers Zeni of Venice, who, between 1388 and 1404, are said to have visited Greenland and Nova Scotia, and to have long resided as the guest of its king in an island called Frisland, the position—indeed the very existence—of which has never been fully proved, although some authorities are of opinion that it was really only one of the Faroe Islands. However that may be, many legends were long current in Venice of the intercourse with the unknown Frisland and islands further west, one of which, called Estotiland, is supposed to have been Newfoundland. Hints, too, are scattered up and down old chronicles, of wandering fishermen sailing southward from Estotiland having come to a country answering in the descriptions given of it to Mexico; the Chinese, Malays, and Polynesians are said to have reached the American coasts; and, to conclude our summary of lore relating to the oldest of the continents, Picigano's map, which is dated 1367, gives indications of a western continent named Antilles, and a yet older map shows an island where Newfoundland ought to be.

Whether America was or was not visited from Europe or from Asia before the time of Columbus, however, the barbarism in which European society was sunk in medieval times prevented any recognition of the true significance of the details of adventures given by returned mariners; and their voyages thus fail to form any real link between the America of the middle ages and that of the present day. If, therefore, we would point out the true precursor of the first hero of discovery in the West, we shall find him, not in the wild Northmen bent on pillage and bloodshed, nor in the brothers Zeni of legend and romance, but in that grand central figure of the scientific annals of the 13th century, Marco Polo, whose book, revealing the existence of vast empires in the East, did much to stimulate the enthusiasm, not only of Columbus, but also of Bartholomew Diaz, Vasco da Gama, and other early heroes of travel, thus indirectly leading to the discovery alike of the Cape of Good Hope and of America.

Although Columbus never set foot on the Northern half of the American continent, with which alone we have, strictly speaking, now to do, no record of travel in any part of the New World would appear to us complete without some account of his first voyage, and of what led to that voyage. For there can be no doubt that, but for the noble steadfastness of purpose which resulted in the achievement of one discovery while its author was bent on another, the revelation of the existence of a quarter of the globe larger than Europe and Asia put together, and which was destined to be the scene of much of the most stirring history of modern times, would have been indefinitely postponed.

CHRISTOPHER COLUMBUS.

Of the early life of Christopher Columbus little is known with any certainty. He is supposed, however, to have been born about 1435, and, as the son of a poor wool-comber of Genoa, to have enjoyed few educational advantages, although, fortunately for him, what little teaching he received seems to have tended to foster his peculiar genius. According to his own account, preserved in the *Historia del Amirante*, he began his maritime career at fourteen, after a brief sojourn at the University of Pavia, enduring great hardships as a sailor employed in the half-commercial, half-nautical cruises of the roving ships which, in the latter part of the 15th century, haunted the Mediterranean and the coasts beyond the Straits of Gibraltar.

In 1459 we hear of a certain " handy sea-captain " named Colombo taking part as a private adventurer in an expedition sent out by John of Genoa against Naples ; and in 1470 we find the same sea-captain—now in the prime of life—settling in Lisbon, and by his marriage with the daughter of Palestrello, the discoverer of Porto Santo, coming into possession of many valuable charts and journals, the study of which is said to have first suggested to him the existence of land to the westward, which land, however, he from first to last erroneously supposed to be, not a new continent, but a continuation of the eastern shores of Asia.

Whether our hero drew his inspiration from one author or another, or, as appears more likely, was led up to the conception of his great design by the spirit of the age in which he lived, affects but little the historical fact that it was about 1474, when the enlightened efforts of Prince Henry of Portugal had ushered in a new era of geographical research, that Columbus first enunciated his belief that there was land in the western part of the ocean; that it could be reached; that it was fertile; and, lastly, that it was inhabited a belief which was shortly afterward converted into a design for seeking a *western* route to India, although eighteen long years elapsed before the first step was taken in the realization of a scheme so totally opposed to all the preconceived notions of cosmographers.

In voyage after voyage made by Columbus in the succeeding years to the Azores, the Canaries, and the coasts of Guinea, then the limits of navigation to the westward, the future discoverer became more and more fully convinced that, with the necessary time and means at his disposal, he might convert his dream into a waking reality; but, alas! all his attempts to obtain a hearing for his scheme from those who were in a position to forward it were met by scorn and ridicule.

The first ray of hope to break upon the despair of Columbus at this ill-success was the invention—or, to be more strictly accurate, the application to navigation—of the astrolabe, the precursor of the modern quadrant, by Martin Behaim, and by Roderigo and Joseph, physicians in the employ of John II. of Portugal. Armed with it and the mariner's compass, as defensive weapons, the nautical explorer needed no longer to fear trusting himself on the trackless paths of the ocean; and, Columbus, full of new hope, asked for and obtained an interview with John II. in 1482 or 1483. We can imagine with what eagerness our hero pleaded his cause, and with what patience he explained every detail of his scheme, winning at last a consent, though but a reluctant one, that his proposition should be referred to a "learned junto, charged with all matters relating to maritime discovery," to which title we may add the saving clause, "of which they were cognizant;" for the minds of king and council alike were set, not on the pushing of discovery westwards, but on further efforts to find a new route to India on the East, and to ascertain the locality of the empire of the fabulous monarch, Prester John.

The council to whose judgment the scheme of Columbus was submitted consisted of the Roderigo and Joseph already mentioned, and of the king's confessor, Diego Oriz de Cazadilla, Bishop of Ceuta, who condemned it without hesitation. The king, however, feeling perhaps not altogether convinced by the arguments adduced against it, privately sent out a vessel to test the route mapped out by Columbus, obtaining no result except that of driving the greatest man of the age away from his court, disgusted with the duplicity which, while openly discrediting their author, could thus seek to use his plans.

COLUMBUS BEFORE THE COUNCIL.

The ignorant pilots commissioned to work out the route conceived by the master-mind of the great mariner, returned to Lisbon without venturing beyond the beaten track; and in the ensuing year Columbus secretly left Lisbon, taking with him his young son Diego. We all know the story of his scornful reception at the court of Genoa, and of his arrival, after long wanderings to and fro, footsore, hungry and disheartened, at the gate of La Rabida, a Franciscan convent in Andalusia, to beg a little bread and water for his starving child.

This simple and pathetic request formed the turning-point of Columbus's career. The prior of the convent, Don Juan Perez de Marchina, whose name deserves to be immortalized in every record of the discovery of the New World, was passing at the moment; and, struck by the manly and dignified bearing of the "beggar," he approached, and asked whence he came and whither he was going.

COLUMBUS AT A CONVENT DOOR.

Columbus, now used to rebuffs, was touched by the kindly interest shown in his forlorn condition, and soon told the whole story of his woes, his dreams of geographical discovery, his conviction that they would some day be realized, if not by himself, and so forth.

The prior, surprised at a reply of so unusual a character from a wayfarer in circumstances so reduced, invited Columbus to be his guest; and, anxious to obtain confirmation for his belief in the genius of his visitor, he sent for his friend, Garcia Fernandez, to whom we are indebted for our knowledge of the circumstances of this portion of our story.

Fernandez, having listened to all that Columbus had to say, was as completely won over as Marchina had been; and, after many conferences at the convent, our hero, no longer in rags, started for the Spanish court, armed with strong letters of recommendation to the then reigning Ferdinand and Isabella. This was in 1486, when the war with the Moors was absorbing alike the energies and the resources of the kingdom; and it is not much wonder that Columbus could at first obtain no encouragement for the prosecution of a scheme of maritime discovery. He was kindly received, however, and in the repeated absences of the sovereigns, who headed their armies in person, he won the ear first of one and then of another influential dignitary of the court, and in 1491, five long years after his first arrival, he obtained a promise from Ferdinand, that, as soon as the war was over, he and his queen "would have time and inclination to treat with him about what he had offered."

A chilling message truly to one who had wasted the best years of his life "about what he had offered ;" and Columbus, more truly disheartened by it than by the absolute silence of the sender, went back to his old friend at the convent of La Rabida, resolved to sever finally his connection with Spain. It is of this sad period of his history that the Laureate represents him as saying, long afterwards—

> "No guess-work ! I was certain of my goal ;
> Some thought it heresy, but that would not hold.
> King David called the heavens a hide, a tent
> Spread over earth, and so this earth was flat ;
> Some cited old Lactantius ; could it be
> That trees grew downward, rain fell upward, men
> Walked like the fly on ceilings ? and, besides,
> The great Augustine wrote that none could breathe
> Within the zone of heat ; so might there be
> Two Adams, two mankinds, and that was clean
> Against God's word : thus was I beaten back,
> And chiefly to my sorrow by the Church,
> And thought to turn my face from Spain, appeal
> Once more to France or England."

But once more Perez and Fernandez cheered his drooping spirits. They would not hear of his deserting their country ; yet another effort should be made to secure to it the glory of sending out the great hero of the age on what they were convinced would be a brilliant and successful enterprise.

With a skill which came of a full heart and a mind not easily to be turned from its purpose, the aged monk pressed his plea, urging the soured Columbus to give Spain another chance ; and, observing that his eyes were turning toward France, whose king had sent him a most cordial letter, the Father Guardian did not fail to remind him how that fickle country had forsaken, in the hour of direst need, one of the most daring and noble of her children, Joan of Arc.

Such arguments slowly made way—the more surely, that the Father quoted several proofs that men of influence were beginning to interest themselves in the undertaking of Columbus. The explorer, therefore, at last consented to wait the issue of a letter which was now sent by Don Perez to the Spanish court, addressed, not to the King, but to the Queen. The answer, which speedily arrived, was cheering beyond all expectation ; and, as it contained an invitation to the writer of the epistle to visit her, the old Prior of the convent of La Rabida at once saddled his mule, and, strong in the faith of his mission, passed fearlessly through the country inhabited by the Moors, whence he soon reached Santa Fé, where Ferdinand and Isabella were.

Perez lost no time in presenting himself to the Queen, and the result of the interview was fitly expressed in the message, full of holy thankfulness, which he sent to Columbus the same day—"I came, I saw, God conquered." The Queen graciously expressed her wish to see the hero himself, and she gave orders that he should be provided with funds sufficient to pay the expenses attendant upon his journey, and upon his appearing before her. In 1492, the would-be discoverer arrived at Grenada, and presented himself at court, being just in time to find himself a witness of the final overthrow of the Moorish power, and the humiliation of Boabdil, the last of the Moorish kings.

PEREZ ON HIS WAY TO SANTA FÉ.

Silent and reserved among the rejoicing and shouting multitudes, sympathizing perhaps more keenly with the broken-hearted Boabdil than with his conquerors, Columbus still bided his time ; and so soon as the excitement of victory had a little subsided, he was admitted to an audience with the sovereigns. It was now decided that Columbus should put his scheme to a practical test ; but fresh difficulties arose in consequence of the "princely conditions" to which alone the humble and poorly-clad adventurer would agree. Not content with the tardy recognition given to the grandeur of his enterprise, he demanded that he should be "invested with the titles and privileges of Admiral and Viceroy over the countries he should discover, with one-tenth of all gains, either by trade or conquest."

Once more the fate of the New World, which had been, so to speak, unconsciously waiting all this time for the arrival of its discoverer, hung in the balance. Courtiers clamored at the insolence of the sorry fellow who wished to be set above their illustrious heads ; and the King looked coldly on, unwilling to break his word, yet anxious to get the matter settled or dropped, that he might give the attention so sorely needed to his kingdom, drained as were its resources by the long wars.

But now Isabella, true to the renown she had won by a long course of noble and disinterested conduct, seemed to have been suddenly inspired with a belief in the great mission of Columbus. That hero had again determined to leave Spain, and, as the story goes, was already on the way to Cordova, whence he intended embarking for France, when, at a meeting of the junto discussing the

ISABELLA.

scheme, the Queen exclaimed—"*I* undertake the enterprise for my own crown of Castile, and will pledge my jewels to raise the necessary funds."

Columbus was at once recalled ; and though the pledging of the Queen's jewels was not found necessary, she aided him now with all the energy and enthusiasm of her character. On the 17th April, 1492, the stipulations granting full powers to Columbus, and conferring on him and his heirs the honors he had demanded, were signed at the city of Santa Fé, in the plain of Grenada : and on the 3d August of the same year, eighteen years after he first conceived the idea of the voyage, our hero—all preliminary difficulties over—at last set sail from the bar of Saltos, near Palos (N. lat. 37° 11', W. long. 6°, 47'), in command of three vessels—the *Santa Maria*, the *Pinta*, and the *Niña*, only one of which, the first, and that on which the Admiral himself embarked, was decked. He was leader of one hundred and twenty men ; but the motley character of his crews, enlisted on compulsion, and thoroughly imbued with all the superstitions of the age with regard to the perils of the deep, caused Columbus much embarrassment from the very first, and he was detained for three weeks at the Canaries by an "accident"— supposed to have been purposely brought about—to the rudder of the *Pinta*. It was not until the 6th September that the actual voyage of discovery can be said to have commenced. Setting sail that day from the island of Gomera he passed Ferro, the last of the Canaries, on the 9th.

As the last traces of land faded from the sight of the untutored mariners, their hearts failed them, and with tears and groans they en-

EMBARKATION OF COLUMBUS.

treated their leader to turn back while there was yet time. The passing of a portion of a wreck on the 11th still further aroused their fears, and it was all that Columbus could do to induce them to obey his orders.

On the 13th September a slight but deeply significant incident occurred. Columbus, watching with eager interest the little compass—which, surrounded as he was by timid, vacillating spirits, must have seemed to him his one steadfast, unchangeable friend—noticed a variation in the needle. To quote the words of Washington Irving, "he perceived about nightfall that the needle, instead of pointing to the north star, varied about half a point, or between five and six degrees, to the northwest, and still more on the following morning."

Knowing how greatly this phenomenon would alarm his people, Columbus at first kept it to himself; but it was soon remarked by the pilots, and their report sent a fresh thrill of horror through the crews. They were entering a new world, where the very laws of nature were changing, and in which even inanimate objects were subject to weird, unearthly influences.

Calm amid the ever-increasing excitement, Columbus, with greater ingenuity than penetration, explained away the strange deviation—the cause of which has not yet been determined, though many great authorities attribute it to solar influence—by saying that it was due, not to any fault in the compass itself, but to the alteration of the position of the north star.

Thus, whether he himself did or did not believe this to be the true solution of the mystery, did our hero once more calm the terrors of his men, who were, a little later, further cheered by the sight of a heron and a water-wagtail, which, as birds supposed never to venture far out to sea, were looked upon as sure harbingers of land. Next were seen floating patches of herbs and weeds, which could only, it was thought, have been washed from river banks, or from rocks by the sea-shore ; and, convinced that their perils were now over, the eager mariners crowded on deck, each anxious to be the first to catch a glimpse of the longed-for country ; but as day after day passed on, and no further indications of the end of the voyage were perceived, all the old fears returned, the men broke out into open mutiny, and Columbus's position became critical in the extreme. Even Martin Alonzo Pinzon, one of the most important members of the squadron, now questioned the wisdom of the Admiral's determined adherence to a western course ; and our hero, though still full of the most intense belief in final success if that course were maintained, was beginning to doubt whether he should himself achieve more than martyrdom in the cause he had so much at heart. Matters were at this stage, when, on the night of the 11th October, 1492, as the weary leader was peering into the darkness of the horizon from the deck of his vessel, hoping against hope to make out some indication of land, no matter how vague, he fancied he saw a light.

Scarcely daring to trust his eyes, he called first one and then another of the companions of his venture, each of whom confirmed his opinion. A light of some kind was undoubtedly moving on the distant waters, but whether it proceeded from some fisherman's bark, or from the long-sought land, it was impossible to determine.

Never was daylight more eagerly longed for than then ; but, hours before it came, the suspense of the three watchers on the *Santa Maria* was relieved by the booming of a gun from the *Pinta*, the signal that others also had seen the significant token of the approach to the promised haven. A little later, the dark outlines of the shores of an island, relieved against white breakers, were distinctly made out ; and when the dawn of the 12th October, 1492, broke at last, "a level and beautiful island, several leagues in extent, of great freshness and verdure, and covered with trees like a continual orchard," lay before the eyes of the astonished mariners. Naked natives were hurrying to and fro, expressing by their gestures their astonishment at the appearance of the ships ; and at once ordering the boats to be manned. Columbus, scarcely able to restrain his emotion, started to take possession, in the name of the monarchs of Castile, of the newly-discovered territory.

No sooner did the hero set foot on shore, than he fell upon his knees, kissed the ground, and with tears of joy gave thanks to God for thus enabling him to complete his work. Then rising, his heart doubtless swelling with exultation, he drew his sword, unfurled the royal banner, named the island "San Salvador," and solemnly declared it to be the property of Ferdinand and Isabella, "calling on all present to take the oath of obedience to him as Admiral and Viceroy representing the persons of the sovereigns."

Although there is some little difference of opinion as to which of the West Indian islands was thus discovered by Columbus, it is generally supposed to have been that now called by the English Cat Island, one of the great Bahama group, and situated in N. lat. 24°, W. long. 74° 30′, of which the native name was Guanahamé. Imagining it to be situated at the extremity of India, the explorer called its people Indians, an appellation which has clung to the aborigines of the New World ever since.

Remaining at Guanahamé only long enough to ascertain the "Indians" to be a gentle, friendly, simple people, with well-formed figures, and pleasant, intelligent faces, Columbus again set sail on the 14th October, and, cruising hither and thither, he discovered several other islands, including the important Cuba and San Domingo, of all of which he took possession in the name of his patrons, planting a small colony on the last named, and meeting everywhere with a cordial welcome from the "savages," though his own people gave him a good deal of trouble by their perpetual rivalries and jealousies.

Among these latter troubles, none perhaps affected the Admiral so painfully as the desertion of Don Alonzo Pinzon. Pinzon had, in the days of the discoverer's despondency, stood toward him as a patron, and, Spanish patrician as he was, his countenance had been of no mean value. The very fact also that he consented to serve under Columbus must have seemed a token of his faithfulness ; but they had not long been out at sea before he showed that subordination was galling to him, and at last, while Columbus was exploring Cuba, he made his escape with *La Pinta*, the second in size of the boats which formed the little fleet. The fact was, that news had come to them of rich lands to the North-west, and Pinzon, disappointed that his superior would not steer in that direction, resolved to steal away, and go in search of a golden empire for himself. But the North-west did as little for him as it did for many who came after him, and Columbus encountered him again on the return journey, without the gold of which he had dreamed, and with his vessel so disabled that it could only reach the shores of Spain with difficulty. Indeed, had it not been for the merciful treatment of Columbus, the craven Pinzon would probably have perished on the waters.

Satisfied with the results of his first trip, and anxious to obtain the necessary supplies for the further prosecution of his discoveries, Columbus set sail for Europe on the 4th January, 1493, arriving at the bar of Saltos on the 15th March of the same year. Among those who were on the shore to welcome the returning hero was Don Perez de Marchina, of whose eager waiting for his home-coming the Marquis de Belloy has drawn a touching picture in his charming *Life of Columbus*. We see him for long months spending his spare moments in his observatory, anxiously watching for the least shadow of a sail upon the horizon. At last he descries a little vessel making its way toward Saltos, and he rushes to the harbor, his sudden appearance giving to the people of the little town the signal that Columbus is at hand. Soon the discoverer is at the shore, and the arms of his " guide, philosopher and friend " are the first to embrace him. From Saltos Columbus made his way to Barcelona, then the residence of the court, where he was received with all the enthusiasm due to one who had added to the kingdom a new empire of undetermined extent and apparently boundless wealth.

More impatient of the delay caused by the rejoicings in his success than he had been of the impediments thrown in his way when he had been unable to obtain a hearing for his embryo scheme, Columbus lost no time in urging on the sovereigns the fitting out of a new expedition, and, six short months after his return home, we find him leaving Cadiz with seventeen ships and 1,500 men. This second voyage resulted in the discovery of the Caribbee Islands and Jamaica.

But in the midst of his work among the West Indian Islands, the Admiral was recalled home to answer terrible charges—of untruthfulness in his descriptions of the countries discovered, and of cruelty to the natives and colonists under his charge—brought against him by his enemies. Although he succeeded in clearing himself for a time, to the satisfaction of Ferdinand and Isabella, from the odious suspicions which had been cast upon him, the

COLUMBUS IN CHAINS.

rest of his life was one long struggle with persecution and adversity. From his third voyage, in which he discovered Trinidad, and landed at Paria, on the coast of South America, he was sent home in chains. We only linger a moment by the manacled hero to quote once more from Tennyson's "Columbus."

> .    .    .    .    .    .   You know
> The flies at home that ever swarm about,
> And cloud the highest heads, and murmur down
> Truth in the distance—these outbuzzed me so,
> That even our prudent king, our righteous queen—
> I prayed them, being so calumniated,
> They would commission one of weight and worth
> To judge between my slandered self and me—
> Fonseca, my main enemy at their court,
> They send me out *his* tool, Bovadilla, one
> As ignorant and impolitic as a beast—
> Blockish irreverence, brainless greed—who sack'd
> My dwelling, seized upon my papers, loos'd
> My captives, fee'd the rebels of the crown,
> Sold the crown-farms for all but nothing, gave
> All but free leave for all to work the mines,
> Drove me and my good brothers home in chains ;
> And gathering ruthless gold—a single piece
> Weighed nigh four thousand castillanos—so
> They tell me—weigh'd him down into the abysm.
> The hurricane of the latitude on him fell,
> The seas of our discovering over-roll
> Him and his gold ; the frailer caravel,
> With what was mine, came happily to the shore.
> *There* was a glimmering of God's hand."

Soon after the conclusion of his fourth and last voyage, Columbus died at Valladolid in poverty and disgrace, leaving others—many of whom he had himself trained to be able navigators—to reap the fruits of his labors.

One of the first explorers to follow in the track of Columbus was Amerigo Vespucci, whose name, for some reason not very clearly made out, was bestowed on the land discovered by his great predecessor. The work of Amerigo was, however, almost entirely confined to the southern half of the vast continent called after him, although he is supposed to have sailed without landing as far north as Chesapeake Bay ; and we therefore pass on to the Cabots, one of whom appears to have been the first European of modern times to set foot in North America.

In 1496, Henry VII. of England, intent on finding that short cut to India which it was so eagerly hoped would open to Europe the commerce of the

AMERIGO VESPUCCI.

East, appointed John Cabot to the command of five vessels, with orders thoroughly to explore the western portion of the Atlantic Ocean, and "find whatsoever isles, countries, regions, or provinces of the heathen and infidels, whatsoever they be, and in what part of the world soever they be, which before this time have been unknown to Christians"—a wide commission truly, which was carried out, so far as we can tell from the masses of conflicting evidence before us, by the sailing from Bristol, in 1497, of a single ship, the *Matthew*, with John Cabot as commander, and his three sons, Ludovico, Sebastiano, and Sanzio, among the subordinate members of the expedition.

Sailing due west, as the most direct mode of carrying out his instructions, John Cabot came in sight, on the 24th June, 1497, of the mainland of America; but whether the portion first seen was Cape Breton, Newfoundland, or Labrador, is undetermined. With-

CABOT BEFORE THE COSMOGRAPHERS.

out making any attempt to land, the navigators contented themselves with sailing along some three hundred leagues of the coast, and returned home to be received with as much enthusiasm as if they had fulfilled the whole of their mission, and to be rewarded for finding the "New Isle" with the munificent sum of £10.

A second and a third voyage appear to have been undertaken by John Cabot, with no better results than the first ; but after his death—about 1499—his son Sebastian, who had long been endeavoring to secure the co-operation of Ferdinand of Spain for an extensive scheme of exploration in the North, came to England, and was appointed by the reigning monarch to the command of an expedition to Labrador.

On this trip Sebastian landed several times on different parts of the north-eastern coast of America, and penetrated as far north as 67 1-2°, in his vain quest for that *ignis fatuus* of his day—the North-west Passage to India ; but at last, his provisions failing him, he was compelled to return to Bristol, bringing with him, as his only trophies, some of the natives of districts visited.

This undoubted discovery of the mainland of America, the date of which is variously given by different authorities, important as it in reality was, led to no very definite results. In 1500, a trip was made from Portugal to the North-east by a certain Gaspar Cortereal, who, though nominally in quest of the north-west passage, seems to have made the acquisition of slaves his main object. He penetrated as far north as 50°, and landed on the shores of what is now New Brunswick, naming it Terra de Labrador, or the "land of laborers," a title subsequently transferred to a strip of the seaboard further north. Enticing some fifty-seven of the natives—who

SEBASTIAN CABOT.

are described as "like gipsies in color, well-made, intelligent, and modest"—on board his vessels, he returned with them to Portugal, and, having sold them, started on a new trip shortly afterward, from which he never returned ; but history is silent as to whether he fell a victim to the perils of the sea or to the vengeance of those he wronged.

In 1502, Miguel Cortereal, a younger brother of the inhuman Gaspar, started in search of the missing vessel, but he too disappeared, leaving no trace behind him ; and when an expedition, sent out by the King of Portugal to ascertain the fate of the voyagers, returned with no tidings of either ship, it was resolved that the fatal latitudes should henceforth be avoided. For the next few years the north-east coasts of the western continent were visited by none but certain venturesome fishermen of Brittany, whose memory still lives in the name of Cape Breton, but who, thinking only of securing to themselves the harvest of the new-found seas, added next to nothing to our geographical knowledge ; though John Denys of Honfleur is said to have explored the whole of the present Gulf of St. Lawrence.

INDIAN BOATS.

# CHAPTER II.

BALBOA DISCOVERING THE PACIFIC OCEAN.

TO atone for the sudden check in the progress of discovery in the North, mentioned in our previous chapter, we find the Spanish vigorously prosecuting their explorations in the Gulf of Mexico, bent, like other nations, on finding a new passage to India, though convinced that it lay, not among the snow and ice of the Arctic regions, but in more southerly latitudes.

Ignorant of the important fact, that the land barring their progress westward formed part of one vast continent, one hardy Spanish mariner after another wasted his strength in seeking for some channel between the so-called islands hemming in his bark on this side and on that, until at last the mystery was solved by a freebooter named Vasco Nunez de Balboa, whose romantic story must be given here, forming as it does an era in the history of the whole of the New World.

Nothing could well have been more inauspicious than the commencement of the voyage of the first European who set eyes on the Pacific Ocean. One of the earliest settlers in San Domingo, Vasco Nunez de Balboa was so unsuccessful in his tilling of the soil that he soon found himself in absolute destitution, and, hoping to elude his creditors, he managed to hide himself in a vessel bound for the Caribbean Sea, at that time a favorite resort of pirates and adventurers of every description.

When out of sight of land, Balboa ventured forth from his cask, and, falling on his knees before the captain, Enciso by name, entreated him to protect him and let him share in the expedition. Enraged at so flagrant a defiance of his authority as the concealment of a man on board his ship, Enciso at first threatened to put our hero ashore on some desert island and abandon him to starve, but finally, softened by his eloquent pleadings, he consented that he should work out his passage. To this leniency Enciso soon afterward owed the safety of himself and all his people. His vessel was wrecked on the coast of the Isthmus of Darien, and Nunez, who had visited the district in his early wanderings, led the Spaniards to a friendly Indian village on the Darien.

Life was, however, all Balboa chose to accord to the man to whom he owed his own rescue from a miserable death. Arrived at the village, he accomplished the deposition of Enciso, and his own appointment to the supreme command. Then, having learned in various preliminary excursions that, six days' journey to the west, there lay another sea, he led his men in the direction indicated, and, after literally fighting his way, step by step, through tribes of hostile Indians, he came, on the 15th of September, 1513, to the foot of a high mountain, from which his guides assured him the sea could be seen.

Imbued, in spite of his rough freebooting nature, with something of the true spirit of an explorer, Balboa now ordered his followers to wait, while he made the ascent alone. Arrived on the brow of the hill, he looked down, and beheld beneath him the wide-stretching ocean, lighted up by the brilliant rays of a tropical sun. Forgetting his lust of gain, and the crimes which had led him to his present position, he now thought only of the solution by his means of the problem which had so long baffled men of science of every nationality, and, falling on his knees, he gave thanks to God that it had pleased Him " to reserve unto that day the victory and praise of so great a thing unto him."

This act of worship over, Nunez summoned his followers to gaze upon the wonderful sight and ordered them to pile up stones, as a token that he took possession of the land in the name of his sovereign, Ferdinand of Castile.

FRANCIS PIZARRO.

His next step was to send twelve of his men—one of whom was the great Pizarro, future conqueror of Peru—to find the best route to the Pacific coast, himself following more leisurely with the body of his forces.

The twelve pioneers quickly came to the beach, and, finding a couple of native canoes floating inshore, two of them, named Alonzo Martin and Blazede Abienza, sprung into them, calling to their comrades to bear witness that they were the first Europeans to embark upon the southern sea. Thus, on September 29, 1513, was completed the first discovery of the great Pacific Ocean, of which Columbus had heard from the natives in his various voyages, though he had never been able to reach it, and which, first crossed by Magellan in 1521, has ever since been an inexhaustible field for the efforts of explorers, and is associated with the names of Cook, Anson, D'Entrecasteaux, Vancouver, Kotzebue, and many other great navigators of modern times.

The discoverer of the Pacific, like so many of the heroes of his day, did not live to reap the fruits of his work. He won the appointment of *Adelantado*, or governor of the ocean he had been the first to see—an office giving him, though neither he nor his sovereign was aware of it, authority over some 80,000,000 square miles of land and sea!   But five short years after the eventful 13th September, he was beheaded by order of the Spanish Governor of Darien, Peter Anias, who appears to have been jealous of his superior popularity, and to have feared his growing power.

DEATH OF MAGELLAN.

As was natural, the work of Balboa led to the fitting out of numerous expeditions, n o t only to the southern seas, but to the districts north of the Isthmus of Darien, which, according to native rumor, were rich in gold and precious stones.   Leaving the story of the progress of discovery southwards for the present, we go on to the first successor of Nunez entitled to rank among the heroes of the North, the Spaniard, Juan Ponce de Leon, who, when Governor of Puerto Rico, was induced, by the traditions afloat among the natives of the West Indies of the existence of a Fountain of Youth in the North, to lead an expedition in that direction, which resulted in the discovery of Florida.

Whether, at the time of his adventure, De Leon was old, and anxious to regain his youth, or young, and eager to retain it, history does not say.  We only know that he made it the object of his life to discover the marvelous region containing the magic fountain, and set sail for that purpose with three caravels on the 3d March, 1512, accompanied by a numerous band of gentlemen, eager to share with their leader the glories of immortality.

After a month's sail in a north-westerly direction, De Leon came in sight of a country, "covered with flowers and verdure," and, as it happened to be Easter Sunday, he named the new land Pasena de Flores, or Pasqua Florida, that being the Spanish name for the festival so inseparably connected with floral decorations. On the 2d April the explorers landed at the point now called Fernandina, considerably further north than the modern boundary between Florida and Georgia—the term Florida having been at first loosely applied to all the districts on the north-east of the Gulf of Mexico. Owing to the hostility of the natives, De Leon and his men were, however, soon

A BAYOU IN FLORIDA.

compelled to return to their ships, but they spent some time in cruising up and down both sides of the peninsula, making flying visits in-shore, in hope of extricating information from the Indians as to the position of the coveted Fountain of Youth. In this quest their failure was complete; but when at last compelled to return to Puerto Rico, they were rewarded for their long wanderings by the discovery of the Bahamas on their voyage back.

As usual in such cases, De Leon received the appointment of Adelantado of the country he had visited, weighted, however, with the condition that he should colonize it. With this end in view, and perhaps also with a hope of yet renewing his strength at the magic well, he returned to Florida in 1521, only to fall a victim in a struggle with some Indians who opposed his landing, and greeted their would-be governor with a shower of poisoned arrows.

Between the first and last visit of De Leon to Florida, several heroes of Central American discovery touched on the coast of the newly-found district, on their way to and from Mexico; and in 1518, Francis Garay, for some time Governor of Jamaica, cruised along the whole of the shores of North America bordering on the Gulf of Mexico, passing the mouths of the Mississippi, called by the Indians the Miche Sepe, or Father of Waters, and by the Spaniards the Rio del Espirito Santo, or the River of the Holy Ghost. Refraining from landing on account of the "little hospitable" appearance of the country, Garay contented himself with drawing a map of the coast-line, which he very accurately describes as "bending like a bow," adding that a line drawn from the most southerly point of Florida to the northernmost headland of Yucatan "would make the string of the bow."

The next European to visit Florida was Lucas Vasquez de Ayllon, who set out with two ships from Cuba, in 1520, bound on a quest for a land called Chicora, said to exist to the north of Florida, and to contain within its limits a sacred stream, whose waters possessed powers similar to those of the Fountain of Youth. Landing between 32° and 33° N. latitude, De Ayllon was hospitably received by the simple natives, who crowded on to his vessels, and gazed with wondering, child-like eyes at all the new wonders before them. Leaving the poor creatures unmolested until he had gained their confidence, the crafty Spaniard amused himself for a time with excursions on the banks of a river to which he gave the name of the Jordan, and when he had induced 130 Indians to go on board, he suddenly returned to the ships, and gave orders for the anchors to be weighed, and set sail for Cuba.

The agony of the captives, when they saw the shores of their native land receding from before them, and realized that return was impossible, passed description. Only dimly did they understand that their fate was to work for the white men; and when a fierce storm arose, and one vessel was swallowed up, with all its inmates, by the waves, the survivors may perhaps have thought that the home from which their strange captors came was beneath the ocean. However that may be, but few of the Indians on the second ship lived to reach New Spain, and when there, their services were of little use to their master, who, disappointed in his first venture, lost no time in organizing a new and more formidable expedition, consisting of several vessels, having on board a force of some five hundred men.

After much beating about on the coast north of Florida, during which one pilot is said to have gone mad with vexation at being unable to find the Jor-

HAVANA HARBOR (CUBA).

dan, De Ayllon landed at a spot near his first encampment, and, to his surprise, was received with enthusiasm by the Indians, who, proving themselves apt pupils of their first European teachers, feasted him and his men until they were completely deceived.

On the fifth day after the landing, when the white men were sleeping off the effects of their orgies, the Indians rose *en masse* and murdered them all. Then, turning their attention to the vessels lying at anchor, they attacked the sailors with their poisoned arrows, killing many of them, but failing to prevent the escape of a little remnant, who carried home the story of the ill-fated expedition. Whether De Ayllon himself perished on land or at sea is unknown; but it is certain that he never returned, and, to quote a quaint old chronicler whose narrative is among those preserved by the Hakluyt Society, "he was lost . . . . leaving nothing done worthy of memorie."

After this tragic conclusion of an unworthy career, Florida and its people were left undisturbed for several years, though some further details of the configuration of its eastern coast were given in 1524 by Verrazano of Florence, who sailed from the point of the peninsula as far north as Cape Breton, and whose experiences on the Atlantic seaboard are given below. The brief respite enjoyed by the unfortunate natives was, however, but a lull before a more terrible storm of invasion than any with which they had yet had to cope, for in 1528, seven years after the death of De Ayllon, Pamphilo de Narvaez, inflamed by the exaggerated accounts given by the survivors of previous expeditions as to the wealth of Florida, obtained permission from Charles V. of Germany to take possession of it in his name.

Leaving Spain in the autumn of 1527, with five ships and a force of some 600 men, Narvaez arrived, after many delays, in the Bay of Tampa, on the west coast of Florida, in February, 1528. Landing with half of his forces, the leader at once commenced his march to the interior, in spite of the remonstrances of some of the chief officers, who feared that if he once lost sight of his vessels he would never see them again. Remembering the experience of Cortes, Narvaez hoped to find a second wealthy nation to plunder; but his disappointment and dismay may be imagined when, instead of any indications of advanced civilization, he met only with vast swamps and forests teeming with naked savages, who, though they melted away at his approach, and eluded his vengeance as if by magic, hung about in the rear of his army, harassing his every movement, and picking up the stragglers for private murder and tortures worse than death.

Buoyed up through all his miseries, however, by the rumors which met him at every turn of the existence in the north of a district called Apalachen, where gold was to be had for the asking, Narvaez still pressed on, to be rewarded at last, after months of weary marching by arriving at a miserable Indian village of some forty houses—supposed to have been somewhere near the mouth of the Apalacha river, flowing from the Apalachian mountains of Georgia—from which all the able-bodied inhabitants had fled. "This," said the Indian guides—who, taken prisoners by the way, had been forced to give their unwilling services to the intruders—"this is Apalachen; it is here that the gold you long for is to be found."

Unwilling even yet to own himself beaten, Narvaez took possession of the village, and gave his men permission to remove their armor and rest, intending the next morning to test the truth of the guides' assurance that game and gold were plentiful in the neighboring woods. But the craft of the Indian had once more supplied his want of strength to cope with the white man. So soon as the Spaniards were asleep in the miserable wigwams they had seized, the savages gathered round them with stealthy tread, and set fire to their temporary resting-places. Many who escaped the flames fell victims to the poisoned arrows let fly with unerring aim from ambushes on every side, and when the morning broke, the few survivors, including Narvaez himself, determined to return to the sea by the shortest route they could find.

A fortnight's hard fighting with enemies and obstacles innumerable brought a still further diminished remnant to the beach, far from the place they had left their five vessels ; and with the savages behind them, and the sea before them, the luckless explorers resolved to build some boats, and trust themselves to the mercy of the waves rather than to that of man. Five crazy barks were constructed with infinite difficulty, and in them the few men still alive embarked.

Not daring to venture into the open sea, the explorers, who knew nothing of navigation, paddled slowly along the shores of the modern state of Alabama, and in about six weeks reached the mouths of the Mississippi in safety ; but there a violent storm overtook them and four of the boats, including that containing Narvaez himself, were lost. The fifth, with Cabeca de Vaca (who was originally treasurer to the expedition) on board, had a narrow escape ; but the greater number of men in her reached the land, where they were, strange to say, kindly received by the natives. A little later, stragglers from the other boats, who had saved their lives by swimming, arrived, and, joining forces, the adventurers started for the western coast on foot, hoping to reach the Mexican province of Sonora, which had already been colonized by the Spaniards.

Four only of the original party survived to reach the western coast, and these four, of whom Cabeca de Vaca—who seems to have borne a charmed life—was one, were held in captivity by the Indians long years before they were able to effect their escape. Great indeed was the surprise of the colonists on the shores of the Gulf of California, when the little party of bronzed and half-naked wanderers, speaking their own tongue, appeared at the outposts of the little mining settlement; and when their identity with the long-lost explorers was proved, enthusiasm knew no bounds.

Eager to return to their own land, however, the heroes lost no time in taking ship for Europe, and on the 13th August, 1537, nine years after the starting of the original expedition, they arrived in Lisbon, to meet there with a yet more eager reception than in Sonora.

The excitement caused by the wonderful tales of their captivity, told by Cabeca and his comrades, was, as may be imagined, intense. Far from damping the ardor of others for exploration and colonization, the pictures called up by their narrative of hairbreadth escapes, of the magic influence exercised on whole tribes of dusky warriors by a single white man, of the weird growths of the tropical forests, and of the wild beauty of the Indian maidens, created a passion for adventure among the youth of Spain. When, therefore, the renowned Hernando de Soto, who had been in close attendance on Pizarro throughout his romantic career in Peru, asked for and obtained permission from Ferdinand of Spain to take possession of Florida in his name, hundreds of volunteers of every rank flocked to his standard. Narvaez had failed for want of knowledge as to how to deal with the natives; doubtless the land of gold could yet be found by those who knew how to wrest the secret of its position from the sons of the soil; and so once more a gallant company set forth from Spain to measure their strength against the craft of the poor Indians of Florida.

De Soto, who was in the first place appointed Governor of Cuba, that he might turn to account the resources of that wealthy island, sailed from Havana, with a fleet of nine vessels and a force of some six or seven hundred

DE SOTO.

men, on the 18th May, 1539, and cast anchor in Tampa Bay on the 30th of the same month. Landing his forces at once, the leader gave orders that they should start for the interior immediately, by the same route as that taken by his unfortunate predecessor; and the men were eagerly plowing their way through the sandy, marshy districts immediately beyond the beach, driving the natives who opposed their progress before them, when

one of those romantic instances occurred, in which the early history of the New World is so remarkably rich.

A white man on horseback rode forward from among the dusky savages, who hailed the approach of the troops with wild gestures of delight, and turned out to be a Spaniard named Juan Ortiz, who had belonged to the Narvaez expedition, and had been unable to effect his escape with his comrades. In his captivity among the Indians he had acquired a thorough knowledge of their language, and his services alike as a mediator and a guide were soon found to be invaluable.

The story of his adventures, as told by Ortiz, rivaled even that of Cabeca in thrilling interest. He had been captured soon after the landing of his party by a chief named Ucita, who decided that he should be burned alive by a slow fire, as a sacrifice to the Evil Spirit. A rough stage was therefore set up on four posts; Ortiz, bound hand and foot, was laid upon it; the fire was kindled beneath him, and he resigned himself to the lingering agonies of a shameful death. Around him on every side gathered his enemies, eager to watch his dying contortions. Their shouts of triumph rung upon his ears, and broke in upon his muttered prayers to the God who alone could help him in his extremity. . . . Was he dreaming that the bitter cries were hushed in answer to his appeal?—that those whose duty it was to feed the flames were pausing in their task? No, it was no dream; the daughter of the chieftain was kneeling at her father's feet, pleading, in tones as soft as ever fell from the lips of Spanish maiden, for the life of the stranger. It was but a little gift she asked, and, in granting it, would not her father win honor among the tribes? Would not a living prisoner of a strange race be a brighter gem in a chieftain's crown than the corpse of a dead enemy? Touched by his child's entreaties, or more convinced by her arguments, Ucita relented. Ortiz was removed from the stage, and informed by signs that he must henceforth consider himself as a slave. In captivity therefore he remained, to be the hero, three years later, of a second romantic adventure, when he was again condemned to be burned, and again rescued by the chieftain's daughter, who warned him of his danger in time, and led him to the camp of another chieftain, under whose protection he remained until the arrival of his fellow-countrymen. How the devotion of the Indian girl was rewarded we have been unable to ascertain, for, with the characteristic egotism of the Spanish adventurers, Ortiz dwells in his narrative only on his own escapes, and with his acceptance of the second chieftain's protection, or rather his entry into his service as a slave, the poor maiden disappears from the story.

Led by Ortiz, De Soto and his army made their way, slowly and with difficulty, in a north-easterly direction, till they came to the east of the Bay of Apalachen, a little beyond the mouth of the Flint, where the peninsula of Florida joins the mainland of the United States. Here the camp was pitched for the winter ; messages were sent to Cuba for fresh supplies of men and provisions, and exploring parties were dispatched to reconnoiter the land on either side. The discovery of the harbor of Pensacola on the west was the only result of any importance achieved, and early in the spring of the following year, 1540, the march was resumed, this time under the guidance of a native, who said he would take the white men to a far country, governed by a woman, and abounding in a yellow metal, which was used for making all manner of ornaments, etc. This metal could be none other than gold ; and, with fresh hope in their hearts, the explorers pressed on.

Following a north-easterly direction, the wanderers soon entered the district now known as Georgia, and, crossing the Altamaha river on its way to the Atlantic, they left the low alluvial lands and swamps of the coast on their right, and struggled on over the rough hilly country gradually sloping up to the Blue Ridge mountains belonging to the Alleghany or Apalachian range, the El Dorado for which they were seeking ever receding as they advanced, while their course was everywhere marked by blood and pillage.

His own conduct to the unfortunate natives giving him no right to expect any thing but treachery from them, De Soto soon began to entertain suspicions of the fidelity of his guide. Perhaps, after all, he was only leading him into an ambush of dusky warriors. He would try and extract further information from some of the captives in his hands. Four poor creatures were therefore brought before the leader for examination, and the first questioned replied that he knew of no such country as that so eagerly sought.

Enraged at this answer, so unlike what he hoped for, De Soto ordered the wretched man to be burned alive, and the sight of his terrible death so inspired his companions that, when their turn came to be examined, they vied with each other in the descriptions they gave of the fertility and wealth of the land on the north. Again deceived, and that with a readiness only to be accounted for by the consuming lust for gold which blinded his understanding, the leader ordered the march to be resumed, and in the spring of 1540 he was met by an Indian queen, who, hearing of his approach, had hastened to welcome him, hoping perhaps to conciliate him, and save herself and her subjects from the usual fate of the natives at the hands of the white men.

Very touching is the account given by the old chroniclers of the meeting between the poor cacica and De Soto. Alighting from the litter in which she had traveled, carried by four of her subjects, the dusky princess came forward with gestures expressive of pleasure at the arrival of her guest, and taking from her own neck a heavy double string of pearls, she hung it on that of the Spaniard. Bowing with courtly grace, De Soto accepted the gift, and for a short time he kept up the semblance of friendship ; but having obtained from the queen all the information he wanted, he made her his prisoner, and robbed her and her people of all the valuables they possessed, including large numbers of pearls found chiefly in the graves of natives of distinction. We are glad to be able to add that the poor queen effected her escape from the guards, taking with her a box of pearls which she had managed to regain, and on which De Soto had set especial store.

The home of the cacica appears to have been situated close to the Atlantic seaboard, and to have been among the villages visited by De Ayllon twenty years previously, the natives having in their possession a dagger and a string of beads, probably a rosary, which they said had belonged to the white men. Unwilling to go over old ground, the Spaniards now determined to alter their course, and taking a north-westerly direction, they reached, in the course of a few months, the first spurs of the lofty Apalachian range, the formidable aspect of which so damped their courage, that they turned back and wandered into the lowlands of what is now Alabama, ignorant that in the very mountains they so much dreaded were hidden large quantities of that yellow metal they had sought so long and so vainly.

The autumn of 1540 found the party, their numbers greatly diminished, at a large village called Mavilla, close to the site of the modern Mobile, (N. lat. 30° 40′, W. long. 80°), where the natives were gathered in considerable force ; and it soon became evident that an attempt would be made to exact vengeance for the long course of oppression of which the white intruders had been guilty in their two years' wanderings.

Intending to take possession of Mavilla in his usual high-handed manner, De Soto and a few of his men entered the palisades forming its defenses, accompanied by the cacique, who, meek enough until he was within reach of his warriors, then turned upon his guests with some insulting speech, and disappeared in a neighboring house. A dispute then ensued between a minor chief and one of the Spaniards. The latter enforced his view of the matter at issue by a blow with his cutlass, and in an instant the town was in a commotion. From every house poured showers of arrows, and in a few minutes nearly all the Christians were slain. De Soto and a few others escaped, and, calling his forces together, the Spanish governor quickly invested the town.

A terrible conflict, lasting nine hours, ensued, in which, as was almost inevitable, the white men were finally victorious, though not until they had lost many valuable lives and nearly all their property. Mavilla was burned to ashes ; and when the battle was over, the Spaniards found themselves in an awful situation—at a distance from their ships, without food or medicines, and surrounded on all sides by enemies rendered desperate by defeat. The common soldiers, too, had by this time had enough of exploration, and were eager to return to the coast, there to await the return of the vessels which had been sent to Cuba for supplies. Evading the poor fellows' questions as to his plans, however, De Soto, who had received secret intelligence that his fleet was even now awaiting him in the Bay of Pensacola, but six days' journey from Mavilla, determined to make one more effort to redeem his honor by a discovery of importance. With this end in view, he led his disheartened forces northward, and in December reached a small village belonging to Chickasaw Indians, in the state of Mississippi, supposed to have been situated about N. lat. 32° 53′, W. long. 90° 23′.

In spite of constant petty hostilities with the Indians, the winter, which was severe enough for snow to fall, passed over peaceably ; but with the beginning of spring, the usual arbitrary proceedings were resorted to by De Soto for procuring porters to carry his baggage in his next trip, and this led to a second terrible fight, in which the Spaniards were worsted, and narrowly escaped extermination. Had the Indians followed up their victory, not a white man would have escaped to tell the tale ; but they seem to have been frightened at their own success, and to have drawn back just as they had their persecutors at their feet.

Rallying the remnant of his forces, and supplying the place of the uniforms which had been carried off by the enemy with skins and mats of ivy leaves, De Soto now led his strangely transformed followers in a northwesterly direction, and, completely crossing the modern state of Mississippi, arrived in May on the banks of the mighty river from which it takes its name, in about N. lat. 35°,

Thus took place the discovery of the great Father of Waters, rolling by in unconscious majesty on its way from its distant birthplace in Minnesota to its final home in the Gulf of Mexico. To De Soto, however, it was no geographical phenomenon, inviting him to trace its course and solve the secret of its origin, but a sheet of water, "half a league over," impeding his progress, and his first care was to obtain boats to get to the other side.

DE SOTO DISCOVERING THE MISSISSIPPI.

The Chickasaw Indians, relieved, doubtless, at the prospect of getting rid of the intruders, gladly led them to one of the ordinary crossing-places, but the native canoes found there were not fit for the transportation of horses, and a month was consumed in building barges, during which visits were paid to the strangers by Aquixo, the cacique of the Dakota tribe dwelling on the other side of the Miche Sepe, who would gladly have made friends with his white brother, had not De Soto met his advances by killing the first of his followers who landed near his camp.

By this short-sighted policy the Spanish leader once more defeated his own purpose, and when the transit of the Mississippi was at last effected, his march along the western banks was harassed by the constant hostility of the natives. In the course of the summer, however, after a dreary struggle through the morasses above the landing-stage, he came to the dryer and loftier regions of Missouri, where the natives took him and his men for Children of the Sun, and brought out their blind to be restored to sight.

For once, De Soto refrained to inflict any injury on the simple believers in his divine mission. Perhaps some dim vision of what he might have been to the untutored savages, had he been true to his own creed, flitted across

SCENE ON THE MISSISSIPPI AT THE PRESENT DAY.

his mind. In any case, we find the stern, unrelenting, bloodthirsty man assuming for a moment the character of a preacher of the Gospel, pointing to a cross he had set up on an Indian mound, and telling the Indians to pray only to God in Heaven for what they needed. Nay more, he condescended to try to explain to them the mystery of the Atonement, and was so far successful, that chief and subjects kneeled with him and his men at the foot of the sign of our redemption, and listened without interruption to the prayers put up to the God of the white men.

The service over, De Soto asked for instructions as to the best route to follow in his untiring quest for gold; and, acting in accordance with the answers he received, he seems to have turned away from the Mississippi, and, in August, 1541, to have reached the highlands of the south-west of Missouri, near the White River, crossing which, he journeyed southward through Arkansas, and set up his camp for the winter about the site of the present Little Rock (N. lat. 34° 45′, W. long. 92° 13′). Bent on resuming his researches in the ensuing spring, though worn out by continual wanderings and warfare, and deprived by death of his chief helper, Juan Ortiz, the indomitable explorer now endeavored to win over the Indians by claiming supernatural powers, and declaring himself immortal; but it was too late to inaugurate a new policy. The spot chosen for encampment turned out to be unhealthy; the white men began to succumb to disease; scouts sent out to explore the neighborhood for a more favorable situation brought back rumors of howling wildernesses, impenetrable woods, and, worst of all, of stealthy bands of Indians creeping up from every side to hem in and destroy the little knot of white men.

Thus driven to bay, De Soto, who was now himself either attacked by disease or broken down by all he had undergone, determined at least to die like a man; and, calling the survivors of his once gallant company about him, he asked pardon for the evils he had brought upon those who had trusted in him, and named Luis Moscoso de Alvarado as his successor.

On the following day, May 21, 1542, the unfortunate hero breathed his last, and was almost immediately buried secretly without the gates of the camp, Alvarado fearing an immediate onslaught from the natives should the death of the hero who had claimed immortality be discovered. The newly-made grave, however, excited suspicion, and, finding it impossible to prevent it from being rifled by the inquisitive savages, Alvarado had the corpse of his predecessor removed from it in the night, wrapped in cloths made heavy with sand, and dropped from a boat into the Mississippi.

The midnight funeral over, all further queries from the natives, as to what had become of the Child of the Sun, were answered by an assurance that he had gone to heaven for a time, but would soon return. Then, while the expected return was still waited for, the camp was broken up as quietly as possible, and Alvarado led his people westward, hoping, as Cabeça had done before him, to reach the Pacific coast.

But long months of wandering in pathless prairies bringing him apparently no nearer to the sea, and dreading to be overtaken in the wilderness by the winter, he turned back and retraced his steps to the Mississippi, where he once more pitched his camp, and spent six months in building boats, in which he hoped to go down the river to its outlet in the Gulf of Mexico. In this bold scheme he was successful. The embarkation into seven roughly-constructed brigantines took place on the 2d July, 1543, and a voyage of seventeen days, between banks lined with hostile Indians, who plied them unceasingly with their poisoned arrows, brought a few haggard, half-naked survivors to the longed-for gulf. Fifty days later, after a weary cruise along the rugged coast of what is now Louisiana and Texas, a party, still further reduced, landed at the Spanish settlement of Panuco, in Mexico, where they were received as men risen from the dead.

In spite of the disastrous conclusion of so many expeditions to the ill-fated "Land of Flowers," there were not wanting many adventurers still eager to try their fortunes in the newly-discovered districts. The first hero of note to succeed De Soto was a Dominican priest named Louis Cancello, who, with a number of his brethren, determined to endeavor to convert the natives to Christianity, and, as an earnest of their peaceful intentions, took with them to Florida a number of natives who had been carried off as slaves by their predecessors. Martyrdom was, however, their only reward. The Indians, who had been taught in a long series of severe lessons to look upon white men as their natural enemies, fell upon the missionaries, who were the first to land, and put them to death. With the fate of their leaders before them, the minor members of the party lost no time in effecting their escape, and the freed slaves alone reaped any profit from the trip. Not more successful was an imposing expedition headed by Don Tristan de Luna in 1559. Although provided with an army of 1,500 men, and accompanied by a large body of missionaries eager to convert the natives; the weapons, alike temporal and spiritual, of the new adventurers were powerless against the prejudices of the Indians and the ravages of fever. Those of the explorers who escaped the evil effects of the climate fell victims to the vengeance of the sons of the soil, and but few survived to tell the tale of the failure of the most carefully organized of all Spanish attempts at colonization north of the Gulf of Mexico.

We shall meet yet again, however, with the Spanish in Florida; but it was now the turn of the French to gain a footing in the New World, and before we complete the tale of Spanish discovery in the North, we must give a brief account of the adventures of the Gauls in the great exodus of the Western nations, in which they bore so important—though so fitful—a part.

# CHAPTER III.

EARLY FRENCH SETTLERS IN NORTH AMERICA, AND THEIR STRUGGLE WITH
THE SPANISH IN FLORIDA.

THE work begun by Vasco Nuñez de Balboa in the great journey already
related, which terminated so disastrously for himself, was completed
in 1522 by the sailing round the globe of one of the ships of the Magellan
expedition, thus proving the existence of a southern oceanic passage to the
East, and stimulating the eagerness with which the European nations sought
to find a shorter north-western route. The French, hitherto indifferent to
what was going on in the New World, seem now to have been suddenly
aroused to a sense of the fact that the English, Portuguese, and Spanish
were contending, not, as was at first supposed, for the possession of scattered
and unimportant islands, but for that of a vast continent of as yet undetermined extent; and Francis I, then smarting under the loss of the Imperial
Crown he had so eagerly coveted, resolved to make up for the priority of
his rivals in the field by new discoveries in the North. "Why," he is reported to have said, "should the Kings of Spain and Portugal divide all
America between them without suffering me to take a share as their brother?
I would fain see the article in Adam's will that bequeaths that vast inheritance to them."

The first result of this new interest in the affairs of the West was the fitting out of an expedition, consisting of four ships, under the command of
Giovanni Verrazano, a native of Florence, already mentioned. Of these
four vessels, three were disabled almost before they set sail, leaving to the
sole survivor, the *Dauphine*, the whole burden of the trip. In that vessel
Verrazano left the Madeiras in January, 1524, with the intention of reaching
the American coast somewhere above Florida, and thence sailing due north
till he came to the North-West Passage.

The first part of this programme was duly carried out, the *Dauphine*
having made land about 34° N. lat., whence she cruised down the coast in
search of a harbor some two hundred leagues, thus passing the most north-

erly point visited by the Spaniards. The natives of the coasts, belonging probably to the same race as those who had so hospitably received De Ayllon before his real character appeared, crowded to the beach to stare at what must have seemed to them a strange monster of the deep; and when they found the "monster" was, after all, the servant of men such as themselves, they beckoned their visitors to land.

One sailor alone had the courage to respond to the invitation, and he was nearly drowned in attempting to swim to the shore. Picked up in an exhausted condition by the Indians, he was, however, restored by their tender treatment. Fires were lighted, by which his clothes were dried ; and when he was completely restored, he was allowed to return to his comrades, who had all the while been watching the proceedings on shore in horror-struck silence, expecting the lighting of the fires to be the preliminary of a human sacrifice. In the hands of a true leader of men this little episode might have been made the foundation of lasting and, eventually, beneficial relations between the Indians and their guests. Verrazano, however, was no exception to the explorers of his day; he rewarded those who had saved the life of his sailor by carrying off a young boy as a slave, and then, weighing anchor, he set sail with his solitary prize for the North, arriving, after a long cruise, in what is supposed to have been the harbor of New York. Then, as now, though its aspect is so materially changed, the mouth of the Hudson presented a beautiful appearance, with what are now known as Staten and Long Islands on one side, and the mag-

MOUTH OF THE HUDSON RIVER.

nificent sheet of water flowing into the sea on the other. Instead of the stately vessels and trim little gun-boats which now guard the approach to the capital of the Metropolis, Indian canoes were shooting here and there on the sunlighted waters, their rowers pausing again and again to look at the strange intruder from the South.

Verrazano remained at anchor off the mouth of the Hudson for about fifteen days, receiving visits on board from the natives — a k i n d l y, cheerful race, with regular features, clear complexions, long, straight hair, and good figures. Then steering up the shores of New England for some forty or fifty leagues, he came to the harbor of Nova Scotia, where he would gladly have rested awhile, but finding his provisions failing him, and the Indians meeting his advances with coldness and suspicion, he turned the *Dauphine's* head eastward-ho, arriving at Dieppe after an absence of only six months.

More important was the work done by Verrazano's successor, Jacques Cartier, of St. Malo, who, at the instigation of Admiral Chabot, was sent out in

JACQUES CARTIER.

April, 1534, with two ships of about 130 men, by Francis I., with orders

to found a colony somewhere in the North-west. Acting on these somewhat vague instructions, Cartier first made the land at Bona Vista Bay (N. lat. 48° 50′, W. long. 53° 20′), on the eastern coast of Newfoundland. With a knowledge of geography scarcely to have been expected at that early date, Cartier lost no time in steering, first north and then northwest, for the straits of Belle Isle, dividing Newfoundland from the Mainland ; and, though his course was considerably impeded by the ice, he passed without accident into the Gulf of St. Lawrence, crossing which, in a southwesterly direction, he entered a bay on the coast of Canada, which he named Chaleur (N. lat. 49° 55,′ W. long. 65° 25′), on account of the heat.

Landing on the shores of what he describes as an inviting country—though the natives were half-naked savages, living on raw fish and flesh, and with no houses but the canoe tents already noticed in speaking of the discoveries of the Northmen—Cartier took possession of the land in the name of the King of France, setting up a huge cross upon the beach, with the *Fleur de Lys* carved upon it, in spite of the deprecatory gestures of the natives, who well knew what the proceeding portended.

By dint of the exercise of a good deal more tact than was usually shown by early explorers, Cartier disarmed the suspicions of the natives, and even persuaded their chief to allow him to take his two sons, Taignoagny and Domagaia, to France, for which country he sailed shortly afterward, to report progress and receive further instructions.

Pleased with the description given of the new country, Francis I. sent Cartier back in the following spring with three well-manned vessels under his command, and full powers to plant French colonies wherever he chose, also to prosecute the search for a short cut to the East, and to convert the natives to the true faith.

With the two Indian lads—whose full confidence he seems to have won—beside him on the deck of the foremost vessel, the future founder of Quebec arrived at the mouth of a large river, the St. Lawrence of the present day, on the 10th August, 1534 ; and being informed by the natives that its name was Hochelaga, and that it came from a far country which no man had ever seen, he determined to ascend it, thinking that it might perhaps be that strait leading to the Indian Ocean which had so long been sought in vain.

CARTIER'S SHIP.

Naming the new river the St. Lawrence, in honor of the saint on whose

festival day he first entered it, Cartier made his way slowly over its broad waters till he came to the point at which it receives the Saguenay, beyond which he anchored off a little island, which he called the Isle aux Coudres, on account of the hazel-trees abounding on it. Eight leagues further on, the island now known as the Isle d'Orleans was reached, and here the natives, reassured by the sight of their two fellow-countrymen, flocked on deck, eager to hear of their adventures in the strange land beyond the sea. De-

ISLANDS AT THE MOUTH OF THE ST. LAWRENCE RIVER.

lighted with their accounts of the kindness shown them in France, Don.nacona, the chief or lord of Saguenay, embraced Cartier, and swore eternal friend-ship with him and his people, little dreaming that the advent of the French meant the death of his own race as a nation.

From the Isle d'Orleans the French vessel sailed on, past the mouth of the St. Croix, now the St. Charles, to the village of Stadacona, on the site of the modern Quebec; thence, undeterred by various stratagems of the na-tives, intended to intimidate the explorers, to the more important town of Hochelaga, where Montreal now stands; and then past Huron, a settlement of some fifty huts, inclosed within a triple barrier of palisades.

Landing at Hochelaga, among crowds of gesticulating natives, Cartier and his chief followers were led into the public square, where they were at once beset by women and girls, who brought children in their arms to be touched by the white men from beyond the sea.   In the center of the square lay the king of the land, Agouhanna, a martyr to the terrible disease of paralysis.   Looking up into the face of his visitor, the monarch, with pathetic confidence in his omnipotence, begged that he might be freed from his sufferings ; and Cartier, touched by the appeal, kneeled down and rubbed the poor shrunken limbs of the sufferer, receiving in return for the momentary relief thus afforded a present of the royal sufferer's own crown of porcupine quills.

The ready help given to their leader was the signal for the bringing into the market-place by the natives of all the lame, halt, blind, and aged ; and Cartier, finding himself the center of an eager group, could think of nothing better to do than to pray for them all, so he read them a chapter from the Bible, and then kneeled down and addressed a petition to Heaven on their behalf in his own language, the Indians imitating every gesture, under the idea that some magic spell was being performed.   We can imagine their disappointment when no immediate result ensued from the ceremony ; and we are glad that the explorer showed so much consideration for their ignorance as to distribute presents of knives, beads, rings, etc., among them, which, we are told, they received with joy.

This town of Hochelaga, which is so prominent in Cartier's narrative, disappeared from history soon after his day ; whether it was annihilated under the attack of some rival tribe, or destroyed through some tremendous physical convulsion, history does not tell us.   But its name has been revived, and invested with a new interest, in our day ; for the geologist—as truly an explorer as the geographer—has been busy upon the site of the ancient town, and has discovered many valuable remains of its strange, forgotten life, which confirm and complete the account given by Cartier.   Principal Dawson, of Montreal, in his book on *Fossil Men*, tells us that he has in his possession from 150 to 200 fragments of earthen vessels found upon the spot where Hochelaga stood ; and there is abundant evidence to prove that its inhabitants were people of no mean mechanical skill.   For instance, traces have been found of pots, in the necks of which are appliances for suspending them, so that the suspending cord might not be burned.   Various relics testify also to their artistic feeling, most notable among which are tobacco-pipes, upon which much fine work must have been spent ; their peculiar at-

tention to the pipe being perhaps traceable rather to their reverence for the
worship in which it had an important place, than to the lighter fancy which
dotes upon meerschaums now-a-days. Their food was that which their sur-
roundings provided ; and Dr. Dawson says that, among the remains excavated, bones of nearly all the wild mammals have been found, as well as of
numerous birds and fishes. Suspicions of cannibalism are roused by the
discovery of part of a woman's jaw among kitchen refuse; and these are,
perhaps, increased by the fact that the Hochelagan skulls which have been

MONTREAL.

discovered bespeak a temperament undoubtedly fierce and cruel ; but on
this point there is nothing to lead to certain conclusions. It might be interesting to follow out this wonderful story of Hochelagan life further, but to
do so here would be aside from the purpose of this chapter, and we therefore content ourselves with adding, that there are not wanting traces of a
religious sense, simple and rude it may be, but real and even beautiful,
among the Canadians of Cartier's day ; while the tokens which accompany

the dead are such as to show that the hope of immortality had shed its soft light upon their hearts.

Naming a hill overlooking Hochelaga Mont Royal—hence the modern name of Montreal—in memory of his visit, Cartier soon returned to the mouth of the St. Charles, where he established his winter quarters and remained until the spring, when, having invited Donnacona and nine other natives on board his vessel, he set sail for France, carrying them with him. All but one little girl died soon after the arrival of the fleet at St. Malo, in July, 1536; but their captain considered he had more than repaid them for their sufferings by their admission into the Roman Catholic Church before the end, and was undeterred by any fear of vengeance for his cruelty to them from undertaking, in 1540, yet another trip to Canada, as the new country was now beginning to be called.

The new expedition consisted of five vessels, and was originally placed under the command of Jean François de la Roque, Seigneur de Roberval of Picardy; but at the last moment, for reasons variously given, he requested Cartier to take his place. Arrived for a third time at his old anchorage off Stadacona, Cartier was at first well received by the natives, who expected now to welcome back their chief and his warriors; but when they heard that they were dead, grief and horror filled their hearts. No longer were they willing to look upon the white men as their brethren, or to aid their settlement among them; and though no open hostilities were resorted to, Cartier found his position throughout the winter so very far from pleasant, that he set sail for France as soon as the weather permitted, meeting De Roberval with reinforcements for the colony—which ought to have been founded —in the harbor of St. John's, Newfoundland.

The Sieur de Roberval, indignant at the failure of his deputy, ordered him to return to the St. Lawrence at once, but Cartier continued his course to his native land in the night, leaving the original commander of the expedition to complete his work as best he could. The new-comers sailed up the St. Lawrence as far as the St. Charles, but De Roberval was almost immediately recalled to France to aid his sovereign in his struggle with Charles V.; and though he left thirty of his men behind him, they failed to gain any real foothold in the country, and returned home in the ensuing spring, some say under the escort of Cartier himself, who was sent to their relief.

Thus, ruined on the very eve of success by a petty act of oppression, ended alike the first attempt at colonization by the French in North America and the first exploration of the St. Lawrence, which, though it formed no short cut to the Indies, was yet destined, as the largest body of fresh water in the world, to play a mighty part in history as a highway from the coast to the interior of North America.

Very different to that of any of his predecessors was the character of our next hero of North American discovery. Driven to bay in France by the long series of treacheries and cruelties which culminated in the awful massacre of St. Bartholomew on the 24th of August, 1572, the French Huguenots hoped to find in the New World a refuge from religious persecution ; and after the failure of an attempt to found a colony in Rio Janeiro in 1555, the good Admiral Coligny sent out an expedition to that "long coast of the West India called La Florida," under the command of John Ribault, of Dieppe.

Trained in the stern school of adversity, Ribault started on his voyage prepared to face any amount of danger and privation in carrying out his mission of founding a little Huguenot Church in the wilderness. He was accompanied by many heretic noblemen imbued with the same spirit, and by a little band of well-tried troops. After a stormy voyage, the little fleet came in sight of the coast of Florida, in about N.

COLIGNY.

lat. 29 1-2°, on the 27th April, 1562, and, after a brief halt, sailed northward till it reached the mouth of "a goodly and great river," the modern St. John's, to which the name of the "River of May" was in the first case given.

Entering the River of May in high delight with the beauty of the scenery lining its banks, the French refugees landed at a little distance from the sea, and set up a stone column bearing the arms of France, on a little hill overlooking the south bank, in token that the land henceforth belonged to his Majesty of France. The natives, who are described as "mild and courteous, well-shaped, of goodly stature, dignified, self-possessed, and of pleasant countenance," gazed with wonder, but with no notion of its significance, on the strange pillar set up among them ; and leaving it as the sole token of their visit, the Frenchmen pressed on up the coast, passing one

river after another, till they came, on the 27th May, to the beautiful harbor of Port Royal, near the southern boundary of the present Carolina, where Ribault determined to plant a colony.

A fort was erected to begin with, and named Fort Charles, or Carolina, in honor of Charles IX. of France; and leaving thirty of his men, under the command of an experienced soldier named Pierria, to form the nucleus of a settlement, Ribault returned to France for reinforcements. On his arrival in his native land, however, he found his co-religionists in greater distress than ever, and not until after the peace of 1562 was the good Coligny able to devote any attention to the affairs of the emigrants in the West.

In 1564 three ships were sent out to their relief, under the command of Captain Renè de Laudonnière, who had been with Ribault on his first trip; but on his arrival at the River of May, he was met with the intelligence that Fort Charles had been abandoned, and by degrees the whole story of the sufferings of his predecessors leaked out. Relying on Ribault's promise of speedy reinforcements, and missing his bracing influence, the unlucky Huguenots forgot all about the primary object of their exile, the founding of a church in the wilderness, and gave themselves up to indolence and luxury. As a result, their provisions quickly failed, and, though the Indians befriended them to the best of their ability, they began to succumb to famine. Discontent and mutiny ensued; Pierria was assassinated in revenge for the severe discipline he endeavored to maintain, and his successor, Nicolas Barre, determined to build a small pinnace, in which to return to France.

With infinite difficulty this plan was carried out. A vessel of some kind was constructed, and in it, with no provisions but a little corn given by the natives, the survivors embarked. For three weeks they tossed about at the mercy of the waves, unable to make any considerable progress eastward; and then, all the corn being consumed, they resorted to the awful expedient of obtaining food by slaying one of their number. Lots were drawn, and the ghastly ceremony resulted in the murder of a certain La Chère, a soldier who had been pre-eminent in insubordination under Captain Pierria, and banished by him to an island outside Port Royal, had been rescued by his comrades, only to meet with a yet more awful fate than death by starvation.

Soon after the awful banquet, the blood-stained cannibals—for such had the zealous sufferers for the Huguenot faith now become—were met by an

English vessel and taken on board, some to be landed in France, others to be carried prisoners to England.

Convinced of the truth of the story told by the Indians of the desertion of Fort Charles, Laudonnière abandoned his scheme of going there, and resolved instead to found a colony on the May ; and for this purpose he selected a spot near the mouth of that river, which is now known as St. John's Bluff. Again a fort was built, to which the now ill-fated name of Carolina was once more given. Again the colonists contented themselves with preparing for imaginary enemies, and neglected to provide against the attacks of famine and fever. Strength and means were wasted in fruitless expeditions in search of that Apalachen, so long the *ignis fatuus* of explorers in Florida, where gold in plenty was ever sought but never found. Moreover, among Laudonnière's men were many reckless adventurers, who, not content with rousing the wrath of the peacefully disposed Indians by unprovoked assaults upon them, varied their occupations by piracies against the Spaniards of the Gulf of Mexico. Retaliations ensued, until at last the colonists, with enemies rising up on every side, were reduced to the greatest extremities.

In vain did Laudonnière endeavor to stem the current of adverse circumstances ; in vain did he strive, by example and by precept, to inaugurate a new policy, by tilling the ground for future support, and conciliating the Indians, with a view to obtaining present supplies. His men, desperate with hunger, clamored for him to seize a neighboring chief, and hold him as a hostage, till his people ransomed him with corn ; and finally, though much against his own judgment, Laudonnière yielded.

Outina, a chieftain of high repute, was carried off, and imprisoned in Fort Carolina. His subjects, at first furious, appeared to acquiesce in the situation, and offered the coveted ransom in corn, to be fetched from a distant village by the Frenchmen. The famished Huguenots fell into the snare. Instead of granaries of the staff of life they found an ambuscade of armed natives, and, after a long and bloody fight, they returned to their camp with diminished numbers, and no trophies of a hard-earned victory but two small bags of corn.

Death now stared the colony in the face, and probably every member of it must have perished miserably, had not Sir John Hawkins, first of the long list of Englishmen who have disgraced their nationality as dealers in slaves, touched at the fort on his way home from a successful cruise. The wealth he had won in his traffic in human flesh enabled Hawkins not only to relieve the present necessities of the French, but to give them a vessel in which to return home; and they were on the eve of a joyful embarkation, when our old friend Ribault appeared on the scene with fresh emigrants and plentiful stores of every variety.

A new era seemed now likely to be ushered in, but its inauguration was saddened by the humiliation of Laudonnière, whose vigorous efforts to carry out the original intentions of his employer, Admiral Coligny, had been misrepresented in France by certain of his insubordinate followers, whom he had sent home in disgrace, and forgotten. When the first enthusiasm at the arrival of his fellow-countryman had subsided, the one man who had striven to avert the evils which had befallen the colony learned that Ribault had come out to supersede him in his command. The fact that the new governor was quickly convinced of the injustice of the charges brought against Laudonnière, and begged him to remain with him as a friend, and to retain the command of Fort Carolina, appears to have done little to soothe the wounded spirit of our hero. He had resolved to return to France at once and stand his trial, when one of those sudden changes in the aspect of affairs, to which early settlements in America have ever been subject, held him to his post.

As we have seen in our previous chapter, the Spanish looked upon Florida, which they took to include the whole of America north of the Gulf of Mexico, as their own peculiar property. The news of the establishment of a settlement of French Protestants in their territory was, therefore, received with a burst of indignation, to which it was difficult to say whether cupidity, religious zeal, or national jealousy most contributed.

After the failure of the expedition of De Luna to Florida in 1561, a certain Pedro Menendez had been appointed by the Spanish monarch to the government of Florida, on the condition of his subduing it in three years. He now received orders to hasten the start of his expedition, and to add to his scheme the destruction of the colony of French heretics.

The rejoicings at the arrival of Ribault were still going on among the unconscious settlers on the May, when the fleet of Menendez was seen creeping into the harbor. A messenger sent to inquire whence it came, and what it wanted, received the laconic answer that Pedro Menendez was in command, and had come, in obedience to the orders of his sovereign, to "burn and destroy such Lutheran French as should be in his dominions."

Of Ribault's fleet of seven vessels, three were just then absent on a trip up the river, and not daring to meet the Spaniards with only four, the

French commander was compelled to put out to sea with them, leaving his colony totally unprotected. From a safe distance he watched his enemies disembark a little to the north of his own settlement, intending, so soon as they were involved in all the confusion of a march through an unknown country, to fall upon their rear and destroy them. But, alas! at the critical moment a terrible storm came on, dispersing the French vessels, and leaving the women, the children, and the disabled in Fort Carolina at the mercy of the ruthless Spaniards.

A terrible massacre ensued, from which but a few, including Laudonnière, escaped, and got on board the only two vessels which had not been wrecked, in which they at once put to sea, arriving in due time in France, to tell the awful tidings of the fate of their comrades. The French Government took but little notice of the matter—for were not the sufferers heretics?—and the Huguenots, though beside themselves with rage, were unable to send any adequate force to avenge their co-religionists, until two years later, when the services were secured of Dominique de Gourgues and 150 men.

Before any reinforcements arrived in Florida, therefore, fresh horrors were enacted. Menendez, having obtained intelligence from the Indians that a number of Frenchmen were still alive on Anastasia Island, a little to the south, where they had taken refuge on the destruction of their vessel, hastened to the spot, and, after a short parley, induced the Frenchmen to surrender themselves unconditionally into his hands. Then, having weeded out from among them the few who professed themselves to be Catholics, and two or three craftsmen whose services he required, he had them all hewn down before his eyes. This new atrocity over, he returned to Florida, but, being met by the intelligence that Ribault himself, with a little remnant of his immediate followers, had survived, and was now probably on the scene of the massacre of his fellow-countrymen, he hurried back to Anastasia to complete his bloody work.

Knowing what he had to expect, Ribault gathered his men about him, and received his executioners with quiet dignity. Asked were he and his companions Catholics or Lutherans, he replied simply that they were all of the Reformed religion, that from the dust they had come and to the dust they must return; twenty years more or less could matter but little; the Adelantado could do with them as he chose. Again the men who might be of use to him in his work of colonization were led apart by Menendez, again the signal for the massacre was given, again the triumphant cries of the victors were mingled with the groans of the dying ; and when all was over, Menendez, with the consciousness of having done his duty, returned thanks to God, and retired to his head-quarters to send home to his king an account of the triumph of the true faith.

Scenes of bloodshed were now exchanged for the peaceful work of founding a Spanish colony. The site chosen was in N. lat. 29° 51', W. long. 81° 30', some miles north of the ill-fated Fort Carolina, and was named St. Augustine, because the Spanish fleet had first come in sight of Florida on the festival day of that saint. The boundaries of the settlement were carefully marked out under the supervision of Menendez himself, and though its foundations were laid in blood, it grew with a rapidity hitherto unequaled, and bid fair to be the first permanent settlement of Europeans in North America. The past was forgotten, and not more unconscious of their coming doom than the poor colonists of Carolina were the Spaniards of St. Augustine, when once more a little fleet appeared upon the coast of Florida, coming, not this time from the South, but from the North ; for De Gourgues, with the foresight of a true soldier, had paused to secure the friendship of the Indians of the May before venturing to approach the Spanish camp.

The outposts of the Spaniards were surprised, the sentinels were slain at their posts, and a force of four hundred men sent out by Menendez against the enemy was completely destroyed, those taken prisoners being hanged on the very trees on which some of the Frenchmen of Carolina had suffered the same fate at the hands of the Spaniards. With this retribution, however, De Gourgues—who, it must be remembered, was acting without the authority of his government—appears to have been content. He made no descent upon St. Augustine itself ; but having destroyed the forts whose garrisons he had massacred, he bade his Indian allies farewell, and left the country. But his work had been more thorough than he knew himself, for the natives, who had hitherto looked upon the Spaniards as invincible, had seen them fall an easy prey to the French, and the remainder of the career of Menendez was one long struggle against the treacherous schemes of the red men. His efforts at exploration on the North were unsuccessful ; the missionaries whom he induced to land on the north-western shores of Florida were led into ambush, and massacred by the natives ; and though summary vengeance was exacted for their fate, the enmity of the Indians continued to hamper all the movements of the Spaniards.

To complete the story of early settlements in Florida, we may add that for thirty years St. Augustine was the only European colony north of the Gulf of Mexico, and that in 1586 a visit was paid to it by Sir Francis Drake, who found it under the command of Pedro Menendez, nephew of its founder, who is thought to have been the first European to enter Chesapeake Bay.

VIEW ON THE COAST OF FLORIDA.

The English being at this date very bitter against the Spanish, Drake thought it a pious duty to carry off the treasure and burn the houses of St. Augustine, the inhabitants of which fled at his approach, with the exception of a certain Frenchman, a fifer, who had been one of the few spared in the massacres of Anastasia, and who now came to meet the English "in a little boate, playing on his Phiph the tune of the Prince of Orange his song."

# CHAPTER IV.

IT was now the turn of the English, who had thus far been slow to realize the great value of the newly-discovered districts, to send out expeditions with a view to the planting of settlements in North-east America. In the early part of the 16th century, several voyages to the North-west were made under British leadership, and some slight knowledge of the limits, though scarcely of the geography, of the western coasts of North America was gained by the brilliant pirate Drake, who sailed as far north as the present state of Oregon ; but it was reserved to the half-brothers, Sir Humphrey Gilbert and Sir Walter Raleigh, to give the first real impulse to the intelligent exploration of the western seaboard of North America.

The brothers appear to have been first roused to take an interest in the New World from the reports given at the court of Elizabeth by some of the unhappy Frenchmen, who, as we have seen, were rescued from a fearful fate by an English vessel after their escape from the colony on the River of May. Sir Humphrey Gilbert, after a long negotiation, obtained a charter from Elizabeth in 1578, granting him full power for six years to discover "remote, heathen and barbarous lands not actually possessed by any Christian prince or people," and to take possession of them for his own benefit ; and Sir Walter was among the earliest to come to his aid with money and advice, though he was forbidden by the maiden monarch to take any personal share in the enterprise.

Gilbert's first attempt to start for the West failed at the very outset, through the loss of one of his vessels and the desertion of many of his followers. The second expedition, which started in 1583, reached St. John's, Newfoundland, in safety, and, landing, Sir Humphrey read aloud his commission to the motley crowd of fishermen of all nations there assembled. A pillar bearing the arms of England was then set up, in token that the land henceforth belonged to the English monarch, and the voyage was resumed ;

but before the fleet had proceeded far down the coast of the United States, the largest vessel was wrecked, and the remainder beat a hasty retreat for England. Gilbert, who had embarked on the smallest of the ships in order to superintend the coast surveys, refused to leave it for the homeward voyage, replying, when urged to do so, "I will not forsake my little company . . . with whom I have passed so many storms and perils." For this noble resolution the unfortunate commander paid with his life, for his little bark, the *Squirrel,* went down, with all on board, in mid-Atlantic.

On receiving the news of the sad fate of his half-brother, and of the total failure of his expedition, so far as any practical results were concerned, Sir Walter Raleigh lost not a moment in obtaining a new patent from the Queen; and though forbidden at the last moment by Her Majesty to sail himself, he succeeded in dispatching two vessels, under the command of Captain Philip Amadas and Captain Barlow, as early as the 27th of April, 1583.

The coast of Florida was sighted on the 2d of July of the same year, and, sailing for some hundred and twenty miles without finding any harbor, the adventurers came in due course to what they took to be an island, but which, so far as can

THE LAST MOMENTS OF SIR HUMPHREY GILBERT.

be made out from the confused and contradictory accounts given of the voyage by old chroniclers, is generally supposed to have been Cape Hatteras (N. lat. 35° 14′, W. long. 75° 32′). Here they disembarked, and were kindly received by the king of the country, a native of "mean stature, of color yellow, and with black hair, worn long on one side only," the latter peculiarity being, as it turned out, a distinctive mark of the male sex of this district, the women alone enjoying the privilege of wearing the hair long on both sides.

The name of the newly-discovered territory was Wingandacoa, and that of its king Wingina; but, with the usual cool disregard of the feelings of the natives shown by all or nearly all early explorers, the visitors took posses-

SIR WALTER RALEIGH.

sion of it, and "of all adjacent countries," in the name of their queen, who, on hearing of its discovery, called it Virginia, after her own most excellent virgin Majesty.

After exchanging presents with Wingina and his brother, Granganameo, of the neighboring "island" of Roanoake, the name of which is still retained by a river of Virginia, the adventurers returned to England, and in the ensuing year, 1585, a second and more important expedition was sent out by Sir Walter Raleigh, under Sir Richard Grenville, with instructions

SIR FRANCIS DRAKE.

to found a colony in Virginia, from which further explorations inland and along the coasts were to be made as opportunity offered.

The colony was duly founded, with Roanoake as its headquarters, and leaving 108 men and women to inhabit the country, under the governorship of Ralph Lane, Sir Richard returned to England, confident that he had sown the seed of an important offshoot of the mother country.  In a short excursion he had made up the coast, however, the governor had planted a thorn in the side of the infant community by the summary vengeance he had taken on a whole village, one member of which had stolen a silver cup. The natives, who had at first been prepared to allow the new-comers to plant and build without molestation, were now eager to get rid of them by fair means or foul, and no course seemed open to Lane but the fatal one of intimidation, which had already led to so many terrible scenes on the fair western coasts of America.

After a trip up the coast resulting in the discovery of Chesapeake Bay, which had, however, long been known to the Spanish, Lane, misled by legends, in which he thought he read signs of the existence, not very far westward, of abundance of pearls, of copper-mines, and, best of all, of the white breakers of the Pacific Ocean, went for some little distance up the Roanoke river, returning disheartened and disgusted, to find his people at daggers drawn with the Indians, who were in their turn embroiled with a neighboring chief. With the prospect of massacre if their enemies triumphed, and death by famine through the failure of native supplies if they were defeated, the unlucky colonists were in despair, when Sir Francis Drake, red-handed from his destruction of St. Augustine, arrived off the coast with a fleet of twenty-six vessels.

Although Drake would have left with Lane men and provisions enough to save them from either of the evils they so much dreaded, the colonists, who had completely lost heart, clamored to be taken home, and one and all embarked for England, taking with them as sole trophy of their brief occupation of Virginia a supply of tobacco, the use of which they had learned from the Indians, who had from time immemorial connected the smoking of it with all their religious or civil ceremonies

DRAKE'S SHIP.

of any importance, and who would probably have looked upon its every-day consumption as little short of sacrilege and mockery of the "Great Spirit."

The fleet of Sir Francis Drake had scarcely left the coast, before a vessel, under the command of Sir Richard Grenville, arrived sent out by Raleigh, with supplies for the colonists.  Finding the settlement deserted, the leader of the relief party left fifteen men at Roanoake to retain possession of it for England, and returned home. Determined not to allow his brother's work to remain unfinished, Sir Walter, in spite of these repeated failures, lost no time in fitting out yet another expedition consisting of 150 men, and commanded by John White as governor, and Simon Ferdinando as admiral. The two leaders quarreled before Virginia was reached, and, as a result their trip was as unsatisfactory as any which had preceded it. No trace could be found of Grenville's fifteen men, and the only incidents of this visit to Virginia worthy of record were the murder by Indians of a Mr. Howe, with the terrible vengeance exacted on some natives *who had had nothing whatever to do with the outrage,* and the birth, on the 18th August, 1587, of Virginia Dare, grand-daughter of White, and the first child of English parents born on North American soil.

ELIZABETH KNIGHTING DRAKE.

Finding himself unable to cope with the difficulties of his position, White soon made excuse for returning to England, and leaving a small detachment of his forces, his daughter, and her infant alluded to above, in the "City of Raleigh," as the new settlement was called, he set sail at the end of August, 1587, promising to return speedily with reinforcements.

Three years elapsed before this promise was fulfilled, and of the history of the deserted colony during that period no details have ever been gathered. Arrived at Roanoake in the spring of 1590, the indefatigable Sir Walter Raleigh again bearing the expense of the expedition, White found no trace of the city of his benefactor. The light of a distant fire was the sole sign of life which met his eyes when he reached the spot where he had expected to find his former comrades, his daughter, and his now three-year old grand-child. Eagerly pressing on in the direction of the fire, some of White's men discovered the letters "C R O " carved on the trunk of a tree on a little hill. The sight of these letters reminded the leader that the colonists had agreed, should they have to leave the City of Raleigh, to carve the name of the place to which they went on some tree or trunk, and, further, to add beneath the name a cross, in the event of any misfortune having befallen them.

What, then, could the three letters mean? Nothing worse, surely, than that the emigrants had removed to some place the name of which began with them. "Cro—Cro—" repeated one after another, until at length the remainder of the word flashed across the minds of all. The friendly village of Croatoan, already known to White, must be now the home of the lost emigrants. There was no cross beneath the initial letters to damp the delight at this discovery, and the march was resumed. A little further on the full word "Croatoan" was found carved upon a tree, still without the cross; but, in spite of this reassuring token, all further efforts to find the colony were unavailing. The fire had been lighted by Indians, who could give no information ; and when after many days of disheartening search, a number of empty chests, frameless pictures, and other relics were found in a trench, White—who seems, to say the least of it, to have been strangely ready to accept the loss of his daughter and grandchild—threw up the search and returned home, without, so far as we can make out, actually visiting the village of Croatoan after all.

This silent disappearance of a colony of white men, including at least one woman and an infant girl, has given rise to many a legend of the presence, among the dusky warriors of the West, of princesses of alien race ruling the simple savages by virtue of their superior intelligence ; but though Raleigh sent out expedition after expedition to scour Virginia and the surrounding districts for traces of his lost people, not one trustworthy word was ever obtained as to their fate, though the name of many another Englishman was added to the already long roll of martyrs to the cause of colonization in the West.

With the death by drowning, off Chesapeake Bay, of his nephew, Bartholomew Gilbert, early in 1602, ended Raleigh's direct connection with North America. In 1603, when the loss of his beloved mistress had converted him from a court favorite into a "spider of hell" and a "viperous traitor"—to quote the forcible language of his prosecutor, Coke—the patent, which he had reserved in his own name on the death of his brother, Sir Humphrey, expired by his attainder for high treason ; but to his influence was due, first, the sending out, in 1602, of the little ship *Concord*, under Bartholomew Gosnold ; and, secondly, the great expedition of 1606, inseparably connected with the names of Captain John Smith and the fair Pocahontas.

To Bartholomew Gosnold we owe the first practical corroboration of the ancient sagas, on which is founded our account of the visits to the western coast of America by the Northmen.

Arriving in his little bark off the modern Cape Ann, in N. lat. 42° 37', our hero sailed southward across Massachusetts Bay, landed on Cape Cod, N. lat. 42° 5', and thence visited some of the adjoining islands, one of which he found so full of vines that he named it Martha's Vineyard, thereby unconsciously following the example of the old sea-kings, who had called it, or some not very distant locality, Vinland.

Unable, with the very limited means at his disposal, himself to found a colony, though he made an unsuccessful attempt to do so in the westernmost of the islands visited, and which he named Elizabeth, Gosnold took home such proofs of the wealth of the newly-discovered districts that the interest of many influential noblemen and merchants was aroused. An association —including the great Richard Hakluyt—whose name still lives in the valuable society to which we owe so much of our knowledge of the progress of geographical research—was quickly formed, and as early as 1606, when Raleigh was expiating his imaginary crimes in the Tower, letters patent were issued in the name of James I. to Sir George Summers, Edward Maria Wingfield, and others, granting them all lands on the American coast, with the adjacent islands, between 34° and 45° N. lat.

Among the conditions annexed to these letters patent was the important one that two companies should be formed—one to be called the Southern, the other the Northern Colony.

While the preliminary steps in the organization of these two companies were being taken, two short though important visits were paid to North America—one by Martin Pring in the *Speedwell*, resulting in the discovery of several of the harbors of Maine, and of the Saco, Kennebec, and York Rivers; the other by George Weymouth, who supplemented his predecessors' work by a thorough survey of the coast of Maine, and the discovery of the Penobscot River.

On the 19th December, 1606, after an unsuccessful attempt by the Plymouth Company to settle a colony in the lands assigned to it, the Lon-

don Company sent forth the expedition destined to obtain the first permanent foothold in the present United States. Three vessels, the _Sarah Con-
stant_, the _God-speed_, and the _Discovery_, bore to the site of their new home
one hundred and five men, of whom the most noteworthy were the commander, Newport, Bartholomew Gosnold, Gabriel Archer, Edward Maria
Wingfield, the Rev. Robert Hunt, George Percy, brother to the Earl of
Northumberland, and the great John Smith.

VIEW ON THE COAST OF MAINE.

The voyage out was rendered harassing by perpetual disputes; and when,
on the 26th April, 1607, the colonists sailed up Chesapeake Bay, the seeds
were already sown of future troubles. Naming the southern extremity of
the bay Cape Henry, and the northern Cape Charles, after the sons of
James I., the explorers landed on the peninsula, about fifty miles from the
mouth of the bay. The sealed instructions which had been brought out by
the commander were now opened, when it was ascertained that the govern-

ment was to be vested in a council, to consist of Gosnold, Smith, Newport, Ratcliffe, Martin, and Kendall, under the presidency of Wingfield, and that, among other minor tasks, the emigrants were to discover the water communication still supposed to exist between Virginia and the Pacific.

Having fixed, on the 13th May, 1607, on the site of the first settlement, which they named Jamestown, in honor of their monarch, the emigrants divided their forces, some setting to work to fell trees and so forth, others joining Captain Newport in fitting out a shallop in which to make the first discovery so eagerly hoped for by all.

Entering the river Powhatan, which they christened James, the exploring party sailed up as far as the now well-known Falls, by which further progress was barred, and after paying a visit to the native chieftain, Pawatah—who received his strange guests with ill-disguised fear—returned disappointed and disgusted to Jamestown within a week of setting out. A little later, Newport set sail for England, and his departure seems to have been the signal for the breaking out of the fire of discontent and jealousy which had long been smoldering.

From the first, Smith had been, according to one account, the ring-leader of the malcontents, and according to his own, the most oppressed among the ill-used colonists. In any case, his name crops up as a bone of contention in all the documents still extant relating to the much-vexed early days of Jamestown. Famine, disease, and quarrels among themselves greatly reduced the original number of the emigrants before the first summer was over, and, but for the kindness of the Indians, all would probably have perished.

Refraining from entering into details of the disputes between Wingfield and Smith, and, when the former had been deposed, between his successors, Ratcliffe and Martin, and the same noted member of the council, we must content ourselves with adding that the supreme power finally passed into the hands of John Smith, and that, whatever may have been his faults as a private individual, he proved himself more than equal to the emergency as the leader of what had now become little more than a forlorn hope.

By his energetic measures, even before he was formally elected president of the council, Smith succeeded in restoring first peace and then prosperity to the almost despairing band of survivors, and the winter of 1607 found him in a position to pursue the geographical explorations so suddenly interrupted, and with which alone we have, strictly speaking, now to do. On the 10th

December he started in a small boat with two Englishmen and two Indian guides, up the little river Chickahominy, which flowed into the James river a few miles above the infant settlement.

ADMIRALL OF NEW ENGLAND. THE PORTRAICTUER OF CAPTAYNE IOHN SMITH

CAPTAIN JOHN SMITH.

Unable to proceed far by water, Smith soon left his boat under charge of his fellow-countrymen, and set off alone through the woods with the natives. His English comrades were almost immediately surprised and killed by savages, and he himself was taken prisoner by a chief named Opechancan-ough and his warriors, who would have slain him had he not suddenly produced his pocket compass, the strange proceedings of which so astonished his captors that they resolved to retain its owner among them, as one likely to bring honor to their tribe. From place to place the unfortunate white man was marched, to be shown to crowds of admiring Indians, paying thus the first visit ever made by a European to the Potomac River, and finally arriving at the encampment of Powhatan—probably the father of the Pawatah mentioned above—then staying on the bank of what is now called York River.

Here occurred, or rather is said to have occurred—for some authorities make no allusion to it—that romantic i n c i d e n t which has formed the theme of so many legends and romances. According to Smith's own account, preserved in his *General History*, he was first received with great respect and ostentation by the Emperor Powhatan, and afterwards a consultation was held between his host

CAPTAIN SMITH TAKEN PRISONER BY THE INDIANS.
(From Smith's " Virginia.")

and his chief men, resulting in the decision that the white man should be slain. Two large stones were then dragged into the presence ; Smith was led to them, and made to lay his head upon them. Three executioners now hastened forward, and were about to beat the victim's brains out with clubs, when Pocahontas, the king's dearest daughter, a lovely girl of about twelve years old, rushed forward, seized Smith's head in her arms, and laid her own down upon it.

The hands of the executioners were stayed, and Pocahontas, turning to her father, pleaded so eloquently for the life of Smith, that her prayer was

POCAHONTAS AND CAPTAIN JOHN SMITH.

granted.   He was restored to liberty, and sent back to Jamestown under an escort of twelve savages, arriving there after an absence of about four weeks, to find the colony again in a state of destitution and anarchy.  The immediate wants of the unlucky emigrants were, however, supplied by Pocahontas, who seems to have determined not to lose sight of the hero she had saved, and to have come constantly to Jamestown with supplies of corn for him and his people.  A little later, her kindly aid was supplemented by the return to Jamestown of Newport, with one hundred and twenty men, provisions, implements, and seeds.

The brief revival of prosperity was, however, to a great extent neutralized by an unfortunate discovery near Jamestown of a quantity of yellow mica, which was mistaken for gold.  Newport and his men threw up for its sake the tilling of the ground and trading for furs with the Indians—which would really have produced a golden harvest—and finally set sail for Europe, with a cargo, to quote Smith's own expression, of the useless dirt.

With Newport departed Smith's rivals, Wingfield, Archer, and Martin, leaving him the chief person in the colony; and so soon as his movements were unhampered, he set to work exploring the neighborhood, quickly gaining a very thorough knowledge of Chesapeake Bay and its tributaries, which he embodied in a map still extant.  On one trip he penetrated far into the present state of Ohio, and heard from the natives something of the doings of the French, who were by this time rapidly gaining ground in Canada. On his return to Jamestown in September, 1608, Smith was formally elected, what he had long been in reality, president of the colonial council; and a little later, Newport again appeared on the scene with fresh emigrants, including two women, Mistress Forrest and Ann Burras, her maid, and supplies of provisions. Newport was also the bearer of instructions from the London Council "to bring home a lump of gold," instead of the worthless stuff sent last time, "to discover the passage to the South Sea, to find the survivors of the Roanoake colony, and to crown the Emperor Powhatan."

Instead of the lump of gold, Smith sent back a cargo of timber, and specimens of tar, pitch, and potash; instead of the discovery of the passage to the South Sea, he reported the existence of a richly-watered land, which would repay tillage a hundredfold; and of the message relating to the survivors of Roanoake he took no notice whatever. The only part of the strange orders received literally carried out was that relating to the crowning of Powhatan, who, convinced of his own importance by the fuss made about him, declared he was not coming to Jamestown, but must be waited on at home.

In this the dusky warrior, whose friendship Newport considered of great importance to the colony, was humored, and the banks of the Potomac witnessed a quaint ceremony, the significance of which the chief actor must have been totally unable to understand.

On Newport's arrival in London, early in 1609, with Smith's unsatisfactory replies to the communications of his employers, it was resolved entirely to alter the character of the administration of the colony. A new charter was asked for and obtained from the king; a governor, Lord De La Warre, whose power was to be absolute, was appointed, with a number of officials with high-sounding titles under him. Five hundred emigrants joined his standard, and early in May the whole party, with the exception of the governor himself, who was to follow shortly afterward, set sail from England in an imposing fleet of nine vessels. But a violent storm off the Bermudas wrought terrible havoc among the ships—two were totally wrecked, and seven only reached Virginia. These seven contained but the more reckless of the emigrants, "gentlemen" who had dissipated their fortunes at home; and while they added greatly to the difficulties of Smith, all those of the original expedition, who were worthy of the great task before them, were struggling for dear life on the shores of the uninhabited but fruitful island on which they had been cast.

For a year, Smith struggled on ; for a year, those who would have brought fresh life to Virginia sustained each other's courage by working hard with heads and hands, until they succeeded in building, out of the wreck of their own, two new vessels, in which they again embarked for their western home. Could Smith but have held out until this wonderful feat was accomplished, he might yet have seen the end attained for which he had so long and patiently labored ; but he was disabled in an explosion of gunpowder, and obliged to return to England to obtain proper surgical treatment, shortly before Sir Thomas Gates, who was to act as Lord De la Warre's deputy till his arrival, set sail from the Bermudas.

With Smith's departure from Virginia, all the evils he had suppressed with a strong hand cropped up anew. The Indians were roused to fury by raids and oppression ; the ground was left untilled, and soon a "starving time" began, which reduced the emigrants from one hundred and ninety to sixty. These sixty—a gaunt and crime-stained crew, huddled together in ruined huts, a prey to disease and misery—came forth to meet Sir Thomas Gates and his hardy followers, entreating with tears and cries to be taken away from the land where they had endured such horrors.

Fearing that his own people might share the fate of the wretches before him, Gates at once resolved to take all the Europeans to Newfoundland, and there await, among the fishermen with whom it was now populated, the arrival of reinforcements from England. On the 7th June, 1609, the two vessels constructed on the Bermudas, and four crazy pinnaces which had belonged to the colonists, weighed anchor, and were dropping slowly from the country of which they had hoped such great things, when a boat was seen advancing to meet them from the sea.

Eagerly did all now crowd to the sides of the vessels to ascertain the meaning of this unexpected phenomenon ; and the rejoicing may be imagined when the little bark turned out to be the boat of Lord De la Warre himself, sent to announce his approach with three vessels laden with new emigrants and provisions ! No need now to flee to Newfoundland ; and, with fresh hope in their hearts, the colonists, old and new, returned to Jamestown, there to await the coming of their governor.

Two days later, the three eagerly expected vessels anchored at the mouth of the James River, and Lord De la Warre came on shore. Falling on his knees as he stepped from his boat, the new leader returned thanks to God for all his mercies—Sir Thomas Gates and the colonists, who were drawn up to receive him, joining earnestly, with bent heads, in this act of worship. The prayer over, eager greetings were exchanged between the new-comers and those whom they had rescued ; Lord De la Warre read his commission, and Sir Thomas Gates resigned his power into the hands of his superior officer.

A new era now began for Virginia ; peace was made with the Indians, and cemented by the marriage of the far-famed Pocahontas with an Englishman named John Rolfe, who in 1616 visited England with his bride. The story goes that Pocahontas, whose heart had long ago been given to John Smith, was only induced to marry Rolfe after being carried off from her home by force by a Captain Argall ; and that, on her presentation at the court of King James, she caught sight of her old hero among the crowd, covered her face with her hands, and burst into tears. However that may be, it seems certain that Pocahontas was converted to Christianity, and baptized under the name of Rebecca, before she left Virginia. She remained in England for a year, and died—after giving birth to a son, from whom some of the best families in Virginia claim descent—just as she was about to embark on her return to her native country.

After the arrival of Lord De la Warre in Virginia, in 1610, the colony enjoyed a long period of prosperity. The mouth of the river, named after its first governor, was discovered by the Captain Argall already mentioned, in one of many exploring expeditions up the coast ; while inland, the huts of the colonists gradually replaced the wigwams of the natives on the Potomac, the Ohio, the Shenandoah, the Rappahannock, etc. In 1619 took place two events, pregnant in results, not only to Virginia, but to the whole of the future Republic of America—the first cargo of slaves was landed at Jamestown, and the first Legislative Assembly met in the same town. In 1622, the growth of the colony was suddenly checked by a terrible disaster, in the shape of a general massacre of the whites at the instigation of the chief Opechancanough, who had then succeeded his brother Powhatan as the leader of the dusky tribes whose homes had been appropriated by the English intruders.

No suspicion of the awful fate awaiting them appears to have dawned upon the unlucky colonists, who, scattered up and down in their farms, were engaged in their usual peaceful avocations, when, on the morning of the 22d March, 1622, the house of every white man was visited by a few armed savages, who, having put to death with horrible tortures all its inmates, sparing neither age nor sex, passed on to aid their brethren in the same terrible work elsewhere. One alone of the many Indians who had been apparently converted to Christianity was true to his adopted creed, and, instead of murdering, warned his master in time for him to make his own escape, and carry the tidings of the approach of the red men to Jamestown.

In a little open boat the two sped down the river, arriving at the capital of the colony in time to avert much bloodshed. Messages were sent to the outlying settlements ; and the Indians, finding themselves outwitted, would have retired to their woods, had not the whites cut off their retreat, and in their turn slain without mercy all who fell into their hands. Throughout the length and breadth of the land desolation now replaced the former plenty, and it soon became evident to the natives that in their wild rising they had sounded their own death-knell. Taught by experience not to trust in the promises of the Indians, the Virginians now gathered more closely together, building large towns, in which the first owners of the soil were only admitted as servants, until at last the fact that they had ever been any thing else passed from the memory of their oppressors.

In 1629, Jamestown was visited, from his little colony of Ferryland, in Newfoundland, by Lord Baltimore, a distinguished Catholic nobleman, who was so charmed with the scenery round Chesapeake Bay, that he asked for and obtained an extensive grant of land on its shores from King Charles I. of England. He died before he could himself take possession of his new territories, but his patent was renewed in 1632 to his son Cecilius, who endeavored to established himself on the south of James River. So bitter, however, was the opposition he met with from the English already in possession of Virginia, that he persuaded King Charles to give him the land on the north instead of the south of the original colony. Here, in that "irregular triangle" formed by the fortieth degree of latitude, the Potomac River and Chesapeake Bay, the second Lord Baltimore planted a little colony of English Roman Catholics, naming their new home Maryland, in honor of Queen Henrietta Maria.

The new emigrants, numbering some three hundred in all, landed on one of the islands at the mouth of the Potomac, now reduced to a mere strip of sand, on the 25th March, 1634, and, after celebrating mass on the beach, planted a cross on the loftiest point within reach, round which a second solemn service was held. From the island, excursions were then made up the river by Leonard Calvert—brother to Lord Baltimore, and first governor of the colony—and a few picked men, with a view to selecting the best spot for a first settlement, resulting in the selection of an Indian village which Calvert succeeded in purchasing from the Indians, with whom also he made an offensive and defensive treaty. To the village thus chosen the name of St. Mary's was given, and to the neck of land in which it was situated that of St. Mary's Point. With truly marvelous rapidity a town of comfortable houses gathered about the native wigwams, and the colony seemed likely shortly to rival in prosperity that of its older neighbor, Virginia, when that neighbor, which had from the first viewed its very existence with jealousy, picked a quarrel with its governor, which finally developed into a bitter war, extending over many years.

As will readily be imagined, this unhappy state of things was terribly detrimental to the progress of an infant community ; but in 1635, peace was so far restored that we find Lord Baltimore making extensive grants of land to new settlers, and in 1637 reference is made in historical documents to the "hundreds" into which the country of St. Mary's had been divided. The loss of the MS. records of Maryland, to which early writers of the colony refer the reader for full details of its growth, renders it impossible to trace the gradual exploration of the country contained within its present boundaries ; but enough has, we trust, been said to account for the presence of the Roman Catholic element in the Southern States of America, and to fit the story of Maryland into that mere outline of the early history of the colonies which is all that the nature of our subject requires. For many touching anecdotes of the ways of the Indians we are indebted to the Jesuit Father White, who, after long ministering to the spiritual necessities of his fellow-countrymen in St. Mary's, wandered about in the wild and beautiful districts on the northern banks of the Potomac, striving to instruct the savages in the mysteries of the Roman Catholic religion. But whatever the discoveries made by him in the various phases of human nature with which he came in contact, he added nothing to our geographical knowledge, and we must, leaving his work and that of many another noble missionary to be recorded elsewhere, turn from the two youngest of the Southern States to tell the romantic story of the planting of sister communities along the rocky shores so long known under the general name of New England.

## CHAPTER V.

WHILE the first germ of the now vast American organization was thus struggling into life in Virginia, the coasts of New England and of Maine were becoming dotted with settlements of different nationalities, and the resources of Canada and the districts bounding it on the north were gradually being revealed by the researches of French and Dutch explorers.

From the time of Jacques Cartier, the French had claimed possession of the Atlantic seaboard from the mouth of the St. Lawrence to the south of the modern province of Maine; and as early as 1536, a certain André Thevet had discovered the mouth of the Penobscot river, and reported very favorably of the capabilities of the districts watered by it, and the friendly disposition of the Indians with whom he had come in contact. No real effort to turn these advantages to account was made, however, until the close of the sixteenth century, when Henri IV. of France sent out the Marquis de la Roche with orders to found a new French empire on the western coast of America. The noble leader of this expedition, charged with so grand a commission, found himself hampered in carrying it out by the fact that the followers who were to form the nucleus of the "empire" were all convicts from the overcrowded French prisons. He contented himself, therefore, with landing them on the desolate shores of Sable Island, off the coast of Nova Scotia, whence they returned home after twelve years of misery, having accomplished literally nothing.

In the following year (1599) a trip far richer in results was made to Canada by a merchant of St. Malo named Pontgravé, and a naval officer named De Chauvin, the latter of whom obtained a commission from Henri IV. similar to that given De la Roche. The sudden death of De Chauvin, after a preliminary trip, prevented him from himself reaping any benefit from the full powers conferred on him; but Pontgravé was so convinced by what he had seen on the St. Lawrence of the commercial capabilities of the country watered by it, that he returned in 1603, this time accompanied by Samuel Champlain, an eager and intelligent student of geography, with whose aid a very thorough survey of the great water highway was made.

Provided with trustworthy maps of Canada, Pontgravé and Champlain soon returned to France, and, as one result of their work, a new expedition was sent out in 1604, led by De Monts, a Huguenot nobleman, who was empowered by Henri IV. to take possession of and colonize in his name, all districts between 40° and 46° N. lat., collectively known as Acadia.

LAKE CHAMPLAIN.

De Monts left France on the 9th March, 1604, taking Champlain with him as a confidential adviser. A short visit to Nova Scotia was succeeded by a cruise in the Bay of Fundy, dividing that Peninsula from the mainland; and after much hesitation, a small island near the mouth of the St. Croix, a river of New Brunswick, was chosen as the site for the first settlement. It turned out an unlucky selection, and as soon as the first winter was over, De Monts and Champlain went down the coast to try and find a more favorable situation. The harbors of Maine were visited one after another, and in any one of them a delightful refuge for the little band of Frenchmen might have been found but for the hostility of the Indians, who, since the time of Thevet, had learned to suspect the sincerity of the white man.

Finally the colony was removed to a port of Nova Scotia now known as **Annapolis**, but then called Port Royal, where it feebly struggled for existence, first under De Monts, and then under his successor, Pourtrincourt, until 1610, when some new life was infused into it by the arrival of certain Jesuit missionaries, who, at the instance of the Marquise de Guercheville, to whom De Monts had resigned his claim to Acadia, proposed making the little colony the nucleus of a church in the wilderness, into which the natives were to be gradually enticed.

The success of the first missionaries was sufficient to induce others to follow their example ; and, in 1613, an earnest Frenchman named La Saussaye arrived at Port Royal, with two more Jesuit priests and thirty-eight men,

MOUNT DESERT ISLE.

with whom, having obtained a guide, he started to sail up the Penobscot, intending to plant a second church at the Indian village of Kadesquit, now Bangor.

A dense fog prevented the mouth of the river being perceived ; and, when it cleared away, La Saussaye found himself opposite the beautiful island of Grand Manan, already visited by Champlain, and called by him Mont Desert, with the mighty rock now known as Great Head standing out against the forest-clad buttresses of the Green and Newport Mountains. So beautiful did Grand Manan appear to the French visitors, and so wide a missionary field seemed opened to them on it and the neighboring islands, that La Saussaye determined to remain there, and having set up a cross as an emblem of his peaceful intentions, he set his men to work to build and plant.

But, alas! Grand Manan was within the limits of the New World already ceded to the English, and before the first crops sown by the French had had time to germinate, Captain Argall—the same who had carried off Pocahontas—sailing up the coast on one of his exploring expeditions from Virginia, heard of the infant settlement, and bore down upon it, bent on its destruction. The French, dreaming of no evil, were, some on land, others, to the number of ten, on board their vessel, at anchor off Bar Harbor.

Boarding the little ship, Argall secretly possessed himself of La Saussaye's papers, including the royal commission under which the Frenchman had acted, and then gave orders for the bombardment of the group of houses which La Saussaye had hoped would have formed the nucleus of the church in the wilderness he had set his heart on founding.

La Saussaye and some of his missionaries were now placed in a boat and sent adrift, to find their way back to Port Royal as best they could. Near the coast of Nova Scotia they were picked up by some fishing vessels, and carried to France. Less fortunate were Father Biard, one of the Jesuit priests, and the secular members of the settlement of Mont Desert, for they were taken to Virginia by Argall, and there thrown into prison by the authorities. They were treated with every possible indignity, until their captor, fearing the consequences to himself, confessed his theft of La Saussaye's commission, and obtained their release.

This was but the beginning of that strife between the French and English for territory belonging to neither, which finally resulted in a world-wide struggle between the two nations. A little later, Argall was sent north, with orders to " remove every landmark of France south of the forty-sixth degree ; " and he accomplished his work with an energy and thoroughness worthy of a better cause. First, every trace of the French occupation was obliterated on Grand Manan ; and then Port Royal, now deserted by all but a little remnant under the leadership of Biencourt, Pourtrincourt's son, was burned to the ground.

The next European visitors to Maine were our old friend John Smith and Thomas Hunt—the shipmaster who, in 1614, made a cruise up its coasts, collecting not only the fish so plentiful in its bays and rivers, but also a number of " savages," who were sent to Spain by Hunt, and there sold for slaves.   Smith—who, as we have seen in our account of his work in Virginia, was a clear-headed and far-sighted man—turned his time to better account than did his comrade, and embodied the results of a careful survey of Maine and the neighboring islands in a map, which he took to England and sub-

CAPTAIN JOHN SMITH'S MAP OF NEW ENGLAND.

mitted to Charles I., urging him to inaugurate a company for the colonization of a country so rich in resources, and to give to that country the name of New England.

The latter part of this advice was followed at once, and the districts now forming the six Eastern States of the Union—namely, Maine, New Hampshire, Vermont, Massachusetts, Rhode Island, and Connecticut—were long collectively known as New England. Its 65,000 square miles of fertile country had already been granted to the Plymouth Company by James I., in 1606, so that no new scheme of colonization was necessary ; but Smith's report so stimulated the zeal of the English that in 1615, Richard Hawkins, then President of the Northern Company, himself sailed to Maine. So terrible a civil war was at that time raging among the natives, that Hawkins effected nothing ; but in the following year, Sir Ferdinando Gorges, one of the most active members of the Company, sent out a physician named Richard Vines at his own expense, with instructions to make a settlement somewhere in New England.

Vines, a hero in the best sense of the term, spent the winter of 1616–17 at a place called Winter Harbor, the exact position of which we have been unable to ascertain, though it was probably somewhere between the mouth of the Penobscot and Cape Cod. He found the Indians afflicted with a terrible disease, which had succeeded, perhaps resulted from, the awful civil war alluded to above ; and by the generous kindness and scientific skill with which he alleviated their sufferings, he so won upon their affections, that he was able to travel alone in the wildest forests, secure of a hospitable reception in every wigwam.

Thus protected by an invisible armor, Vines went up the Saco River till he came to its source at Crawford's Notch in the White Mountains of New Hampshire ; and, when the spring permitted navigation, he cruised in and out of the harbors of Maine till he had acquired a thorough knowledge of their geography.

In 1619, while Vines was still peacefully at work among the Indians, a Captain Dermer was sent out by Gorges to explore the coast of New England. Leaving his vessel at the island of Monhegan, situate about twenty miles South-west of the mouth of the Penobscot, Dermer made his coast-survey in an open pinnace, discovering and passing through the now celebrated Long Island Sound, which divides Long Island from New York and Connecticut. On his return trip, Dermer landed on Martha's Vineyard, where he was severely wounded in a skirmish with the natives, and crossed the strip of country near Cape Cod destined to be the first home of the Pilgrim Fathers ; but he did nothing to further the cause of colonization, and of his career after his voyage nothing is known beyond the fact that he died in obscurity in Virginia soon after its completion.

In 1620, the indefatigable Sir Ferdinando Gorges succeeded in obtaining a new patent for the Plymouth Company from the King, which dissolved its connection with the South Virginia Company, and gave to it all lands between the 40th and 48th degrees of north latitude; thus, as those who have carefully followed the course of our narrative will recognize at once, encroaching alike on the rights of the Southern English Company and of the French, who were now firmly establishing themselves in Canada. Regardless, however, of the clamor and excitement caused by the concession it had won from the English monarch, the new Plymouth Company lost not a moment in availing itself of its extended privileges; and in 1621, the year of the arrival in New England of the Pilgrim Fathers, a grant, to which the name of Nova Scotia was given, was made by it to Sir William Alexander of all lands between Cape Sable and the St. Lawrence.

The Scotch colonists sent out by Sir William to people his new territory, found the spots most suitable for settlement already occupied by fishermen of different nationalities; and, failing to obtain any recognition of their claims, they shortly returned to their native country. The sea-coasts of Maine, New Hampshire, and Massachusetts were, however, still free to the emigrant: and in 1623, Sir Ferdinando Gorges, who had hitherto reaped no personal benefit in return for all his efforts on behalf of his Company, obtained from it, in conjunction with John Mason, a grant called Laconia, embracing all lands between the Merrimac and Kennebec, and stretching away to the great Canadian lakes, of which the first had been discovered by the Frenchman, Champlain, in 1608. A vessel bearing a number of emigrants started for New England in the summer of 1623, and, disembarking on the shores of New Hampshire, founded the two settlements of Portsmouth and Dover.

In the same year, Robert Gorges, a son of Ferdinando, was appointed governor-general over the whole of the lands belonging to the Plymouth Company, and received as his private share in these lands three hundred square miles on Massachusetts Bay. The governor did not, however, care for his new possessions, and, after a flying visit to them, ceded them to Captain Levett, one of his assistants, who made a thorough exploration of Maine, and built a house on its shores, to which he gave the name of York. A permanent English settlement was also founded in Maine, in 1625, by two merchants of Bristol, Robert Aldworth and Giles Eldridge by name, who, having bought the Monhegan Island and a neighboring point of the mainland, quickly converted their desolate shores into flourishing colonies. In 1630, too, we find our old friend, Richard Vines, rewarded at last for his long years of work among the Indians by a grant of land on the Saco, while an estate of similar extent on the other side of the river was given to his comrade, John Oldham. From these two concessions sprung the towns of Biddeford and Saco ; and looking round upon the results obtained at various points by different members of the Plymouth Company, under the energetic superintendence of Sir Ferdinando Gorges, before the expiration of its patent in 1635, we find English communities growing up throughout the length and breadth of Maine. It is round the little band of Puritans, however, who settled, by sufferance as it were, on the rocky shores of Cape Cod, in the neighboring province of Massachusetts, that the most absorbing interest gathers ; and their history—as that of men who founded religious and political liberty in the future United States, and who are proudly claimed as ancestors by the noblest of our American cousins—must be given in some detail here.

To account for the presence of English Puritans on American shores, it is necessary to go back a few years, to the beginning of the reign of James I., when the brief respite from persecution, enjoyed during the closing years of Elizabeth's life by the aspirants after a purer ritual than that sanctioned by the State, was succeeded by yet greater oppression than any hitherto endured.

At the little village of Scrooby, in the midland counties of England, a small body of separatists, under the ministry of William Brewster, were in the habit of meeting regularly for worship, and by their zeal and good works were winning to their own persuasion large numbers of the common people, when their elder and two of their chief members were summoned before the Ecclesiastical Commission of York for heresy, and condemned to pay a fine of £20 each. This was but the beginning of evils ; fines were succeeded by imprisonment and indignities of every kind ; and warned by previous experience—some of their co-religionists had fled to Holland a few years before—the Scrooby separatists resolved, like them, to seek a refuge in the Protestant Republic. To the number of 200, the Puritans, most of them well-to-do men, disposed as quietly as they could of their lands and houses, and agreeing to meet at Boston, in Lincolnshire, stealthily made their way from the homes they were willing to forsake rather than abjure their belief.

A large number succeeded in embarking on board a vessel bound for Holland in Boston Harbor, but they were betrayed by the captain, who handed them over to some officers in quest of them. They were searched, robbed of all their valuables, and marched back to Boston. A month's imprisonment was succeeded by a second attempt at escape, ending even more disastrously than the first. A Dutch ship was this time engaged to convey the sufferers for their faith to Holland, and it was arranged that the embarkation should take place at a lonely spot somewhere between Grimsby and Hull. The women and children were sent to the rendezvous in a small vessel ; the men marched thither in small parties by land. All seemed likely to go well. The two detachments met on the low sands of the Lincoln shores, and eager greetings were exchanged between husbands and wives, fathers and little ones. The men were embarking on the Dutch vessel, on which their families were to join them immediately, when a loud tumult suddenly arose on the beach, and down rushed a mob of country people, wild with delight at having arrived in time to cut off the heretics.

The few men already on the Dutch vessel were carried off, whether they would or no, by its affrighted master ; and of the remainder, some endeavored to protect the women and children, while others hurried off in different directions and escaped. From one magistrate to another the luckless emigrants who had been taken prisoners were marched, bearing themselves so nobly and simply in their trial, that many were won over to their belief, and the hearts of others, even in those unrelenting days, were touched. No magistrate would convict them of any worse crime than a desire to be with those belonging to them, and, after much wandering to and fro, a public subscription was got up on their behalf, which enabled them to take ship for Amsterdam, where, in the winter of 1608, nearly the whole of the original Scrooby congregation met once more. Even in Amsterdam, however, their rest was not to be ; for, in the little English community which had already settled there, disputes, some of them most trivial in their character, had arisen, and the Scrooby people had therefore little heart to join it. They had had enough of conflict with foes at home to make them sick of strife, and more than sick of strife among brethren ; and so, with their pastor at their head, they moved on to Leyden.

For a time the sufferers enjoyed peace in the land of their exilé. Their pastor, Brewster, and his able coadjutor, Robinson, administered the affairs of the little community with gentle wisdom. The names of Carver, Cushman, and Winslow stood out as those of burning and shining lights in a congregation where all were earnest and zealous. But, as in all human institutions, there came a change. Not suddenly, but gradually, almost imperceptibly, error crept in. The purity of the faith was threatened by foreign error. The young folks growing up, who had but a dim recollection of the native land where they had unconsciously borne witness for the truth, were showing an undue appreciation of the delights of the world.

After many a solemn consultation, it was resolved that the little church should be transplanted, if possible, to the virgin soil of America, where it would have room to grow and spread, unhampered by any of the restrictions by which it was, in the very nature of things, hedged in in Leyden.

In 1617, when Virginia had already been settled for several years, and the Dutch had successfully colonized a considerable portion of New England, Robert Cushman and John Carver were sent to England to try and obtain from James I. a patent, granting to the Scrooby Puritans lands in North Virginia, with the assurance of religious liberty. A whole year was consumed in unsatisfactory negotiations; and finally, the deputies from Holland were compelled to be content with a private message from James, that he would connive at the settlement in America of their brethren, though he could not give them his public sanction. On the strength of this, however, a patent was obtained from the Virginia Company in 1619, granting to a certain Mr. John Wincob—who was to be a kind of lay figure in the transaction, taking no active share in the matter—some lands on the Hudson. As the Dutch were already in possession on either side of that river, the Pilgrim Fathers endeavored to obtain, in addition, some sanction from them for their presence among them, but they were entirely unsuccessful; and it was finally agreed that one hundred members of the congregation, many of them women and children, should embark, under the care of Brewster as their spiritual pastor, and Carver as their civil governor, and take their chance

THE MAYFLOWER AT NEW PLYMOUTH.

of finding a home in the New World. When they had done so, the remainder of their brethren, with the beloved Elder Robinson, were to join
them.

Two vessels were chartered for this apparently humble enterprise—the
*Speedwell*, which was to convey the pilgrims from Holland to Southampton,
and the *Mayflower*, which was to await their arrival at the English port.
On the 22d July, 1620, after a day of solemn humiliation and prayer, the
advance guard of the deserted little church marched out among their breth

LANDING PLACE OF THE PIL-
GRIMS, AT PLYMOUTH.

ren, and embarked on the *Speedwell* in Delft harbor, arriving in due
course at Southampton, where the *Mayflower* lay at anchor.

A fortnight later, both vessels set sail for America; but, before much
progress had been made, the *Speedwell* was compelled to put into Plymouth
Harbor, being found utterly unseaworthy. This caused a delay of a month;
and it was not until the autumn had begun that the *Mayflower* made her
final and solitary departure from Plymouth, with all who remained faithful
to their purpose on board. A stormy voyage of sixty-five days brought the
now world-famous little vessel in sight of Cape Cod, and, after an unsuccess-

ful attempt to bear southward for the mouth of the Hudson, anchor was cast opposite the low coast, which had already been the refuge of so many tempest-tossed wanderers to the West.

On the 11th November, 1620, after a solemn agreement among all the pilgrims to hold to each other and submit to their governor, John Carver, the first landing was effected. Falling on their knees upon the beach, the emigrants now returned thanks to God for their merciful deliverance from the perils of the deep, and, this pious duty over, sixteen men, under the doughty Captain Miles Standish, were sent forth on a reconnaissance, while the women busied themselves in washing their travel-soiled garments, and making preparations for the general comfort.

The result of the reconnaissance was far from satisfactory. Standish and his men had to cut their way through dense underwood, and were unable to open any communication with the natives, who fled at their approach. A little maize which had been buried by the Indians as their store for the winter was all the wanderers brought back to the vessel from the promised land.

Later trips being equally unsuccessful, the emigrants re-embarked, and the *Mayflower* was taken a little further up the western coast of Cape Cod, whence excursions were made to different points in an open boat by a few sturdy explorers, who landed on Clark's Island—so called after the first man to step on its shores—and finally, on the 11th December, crossed the modern harbor of Plymouth, and landed on or near the rock which has since been revered as the

BIBLE BROUGHT OVER IN THE MAYFLOWER, IN PILGRIM HALL, PLYMOUTH.

sacred "corner-stone of a nation," the "altar and bulwark of religion and liberty."

Convinced that the fertile, well-watered tract stretching away from the sea to the pine-clad hills was the very site for a settlement, the men hastened to report their discovery to their expectant comrades on board ship, and on the 15th December, the *Mayflower* left her anchorage off Cape Cod to sail to Clark's Island and halt half between it and the rock of Plymouth, so-called in remembrance of the port in the south of England from which the little vessel had made her final start.

On Christmas Day, 1620, after the site for the erection of the first house of the new settlement had been chosen at a spot called by the Indians Pa-

tuxet, and christened Plymouth by the new-comers, the main body of the emigrants went on shore. Many are the traditions which have gathered round the rock—of which a portion is still shown to visitors—on which these founders of a great nation first set foot, and in all of them the names of the governor, Carver, and the military captain, Standish, stand out as those of men who were equal to every emergency. A dreary winter, with starvation and disease staring the settlers in the face at home, and hostile Indians hovering about in the outskirts of the little encampment, ready to take advantage of any

TOMB OF THE MATE OF THE "MAYFLOWER."

sign of weakness, was succeeded by a somewhat brighter spring, and toward the end of March, 1621, as the leaders of the colony were discussing their future plans in full conclave, an incident occurred which inspired them with new hope of the successful realization of those plans.

A naked Indian suddenly stalked into the midst of the white men, and greeted them in their native tongue with the words, "Welcome, Englishmen!" The sensation caused by this may be imagined. The Indian, who said his name was Samoset, was eagerly plied with questions, and told how he had been one of the men carried into slavery by Hunt, who, it will be remembered, had accompanied John Smith on his visit to Maine. After many vicissitudes, Samoset had got back to his native land, and, hearing from his comrades that some white men had settled at Patuxet, he had come to make their acquaintance, and to inquire if they came with peaceable intent or as man-stealers. Convinced that they were certainly not the latter, though probably a little puzzled at the explanations given of their presence so far from home, Samoset promised to be their messenger to the Wampanoags and Nansets of the neighborhood, assuring the chiefs of the colony that

the hostile attitude of these tribes had been the result of the ill-treatment they had received at the hands of Hunt and Dermer.

A few days after this first interview, Samoset b r o u g h t some other friendly Indians to Plymouth, including a certain Squanto, who had been taken to England by Weymouth fifteen long years before, and brought back by Sir Ferdinando Gorges. The presence of Samoset and Squanto in their midst w a s fruitful of the best results to the colonists. By t h e i r means, a treaty, offensive and de-

WINSLOW'S VISIT TO MASSASOIT.

fensive, was made between the white men and the greatest chief of the neighborhood, a stately warrior named Massasoit, dwelling at a village on Rhode Island ; and, free from the fear of surprises, the colonists were now able to extend their plantations and sow seed for future needs. Small parties were detailed to explore the bay, the site of the modern Boston was visited, and the close of the first summer found the affairs of Plymouth in a very flourishing condition.

In November, 1621, a reinforcement of thirty-five emigrants arrived from England in the ship *Fortune*, and the first fruits of the labors of the early colonists, consisting of timber and furs, were sent home in her. The second winter passed over successfully, but the spring of 1622 opened gloomily. A terrible massacre of the whites had taken place in Virginia, and, encouraged by the success of their brethren in the south, the Narragansetts of Massachusetts sent a message of defiance to the colonists of Plymouth, thinking that the time had come to possess themselves of the goods of the intruders in their land. The war-challenge of the red men consisted in the sending to the camp of the enemy of a bundle of arrows bound together with a rattlesnake's skin ; the reply of the English was the return of the same skin full of powder and ball—a silent indication that they were ready for the arrows, which the Indians did not fail rightly to interpret.

A lull ensued, and the English were beginning to hope that the real exchange of arrows and shot would not come off, when there arrived from England a little party of emigrants who were not Puritans, and who, while they consumed the stores of their fellow-countrymen, did nothing to help to replace them, and, moreover, imbittered their relations with the Indians by stealing their corn and carrying off their women. After much mischief had been done, the governor, Bradford, who had taken the place of Carver on his death in the previous spring, succeeded in weeding out the evil-doers from among his flock, but not, unfortunately, in warding off the results of their misconduct. At their young settlement of Weymouth, on the northern shores of the Bay of Plymouth, the new colonists behaved in a manner which excited alike the anger and contempt of the natives. It was decided that they should be exterminated, and as their white comrades at Plymouth would doubtless try to avenge them, these must be slain at the same time.

All was ready for the massacre of both parties, when Massasoit, who had made the first treaty with Carver, was taken dangerously ill. Knowing nothing of the plot laid by him against them, the English of Plymouth sent two of their members, Edward Winslow and John Hamden, to express their sympathy with him, and, if possible, relieve his sufferings. Arrived, all unsuspicious of the danger they were running, at the village of Pokanoket, on Rhode Island, the two Christian emissaries found Massasoit in what seemed a dying condition, but Winslow suggested several remedies, which had an apparently miraculous effect. The strength of the dying chief returned to him, and, to the astonishment of all, he sat up and called for food, which he had not been able to swallow for several days. In a short time he was completely restored to health, and in his gratitude to his visitors he revealed to them the plot against the two colonies, adding that he had been urged to join in it himself, but had refused. He recommended the white men to return home without delay, and to defeat the plot against their people by slaying the ringleaders, whose names he gave at once.

Back again in their camp, Winslow and Hamden lost no time in laying the information of which they were possessed before their leaders, and it was at once resolved to send out a small party under Miles Standish, first to warn the colonists at Weymouth, and then to get the Indians named by Massasoit into their power.

With eight men—he refused to take more, lest his object should be guessed at by the natives—Miles Standish started on his hazardous enterprise in a little shallop, and went by sea to Weymouth, where he found the colonists in a terrible condition, scarcely able to subsist on the scanty supplies which were all they had brought with them, and subject to perpetual insults from the Indians, who appeared to be determined to get as much sport as possible out of them before the final blow was struck.

Having relieved the immediate necessities of his unlucky fellow-countrymen, and directed them to keep together as much as possible, Standish endeavored to open negotiations with the Indians, but they had lost all fear of the white men, and met his advances with ridicule. See-

MILES STANDISH'S SWORD, POT, AND PLATTER—PRESERVED IN PILGRIM HALL, NEW PLYMOUTH.

ing that it was absolutely necessary to make an example, although hitherto no blood had been shed by the

Puritans, the Christian captain succeeded in enticing two of the ringleaders, Pecksuot and Wituwamat by name, into a house, and there slew them, assisted by two or three of his men. The result was what he had anticipated— the heads being gone, the minor members of the conspiracy fled. A few English, who had neglected the advice to keep together, were murdered, and one or two other Indians fell in a fitful struggle between scattered parties at isolated points. The general massacre was averted, however, and out of

FANEUIL HALL, BOSTON.

consideration for the benefit to all obtained by his severe measure, Captain Miles Standish was forgiven by his superiors for the shedding of blood, though, on hearing of the affair, Mr. Robinson wrote from Holland, "Concerning the killing of those poor Indians . . . oh, how happy a thing had it been if you had converted some before you had killed any."

The energetic conduct of Standish, however it may have been judged by those who were not on the spot, was, so to speak, the foundation-stone of the prosperity of the Plymouth colony, which henceforth grew with wonderful rapidity, sending out offshoots in various directions, which in their turn, became in due course parent communities. Internal difficulties with certain schismatic members, named Lyford and Oldham, were dealt with in the same rigorous manner as those with the Indians ; and though the first result—condemnation of the conduct of the settlers by the London members of the Plymouth Company—seemed, by cutting off their supplies, to threaten their very existence, it resulted in the breaking up of a confederation which had long held within its heterogeneous elements the seeds of dissolution. Left entirely to their own resources, the Puritans developed new energies ; and they were already carrying on a brisk trade with the Indians, when there came news of the settlement of some rival colonists on Cape Ann, which the Plymouth people considered to be within their territory.

Captain Standish was sent out to deal with the intruders, and found that they consisted of a little band of fishermen sent out by an obscure Company known as the Dorchester, and included among them, not only Lyford and Oldham of troublous memory, but also the sufferer for righteousness' sake, Roger Conant, who had long ago left Plymouth on account of his religious opinions, and was now a leader among the new colonists. Brought face to face with his fellow-countrymen, Standish seems to have hesitated how best to deal with them, and to have been persuaded by Conant to leave them un-molested. From this slight incident arose great results. No longer in dread of their lives, Conant and his companions presently removed from the dreary shores of Cape Ann to Naumkeag, now Salem, on the mainland, and there throve so well, that the Dorchester Company was moved to send forth others to their assistance. A patent was obtained from the original New England Company, granting to its rival a tract of country between the rivers Charles and Merrimac, and to this new home a sturdy reformer named John Endi-cott led forth a few Puritan pilgrims in 1628. In 1629—by which time the numbers of his colony had been doubled, though by what means is not ex-plained—Endicott was joined by John Winthrop with no less than 800 emi-grants, who, after resting a while at Salem, dispersed in small parties in various directions within the limits of the territory assigned to them, some among them settling at the Indian village of Mishawan, or the Great Spring, to which the name of Charlestown had been given by a few of Endicott's settlers a year or two before.

In the course of the ensuing year, 1630, when the Dorchester had devel-oped into the more imposing Massachusetts Bay Company, the emigrants received many fresh additions to their numbers ; and early in the summer a little party moved from Charlestown to Shawmut Point, where the modern city of Boston now stands. The capital of Massachusetts—which still re-

tains in its quaint, irregular streets something of the impress of its rugged
founders, the Puritans—was begun, says Bryant, in a frolic, the first settlers
to land on its beach having been a boat-load of young people, who, after a
playful struggle as to who should first disembark, yielded that honor to
"Anne Pollard, a lively young girl, the first white woman who ever stepped
on the spot" so memorable in the history of the United States.

The earliest settlement of Europeans at Shawmut was begun in August,

HOUSE IN BOSTON WHERE THE TEA PLOT IS SUPPOSED
TO HAVE ORIGINATED.

1630, and was at first called Tri-mountain, on account of the three summits
then crowning one of the high hills overlooking the harbor, and which, now
known as Beacon Hill, bears the imposing State House. On the 7th September, the settlement being then considerably advanced, it was resolved that
it should be called Boston, in memory of the city of that name in Lincolnshire, from which many of its inhabitants had come.   To complete the early
history of Boston, we must add that its site, with all the surrounding country, was claimed by a certain Blackstone, an Englishman, who had long

before settled near a "fountain of sweet waters," which in those days bubbled up somewhere on the present Common. His title as original occupier was considered to be superseded by the royal grant to the Pilgrims, but in many accounts of the matter we find it recorded that in 1635 John Blackstone received £35 for the relinquishment of his "right."

The foundation of Boston was succeeded by that of many other now famous towns of Massachusetts, and, ten years after the arrival of Conant at Salem, 21,000 emigrants are said to have settled in New England, one and all being Puritans, most of whom had been driven from their homes in their native land by the intolerance of the Government. Among those Puritans, however, were many who were unable to conform to the rigid practices or subscribe to the stern tenets of the Massachusetts churches, and to this fact was due the foundation of the first settlement in the neighboring state of Rhode Island. In 1631, a certain "godly minister," named Roger Williams, arrived at Boston with his wife, Mary, and, finding the congregation there not entirely to his taste, he repaired to the older community of Salem, and for some little time acted there as assistant preacher, winning much love from the people by his earnest zeal and loving sympathy, but shortly becoming involved in serious trouble with the elders of the church on account of his heretical opinions.

Banished to Plymouth, and there but coldly received, Williams employed his exile in learning the Indian dialects, and printing a work on them which created great astonishment in England. In 1634 he returned to Salem, where he was eagerly received by his people, but was soon again compelled to flee, for questioning the right of the settlers to take the lands of the Indians without purchase. Our old acquaintance, Winthrop, now Governor of Massachusetts, who appears to have had a private leaning toward the en-

thusiastic young reformer, gave him a hint that he would do well to go to
Narragansett Bay in the South, that being without the jurisdiction of any
English Company, while it was within reach of the Indians, whose love he
had won by his championship of their cause. To the Bay, therefore, though
it was now mid-winter, Roger directed his course, and, early in 1636, he
found a refuge with the chief, Massasoit, whose life had been saved by the
English nine years before, and who now gave his white brother some land

PROVIDENCE, RHODE ISLAND.

on the Seekonk River, east of the modern Providence, where in the early
spring the lonely hero built himself a home. He was soon joined by a few
friends from Salem; and, having received a kindly hint from Governor
Williams of Plymouth, that he would be less likely to be interfered with on
the other side of the river, the site of his house being within the original
grant to the Pilgrim Fathers, he removed with his companions to the Indian
village of Mooshausick, to which he gave the name of Providence, in "gratitude to God's merciful providence to him in his distress, and also because

he hoped his new home might be a shelter for those distressed in conscience."

The dream of Williams was realized. "Slate Rock," as the stone on which he landed from his boat on the Seekonk in his search for a new home was called, soon became worn with the tread of the oppressed, who came to him for help in their troubles, fleeing, some from the bigotry of the Boston Puritans, some from the vengeance of the authorities for civil offenses. As a matter of necessity, the Providence colony, recruited from such sources, was not only a thorn in the side of the Massachusetts Company, but one presenting special difficulties to its founder, who, however, in spite of much trouble in the flesh, was pre-eminently successful in all he undertook. Two years after his first arrival, he bought extensive tracts of land on Rhode Island, and in 1642 his little community was so prosperous, that he went to England to obtain a charter for the colony he had founded. On his return to Providence, he was able to be of great use to the other colonies in their dissensions with the Indians, who looked upon him as their champion ; but his heresy was never forgiven, and when, in 1643, a confederation for mutual protection was made between the New England colonies, Rhode Island was left out.

Roger Williams was, however, but one of many to go forth from the original Massachusetts colonies and found new communities, each of which, while sharing the general character of the Puritan settlements, was distinguished by some special religious peculiarity, into the nature of which none but the initiated could enter with full appreciation. In 1631, intercourse with the Indians of the Connecticut Valley—already, as we shall presently see, colonized by the Dutch—was opened by a visit to Boston of Wahginnacut, a sagamore, or chief, from the river Quonchtacut, on the west of Narragansett, who gave the whites a general invitation to settle in his country, which he reported to be very fruitful.

In 1633, one William Holmes, taking with him a few sturdy followers, and also the frame of a house ready to set up in a suitable locality, left Plymouth in obedience to the call of the sagamore, and, in spite of the opposition of the Dutch, opened a successful trade with the Indians, although, so far as we have been able to ascertain, he failed to make any permanent settlement in the new district. This was, however, atoned for by the emigration to the Connecticut Valley, in the fall and winter of 1634, of several different parties from Massachusetts, who made their way on foot, (driving their cattle before them through the pathless forests, and settled on the various rivers, enduring terrible hardships in the first winter, but holding their own through privations which would have daunted any but the stern Pilgrim Fathers, already inured to suffering.

The little town of Windsor was already a thriving community, carrying on a brisk trade with the natives in furs, when, in 1635, John Winthrop, son of the Governor of Massachusetts, arrived from England, bearing a commission as Governor of Connecticut under the patent of Lord Say and Seal, Lord Brook, and others, to whom the district had previously been granted. Winthrop's first care was to build a fort at the mouth of the Connecticut, to which he gave the name of Saybrook, in honor of his two noble patrons. The Dutch, who claimed the whole of Connecticut—in right of prior discovery and possession, and, best title of all, purchase from the Indians—had, three years previously, fastened the arms of the States-General to a tree, at a spot they had named Kievit's Hoeck and now dispatched two vessels from the South to maintain their rights.

Before the vessels could arrive, however, the Dutch arms had been torn down, and a hideous, grinning face carved on the tree-trunk in their stead, while the landing-place was defended by two cannon, which were enough, in those primitive days, to scare away a whole party of warriors.

This energetic beginning was followed up by other vigorous proceedings, and so prosperous did the colonies founded by Winthrop become, that a tide of emigration to Connecticut rapidly set in, alike from the mother country and from her dependencies. In the latter end of 1635, thousands of pilgrims arrived from England, and in June, 1636, the whole of the church of Newton, one of the later communities of Massachusetts, led by its ministers, Hooker and Stone, went forth to seek, in the fruitful lands in the South, a freer field for their spiritual growth. The narrative of their journey reads like a chapter of romance. Their cattle were driven before them, and Mrs. Hooker, who was an invalid, was carried in a litter in their midst. The leaders on horseback, the remainder on foot, threaded their way slowly through the vast forests of Massachusetts, and, after a tramp of many weeks, they reached the site of the present town of Hartford, so called after the English home of Stone.

Here a final halt was made. Building and cultivating at once began, and Hartford bid fair soon to rival Windsor in prosperity, when the first low muttering of the storm which was to involve old and new settlements in one common ruin was heard in the distance. The natives, alarmed by the rapid growth of the power of the English, began that series of aggressions which resulted in the first great Indian war; but before we enter into its details, we must turn for a moment to the South, and account for the presence of the Dutch as neighbors of the New England settlers.

The close of the sixteenth century witnessed the overthrow of the Spanish power in the Netherlands, and, relieved from the oppression under which it had so long groaned, the Dutch republic was able, like the rest of the world, to turn its attention to that golden prize, the short passage to India, the supposed existence of which had instigated so many important expeditions from other countries. Already, long before their independence was acknowledged by the Spanish, the United Netherlands possessed a navy second to none in Europe, and, in the very year (1597) of the signing of the Treaty of Utrecht, the advanced guard of Dutch geographers were struggling for their lives in the dreary solitudes of Nova Zembla.

Leaving the adventures of Barentz, Heemskerk, and others, we join, as the first Dutchman to travel in the districts now under consideration, the celebrated Henry Hudson, who, after one or two unsuccessful voyages to the North-east, under the auspices of the English Muscovy Company, was invited, in 1609, to take service with the Dutch East India Company. He consented, and was appointed by his new employers to the command of yet another expedition to the extreme North, his instructions, however, being this time of a sufficiently elastic nature to admit of his altering his course if desirable.

Hudson set sail from Amsterdam on his new trip, on the 4th April, 1609, in a modest little vessel named the *Half Moon*, with a crew of some sixteen or eighteen Dutch and English sailors, and, having crossed the Atlantic in safety, he steered due north for Nova Zembla. Before long, the ice, as he had expected, effectually barred his progress, and, after a consultation with his men, he determined to alter his course, and seek for a south-west passage somewhere to the north of the English colony of Virginia. A flying visit for fresh water was then paid to the Faroe Islands, and, after touching at Newfoundland, the *Half Moon* sailed down the coast of North America, anchoring on the 18th July, in a large bay, probably that of Penobscot. Here a party of Indians, already used to peaceful trading with the French, came out in two canoes to make acquaintance with their visitors, and were met—to the shame of the Dutch be it spoken—by a boat-load of armed sailors, who took many of them prisoners, and afterward burned their village. This outrage completed, the *Half Moon* proceeded on her voyage, passing Nantucket and Martha's Vineyard, and even, it is supposed, entering Chesapeake Bay, though without holding any intercourse with the Europeans there established.

At Chesapeake Bay, Hudson once more turned his vessel's head northward, and, cruising along the coast, discovered what was afterward, in honor of the first governor of Virginia, called Delaware Bay. No south-west passage had yet been found, but on the 3d August the watchers on deck saw what they took to be the mouth of three rivers, and which turned out to be the beautiful harbor now forming the entrance to the capital of the New World.

Foiled in his attempt to enter the broadest of the three "rivers" by the bar at its mouth, Hudson ordered the *Half Moon* to be steered into the deeper bay, now known as Sandy Hook, and there passed the night in anxious expectation as to what the morning would bring to light. That morning dawned on a scene of exquisite, and still, in spite of its changed aspect, of world-famous beauty. The island of Manhattan, Long Island, the Narrows, and many another familiar physical feature of the Bay of New York, were there; but instead of the bristling fortifications and the well-built residences of wealthy citizens of New York of the present day, the shores of mainland and islands were dotted with native wigwams—instead of the fiery little gunboats and stately men-of-war now guarding the entrance to the great metropolis, the canoes of Indians were shooting hither and thither, in undisguised astonishment at the sudden apparition of the *Half Moon*.

A quarrel with the Indians inaugurated the first day's work at the mouth of the Hudson, as it had done that on the Penobscot; but the death of one Englishman, a certain John Colman, was in this case the only untoward result. The whole of the shores of the Bay of New York were thoroughly explored, and the great river itself, named after its discoverer, was then entered.

Past the low shores of Manhattan Island, and into the vast expanses of the Tappan Zee and Haverstroo, sailed the *Half Moon*, entering beyond them the lovely scenery of the Highlands, which rise abruptly to a height of some 1,200 to 1,600 feet on either side of the broad waters of the Hudson, until at last the mighty Catskill Mountains, stretching away in silent grandeur on the right bank of the river near its junction with the Mohawk, were sighted, and navigation became difficult, the stream daily growing shallower and shallower.

On the 18th August, 1609, Hudson landed near the site of a town now bearing his name, where he was most hospitably entertained by an old chieftain. On the 19th he passed the site of the present Albany, and on the 22d he came to the rocky promontory close to which the modern village of *Half Moon* now stands, at which point he decided to retrace his steps, the river being apparently too shallow for further navigation.

The return trip down the Hudson was, alas! darkened by a terrible act of

THE HALF MOON AT THE MOUTH OF THE HUDSON.

oppression on the part of the white men. An Indian, one of a crowd of visitors who had come down from the mountain to see the wonders on board the *Half Moon*, was carrying off a few trifling articles he had stolen, when he was detected by the mate, who at once shot him dead. A general *mêlèe* ensued, the natives were hotly pursued by Hudson's men, and, though only one other was then killed, the next day a party of dusky warriors bore down upon the European vessel; a fierce struggle took place, and though the Dutch were victorious, all hope of further exploration was at an end. Differences with his superior officers, and quarrels among his crew, added to the difficulties of Hudson; and when, in November, 1609, he put into Dartmouth Harbor after having made one of the greatest discoveries of the day, he found himself in disgrace both with the English Government and his Dutch employers, who were each jealous of the other.

To make our story complete, we may add that, after a vexatious delay at Dartmouth, Hudson resumed service under the Muscovy Company, and, with its sanction, sailed in the spring of 1610 on the fatal voyage which resulted in the discovery of the great bay bearing his name. Sailing northwestward, in an English vessel, with a crew of twenty-three men, Hudson reached Greenland in June, and made his way thence without delay to the wide strait giving access to the vast inland sea now known as Hudson's Bay.

Astonished at a discovery so little expected, and convinced that great results might ensue from the thorough exploration of the country around, our hero resolved to winter in these desolate latitudes, and pursue his work in the spring of 1611. The failure of his provisions compelled him, however, to relinquish this grand scheme, and the belief which obtained among his men, that he intended to return home, leaving some of them behind to perish miserably, caused a mutiny. Hudson, his young son, and one or two sailors who remained true to him, were overpowered, placed in a boat, and cast adrift on the waters of the bay he had discovered at so terrible a cost; and of his further sufferings, or of his final fate, no rumor has ever reached Europe, though an expedition was sent in quest of him from England.

Meanwhile the Dutch, eager to precede the English in taking possession of the fertile districts watered by the Hudson, lost not a moment in following up the discoveries inaugurated by their Government, and in the three years succeeding Hudson's first voyages, one private merchant after another sent out agents to trade with the natives and found colonies among them. As early as 1613, Manhattan Island owned its Dutch fort and surrounding buildings, and was chief among many stations for the collection of peltries, or furs, and their dispatch to European ports; while the bays of the mainland as far south as the mouth of the Delaware, were dotted with clusters of the huts of the Dutch fishermen.

Among the leaders of the various early Dutch enterprises in these regions, Hendrick Christansen, Adriaen Block, and Cornelis Jacobsen May stand out pre-eminent: the first as having founded the first large fort—that called Nassau—on the Hudson; the second for his exploration of Long Island

Sound, and discovery of the Connecticut river ; and the third for his survey of the coast of New Jersey, still commemorated by the name given to New Jersey's southern headland—Cape May.

On the 11th October, 1614, after long and tedious preliminary negotiations, a charter, insuring to them a monopoly of the fur trade for three years, was granted to the Dutch, and the name of New Netherland given to the region between New France and Virginia—*i.e.*, the Atlantic seaboard between 40° and 45° N. lat. These three years, during which no rival European power interfered, were turned to the best account by the sturdy colonists from Holland, and their scouts penetrated far into the interior on the west, one party, it is supposed, having reached the upper waters of the Delaware, and descended it in native canoes to the mouth of its tributary, the Schuylkill, which is now known to rise in the carboniferous highlands of Pennsylvania, and to join the Delaware five miles below the capital of that state.

The story goes, that, on this last named expedition, three traders were taken prisoners by the Indians, and held by them as hostages, until their prolonged absence exciting the anxiety of their comrades, an expedition was sent in quest of them, under the command of Cornelis Hendricksen, who, in a little yacht named the *Restless*, explored the whole of Delaware Bay, ascended one of the rivers flowing into it, and brought back his fellow-countrymen in triumph.

On Hendricksen's return to the parent settlement, he gave such glowing accounts of the capabilities of the new " havens, lands, and places " visited, that his employers—their original charter being then on the eve of expiration—determined if possible to obtain another, giving them more ample powers. Their petition was refused ; but, in 1621, a far more important enterprise than theirs was sanctioned by the States-General of the Netherlands, who granted to the now famous West India Company a monopoly of all the lands known by the Dutch as New Netherland, and which included much of the territory to which the English had given the name of New England.

The first emigrants to take advantage of the extensive privileges of the West India Company were a little band of Walloons, members of that much-persecuted and sturdy race, descended from the old Gallic Belgæ, whose brave struggle against the Germans in the old mountain fastnesses of the Ardennes had saved them from extermination. The same constitutional impulsiveness and perseverance, activity and skill, which kept the Walloons alive and prosperous throughout all subsequent changes in their native land, rendered them well fitted to fight their own battle in a new scene ; and when the Dutch authorities heard of their expulsion from their homes on account of their religious opinions, they most wisely invited them to settle in New Netherland.

The first city founded by the Dutch under the new charter—or, to be more strictly accurate, by the Walloons, under the West India Company—was the modern Albany, the capital of the present State of New York, which was at first called Fort Orange, and was the second town of importance built within the limits of the United States, Jamestown having been the first. The foundations were laid in 1623, and in less than a year it had become a flourishing settlement, while trading stations established at the same time on Manhattan Island, the Delaware, Connecticut, and other rivers, grew with equal rapidity. In course of time, difficulties with the Indians led to the temporary abandonment of Fort Orange, and the building on Manhattan Island, on a site purchased for twenty-four dollars, of Fort Amsterdam, round which clustered the town long known as New Amsterdam, and now under its English name of New York—it having been taken by the British in 1664—the chief city and most important seaport of America.

The climax of Dutch prosperity in America was reached about 1635, when the settlers in New Amsterdam became involved in difficulties with the English of Connecticut, who drove them, step by step, and little by little, from every outpost they had gained. In 1636 began the terrible Indian war in which the English and Dutch were alike involved, and all the Dutch inhabitants of Staten Island were murdered by the fierce Algonquins ; and in 1637 a company of Swedes and Finns, most of them religious refugees, arrived in Delaware Bay, where, having purchased extensive territories from the Indians, they quietly established themselves, calling their American home New Sweden, and their first fort, built at the mouth of the Delaware, Fort Christiana, after the young Swedish Queen.

In vain did the Dutch protest against what they looked upon as an invasion of their rights. Settlement after settlement of Swedes was established on both banks of the Delaware, and not until 1655 were the Dutch able to gain possession of New Sweden, which, however, ten years later, fell, with the whole of the Dutch territories of America, into the hands of the English.

INTERIOR OF A DUTCH HOUSEHOLD IN EARLY NEW YORK.

# CHAPTER VI.

WHILE the English were firmly establishing themselves in New England, and the Dutch and Swedes were struggling for the mastery in the present states of New York and Delaware, discoveries of vital importance were being made by the French in Canada, or as it was then called, New France. We have already mentioned Samuel Champlain, who accompanied both Pontgravé and De Monts in their early expedition to Maine, and was the author of the first scientific map of the St. Lawrence. It was this Champlain, a true hero of geographical discovery, who paved the way for the establishment of French power in Canada, and to whom we, as the successors of the French, owe an undying debt of gratitude.

In the winter of 1604, when the little settlement at Port Royal was struggling in that feeble infancy destined to be its only existence, Champlain made it the starting point for many a trip to the South, visiting Cape Cod—which his men named Cape Blanc, from its far-stretching white sands—long before the landing of the Pilgrim Fathers. In 1608, when Pourtrincourt, the successor of De Monts, had returned to France in disgust, and Henry Hudson was preparing for the great voyage resulting in the discovery of the river named after him, Champlain was starting with a few faithful followers on an overland journey through perfectly untrodden districts watered by the St. Lawrence.

On the 3d July, after crossing the whole of Maine in a north-westerly direction, so far as we can make out from fragmentary records of his work, Champlain reached Stadacona, where, it will be remembered, Cartier spent his first winter on the St. Lawrence, and at once set to work to erect a fort, to which the name of Quebec was given, either then or very shortly afterward.

The winter was spent in winning the friendship of the Algonquin Indians, chief of the three races then occupying the basin of the St. Lawrence, and in learning from them the capabilities of their country. In a terrible struggle then going on between the Algonquins and their neighbors, the Iroquois, or Five Nations, Champlain was able to give both advice and material assistance, and, as a reward, he was escorted by the former, in the spring of 1610, up the St. Lawrence as far as its junction with the Iroquois, now the Richelieu River, ascending which he discovered Lake Peter, and came, after some little difficulty with the rapids, so characteristic of the tributaries of the

THE FIRST HOUSE ERECTED IN QUEBEC.

great river, to the beautiful sheet of water now bearing his own name, and which has so often figured in the history of the struggle between the French and English in Canada.

Though prevented by the hostility of the Iroquois, or Five Nations—occupying the whole of the South-west of Canada—from actually visiting them, Champlain, on this trip, approached very nearly the sources of the Hudson in the lofty Adirondack Mountains, on the south-west of the great lake, and in the north-eastern corner of the present State of New York, thus connecting his own work with that of his great Dutch contemporary.

The discovery of Lakes Peter and Champlain may be said to have closed the first chapter of our energetic hero's career. On his return to Quebec, he found that De Monts's commission, under which he had been acting, was revoked, compelling him to return to France to obtain fresh powers. In this he was unsuccessful; but he agreed with De Monts to persevere in his undertaking without royal patronage, and in 1610 we find him again on the St. Lawrence, prevented from pursuing his geographical researches by the fierce struggles still going on between the two native tribes, but binding the Algonquins yet further to his service by the efficient aid he was able to render to their cause.

QUEBEC.

On the restoration of peace in 1611, Champlain, after having paid a second flying visit to France for supplies, ascended the St. Lawrence as far as its junction with the Ottawa, and founded the modern city of Montreal, near the hill which had been named Mont Royal by his predecessors. In 1613, leaving both his infant settlements in a flourishing condition, he started, accompanied by several Frenchmen and an Indian escort, on an exploring expedition up the Ottawa, having heard rumors that it came from a lake connected with the North Sea.

The early part of the voyage up the great tributary of the St. Lawrence was full of difficulty, owing to the number and force of the cataracts and rapids impeding navigation ; but, now carrying their canoes through the woods, now dragging them with ropes through the foaming current, the explorers reached the home of a friendly chief, named Tessouant, only to learn from him that the information on which they had acted was false.

Returning to Quebec after this disappointing trip, Champlain again sailed to France in the hope of obtaining fresh recruits for his infant colonies. Aided by the powerful co-operation of the Prince of Condé, he succeeded in equipping a little fleet of four vessels. These, filled with emigrants—including four fathers of the Recollet order, the first missionaries to settle in Canada—all well provided with supplies for the ensuing winter, arrived safely at the mouth of the St. Lawrence early in May, 1615, and on the 25th of that month we find the indefatigable explorer pushing on with a few picked men to the Lachine rapids, which had been fixed on as the rendezvous of the Indian tribes, who were again about to push forward against the Iroquois, encamped among the Great Lakes on the west, never yet visited by a European.

Here was an opportunity not to be lost, and Champlain at once offered to aid the Algonquins and Hurons in making the best disposition of their forces, if they on their part would allow him to join them. The compact was made, and, surrounded by the wild red-skins in their picturesque war-paint and other martial trappings, the white men marched in a north-westerly direction—first up the Ottawa, and then, turning due west, past a number of small lagoons—till they came to Lake Nipissing (N. lat. 46° 16' W. long. 80°), where the natives received them with eager hospitality.

After a rest of a couple of days, the dusky warriors and their pale-faced guests resumed their march, and following the course of a stream now known as the French river, they came to the present Georgian Bay, forming the eastern side of the great Lake Huron, called by the French traders of more modern times the Mer Douce, on account of the remarkable freshness and clearness of its waters. Crossing Georgian Bay in the native canoes near the island of Great Manitoulin, or the Sacred Island, running parallel with the western half of the northern coast, the invaders landed, and, marching northward, were soon joined by a fresh body of Algonquin warriors, with whom they passed several days in feasting and dancing, after which the combined forces turned their steps southward, reaching Lake St. Clair, lying between Lakes Huron and Erie, near the modern city of Detroit, in a few days.    Here they came in sight of the first Iroquois fort, a primitive but well-built structure, skillfully defended by rows of modern palisades.

A fierce struggle ensued, in which Champlain was twice wounded, and the Iroquois warriors defended their town with such skill and bravery that the Canadian Indians were compelled to retreat.    In this retreat Champlain suffered terribly, having been carried, as was each of the disabled warriors, in a small basket, his body being bound into a circular form with strong cords to make it fit into the cramped space.    Released from this unusual position on arrival in the friendly Huron country, our hero and his men begged to be provided with guides and canoes for the return journey to Quebec ; but they were refused, and the white men had to spend the whole of the winter among the frozen lakes.

In the spring of 1616, after making themselves well acquainted with the resources of the neighborhood in the frequent hunting excursions in which they took part, the little band of explorers managed to effect their escape, and, accompanied by a few friendly natives, made their way back to Quebec, where, for a time, Champlain had to give all his attention to the internal affairs of the colonies, now large communities, holding within their heterogeneous elements many a seed of discord.    Trip after trip to France for supplies resulted in the arrival of many new emigrants, but it was long before peace was sufficiently established for any fresh exploring expeditions to be undertaken.    Moreover, the Mohawks, Oneidas, Onondagas, Senecas, and Cayugas, the five nations forming the great Iroquois confederacy, elated by their victory, in spite of the well-organized expedition against them, advanced from their quarters on Lakes Erie and Champlain to within a short distance of the French outposts, resolving to involve the Algonquins and their white allies in one common doom.

In 1626 a noble, but, as it turned out, mistaken attempt at conciliation, made by Champlain, resulted in a terrible tragedy.    Some captive Iroquois, who were about to be tortured by the Algonquins, were sent back to their own people uninjured, accompanied by an Algonquin chief and a Frenchman named Magnan, who had instructions to negotiate a peace between the rival tribes.    This did not, unfortunately, suit the Algonquins, who had hoped with the aid of the French to exterminate the Iroquois, and they therefore sent a message to the latter, warning them that treachery was intended, and that the Frenchman and his companion were spies.

Arrived at the Iroquois camp, the two unlucky emissaries found a large pot boiling over a fire, and were invited to be seated. The chief was then asked if he was hungry, and on his saying yes, a number of armed Iroquois rushed upon him, cut slices from his body, and threw them into the pot. This awful torture was continued till he died in the greatest agony, when the Frenchman was put to death with torture, though of a somewhat less revolting form.

Gladly would Champlain, convinced of the fatal mistake he had made, have taken summary vengeance on the savage warriors, but, alas! he was

INDIAN WARRIORS.

powerless to do so. The few settlements at Ladoussac, Three Rivers, and other advanced points on the St. Lawrence, would have presented an easy prey to the Iroquois, and there were no forces at Quebec or Montreal fit to cope with the thousands who would have swept down upon the whites from the Lakes, at the first sign of weakness among them. At this very time, too, the English were casting longing eyes at the rich fur-yielding grounds of the Canadian backwoods, and would gladly have shared in the cod and whale fisheries of the Gulf of St. Lawrence. A Huguenot refugee, named

Kirk, actually obtained a commission from Charles I. to conquer Canada, and for that purpose anchored a little squadron at the mouth of the St. Lawrence in the summer of 1628, sending a summons to Quebec to surrender.

As a matter of course, Champlain, although literally driven to bay, with the Indians on one side and the English on the other, returned a spirited answer of defiance, which, to his surprise, resulted in the withdrawal of his enemies, who were totally ignorant of the real state of affairs. A year later, however, Kirk returned, this time sailing up the St. Lawrence, and casting anchor off Quebec. Resistance was hopeless, and Champlain was compelled to surrender his "capital;" but, struck by the noble bearing of his opponent, and by the courage with which he had evidently so long been waging a hopeless contest with the natives, Kirk granted the most liberal terms to the French, who were allowed to remain undisturbed in their homes, which were, moreover, now secured to them by English troops from the raids of the savages.

In the autumn of the year of the taking of Quebec, Kirk left that city under the charge of his brother Lewis, and returned to England, accompanied by Champlain, who hoped to obtain by diplomacy what he had been unable to gain by force; and so earnestly did he plead his cause with the French ambassador in London, that the affairs of New France were brought before the then all-powerful Cardinal Richelieu.

Convinced of the vast importance to his country of the fur-trade and fisheries of Canada, the French Minister negotiated with the English Court for the restoration of Canada, Acadia, and Cape Breton, and after much discussion they were transferred to the French Crown by the treaty of St. Germain de Sage, which put off for more than a century the establishment of the British dominion in Canada.

A year or two before this event, so auspicious to French interests in the West, a new association had been formed in France, known as the "Company of the Hundred Associates," to whom Louis XIII. had given the whole of Canada and of Florida—though the latter, as we are aware, was already claimed by Spain—together with a monopoly of the fur-trade. The cod and whale fisheries of the Gulf of St. Lawrence, however, the French monarch reserved for himself.

The joy of the Company of the Hundred Associates, on the restoration of the privileges which had so suddenly been snatched away from them by Kirk, may be imagined. They at once elected Champlain Governor of New

France, and he returned to his old home at Quebec in 1633, taking with him a large party of new settlers, including many Jesuits, who were to form the nucleus of a college for the education of the youth of Canada, from which missionaries were to be sent forth for the conversion of the natives.

Having patched up something of a peace with the Indians, and founded his college, Champlain prepared to continue that part of his work which was nearest his heart—the further exploration of the country ; but before he could organize an expedition to the West, his career was cut short by death. He expired in December, 1635, having sown the seeds of the future greatness of Canada, and inaugurated a new era of geographical discovery.

Champlain was succeeded as Governor of Canada by M. de Montonaguy, a man of a very different stamp, who, while displaying great ability and address in his management of the internal affairs of the colony and his dealings with the treacherous Iroquois, did little to extend our knowledge of the country under his charge.

To continue our narrative of the progress of discovery in French America, we must leave the ruling powers to join two obscure Jesuit missionaries, named Brébœuf and Daniel, the advance guard of that heroic band of laborers for the faith of Christ who led the way in every early expedition from Canada, and with whose names is associated the origin of every great town on the vast inland seas which are now among the proudest possessions of England.

Brébœuf and Daniel, who had both already done good work among the natives, left Quebec on their joint mission in 1634, with a party of Huron Indians, and after just such another arduous journey through the forest and up the Ottawa as that taken by Champlain a few years before, they arrived safely on the banks of Georgian Bay. Here they pitched their tents, and in a short time they gathered about them a little band of converts to the Roman Catholic faith, for whose use a little chapel, built of the trunks of trees, was presently erected, which was dedicated to St. Joseph.

To this little center of civilization in the wilderness flocked many natives and Europeans alike, who were eager to lead a new life—the former won over by the hopes held out to them for the future, the latter eager to forget the past. First one and then another Christian village arose on the banks of the stream connecting Lakes Huron and Ontario, from which every now and then some worn father of the faith would pay a flying visit to Quebec, to return with fresh recruits. Such was the origin of St. Louis, St.

Ignatius, St. Mary's, and many another now flourishing town of Canada, which were yet in their infancy when the news of the great work going forward in the West reached the ears of the Pope himself. Struck by the vast field thus opened for the extension of the Roman Catholic religion, the Holy Father expressed his loving approval of the work of his children in the land of their exile. The King of France followed suit ; the enthusiasm spread to his nobles, and, eager to win the favor of the heads of their church and of their native land, numbers of young French gentlemen of rank joined the missionary band, and devoted their wealth to its cause. The result was what might have been expected. Montreal became the headquarters of the Indian church, St. Mary's, lying about half-way between it and Lake Huron, the rendezvous of the missionaries from distant points, who met three times a year to give an account of their progress.

Six years after the first arrival of Fathers Brébœuf and Daniel on Lake Huron, the missionary outposts had extended as far west as Green Bay, on the north-west of Lake Michigan ; and though the iron belt of the Five Nations still kept the French from the shores of Lakes Ontario and Erie, Brébœuf was able in 1641, accompanied by Father Joseph Marie Chaumonot, to visit the Onguiaharas, a neutral tribe living on a river of the same name, now the Niagara.

The Onguiaharas—who appear to have acted as mediators between the Iroquois and the Hurons and Algonquins, members of the rival tribes meeting in peace in their huts—informed Brébœuf that they were themselves at deadly war with a fierce nation living on the west, which they called the Fire Nation, and described as so reckless of human life, that the French did not care to venture among them while so much still remained to be done around the Great Lakes.

Though so near on this occasion to the now world-famous Falls of Niagara, Brébœuf does not appear either to have heard of them or to have visited them. He collected, however, a good deal of information respecting the habits of the natives, which are embodied in the charming *Relations des Jesuites*, from which the greater part of our early knowledge of the Canadian Indians is derived. In the same year (1641) of this first visit to the Niagara River, two missionaries, named Charles Raymbault and Claude Pigart, made their way to Lake Nipissing—the most north-westerly point reached by Champlain—arriving there just in time to witness a grand native ceremony in honor of the dead, which they describe as extremely imposing.

NIAGARA FALLS,

Lake Nipissing was on this occasion almost covered with the canoes of the warriors, moving solemnly toward that point of the shore where the souls of the departed were to be fêted. Under a long, rough shed, in coffins of bark, wrapped in costly furs, lay the decaying bones of those who had gone to the other world ; and over them a song, half of triumph, half of regret, was sung by the warriors, the women accompanying them with a wailing cry, full of unutterable melancholy.

INDIAN BURIAL GROUND.

When these heathen rites were over, the Jesuit fathers, who, with that earnestness and thoroughness which characterized their whole body, had prepared themselves for their mission by the study of the Nipissing language and the Nipissing mode of thought, came forward and addressed the assembled multitudes. They spoke of the Saviour of the white man and of the red, who came back from the grave after laying down His life for all mankind ; and so worked upon the already melting mood of the hardy warriors of the West, that they obtained permission to dwell on the shores of Lake Nipissing—nay, more, an eager invitation from some Chippeway guests to visit them in their own homes beyond Lake Superior.

The eagerness with which this opening was seized may be imagined. The Chippewayans, or Athabascas, one of the four families of the great Finnish nation, occupied that great lone land stretching away beyond the north-western banks of Hudson Bay, which has even yet not been fully explored. In those vast solitudes, though the missionaries knew it not, dwelt many a strange tribe, living out its destiny in unconscious simplicity. There roamed the Copper, the Horn Mountain, and the Beaver Indians; the Strong-bows, the Dog-ribs, the Hares, the Red Knives, the Sheep, the Sarsis, the Brush-wood, the Nagailer, and the Rocky Mountain Indians, waiting the advent of the fur-trader, from whom they were to receive their distinctive appella-tions, and to whom they were to yield up the treasures of their deserts and of their mountain fastnesses.

Taking a Jesuit named Isaac Jogues, as his companion, and leaving Pigart to continue his work among the Nipissings, Raymbault started for the North-west, and, crossing Lake Huron in a native canoe, the voyage occu-pying seventeen days, he arrived safely at the mouth of the straits connect-ing it with Lake Superior, where two thousand natives were eagerly await-ing his arrival.

The point of land on Lake Superior where the white men first stepped ashore appears to have been near the rapid known as the Sault Ste. Marie, at the beginning of the river St. Mary, through which the waters of Lake Superior flow into Lake Huron; and it was probably within sight of the gray and red sandstone cliffs called the Pictured Rocks, which now look down upon the boundary-line between British America and the United States, that Father Raymbault took up his abode, to begin his ministrations among the Chippewayans. Unfortunately, however, his health began to fail him before he had been at work a year, and, after a farewell visit to the Nipissing converts, he retired to Quebec to die.

Jogues, meanwhile, on whom his superior's mantle should naturally have fallen, was working out a very different mission; and though the Chippe-wayans were not forgotten, and we find Ste. Marie again a missionary station a few years later, it was the fierce Iroquois who were next to receive a Christian minister among them. Sent down the St. Lawrence on a message connected with Raymbault's work, the second missionary, a friendly Huron chief named Ahasisteri, two young French laymen, and some twenty-six Hurons, fell into the hands of a party of Mohawks, who had long been eager for a feast of human flesh, and looked upon the whites and their escort as lawful prey. To quote the quaint Father who sent home an account of the matter, if peace could not be made with the Iroquois, no Frenchman would be safe from "finding a tomb in the stomachs of these savages."

That Jogues this time escaped this awful fate was indeed little short of a miracle. He was marched with his companions in misfortune through three Mohawk villages ; he saw Ahasisteri burned to death, and one of his own young Indian converts tomahawked for making the sign of the cross on a baby's forehead ; yet, for some reason unexplained, his own life was spared, and having managed to get away from his party, he wandered about in the woods, carving the name of Christ on the bark of the trees, till he came in sight of the Dutch fort at Albany, and was received by its commandant, Van Cuyler, having been the first white man to cross the northern half of the present state of New York.

From Albany, Jogues was unable to return direct to Canada, either by sea or by land, and he therefore took ship for England, whence, after suffering many things at the hands of Falmouth wreckers, he managed to get back to the land of his adoption. Here he found all the French stations in a state of horror-struck excitement, owing to the increasing hostility of the Iroquois. A Father Bressain, who had fallen into one of their ambushes, had seen his Huron comrades killed and eaten, and had himself been rescued only at the last moment by Dutch traders. Other horrors, too terrible to be related, had been inflicted on the native converts to Christianity, and in 1645 a solemn assembly of all the French authorities was held at Three Rivers, with a view to the negotiation of peace with the terrible enemy. After much private consultation among themselves, and many a picturesque palaver with the Indian sachems, who came to the meeting decked out in all their finery, the French were cheered by the conclusion of "eternal peace" with the Five Nations. This peace actually lasted a whole year, and at the end of that year seemed so little likely to be broken, that Jogues, in spite of all his previous sufferings, resolved to venture again to the south of the St. Lawrence, and try to win over some of the Iroquois to Christianity.

In June, 1646, we find the heroic Jesuit embarking on the Iroquois, now the Richelieu, escorted by four warriors of that nation and two young Algonquins, his object being to found a church among the Onondagas. He arrived safely at a little village at the head of a small sheet of water connected with Lake Champlain, called by the natives Andiatarocté, or the Gate of the Lake, to which he gave the name of St. Sacrement. After a short cruise on the "Gate," and the presentation of gifts to the Iroquois chiefs and elders who happened to be assembled on its banks, Jogues returned to the St. Lawrence to report progress, and in September of the same year—this time accompanied by a young Frenchman—he once more visited the Iroquois, intending to settle among them and teach them Christianity.

All went well at first, but at the beginning of 1647 Jogues received instructions from his superiors to go to the Mohawk country, with a view to insuring peace with its savage warriors, who were showing signs of breaking the solemn treaty made at Three Rivers. The Jesuit obeyed, though he is reported to have said, "I shall go, but I shall never return." He was right. He had scarcely set foot among the Mohawks, before he and his fellow-countryman were taken prisoners, charged with having blighted the corn and caused a famine. Stripped half naked, they were dragged into a neighboring village and there put to death. Not until long afterward did any details of the tragedy reach Quebec. A Mohawk prisoner, taken in a struggle with the French on the St. Lawrence, and condemned to death for his share in an ambush into which the white men and some of their Algonquin allies had fallen, confessed before his torture began that he had himself killed Jogues, and another member of his tribe the missionary's companion.

No more vivid picture of the struggle between savagery and civilization in the early days of Canada could be conceived, than the account sent home by a Jesuit of the young Mohawk's death. This Mohawk had told how he and another had invited Jogues to supper, and when he arrived in the half-naked state to which he had been reduced, a savage, who had hidden behind the door of the tent where supper was prepared, started out and struck off the head of the unsuspecting guest. The head was stuck on the palisades of the village, as a warning to all other Europeans, and on the following day that of the young French layman was placed beside it.

One would have thought that, after this frank acknowledgment of his own share in the murder, no mercy would have been shown to the Mohawk. But here the true character of the Jesuits came out. Die he still must, and that at the hands of the Algonquins, with all the subtle cruelties in which they were adepts ; but there was no reason for him to die in his sins. The short time before the execution was to take place was devoted to converting him to Christianity ; and just before he was given up to the native chief who was to preside at his death, he was baptized Isaac, in memory of the man he had helped to martyr. Poor Isaac is said to have cried again and again on our Saviour in his agony, and to have said, when dying, "I have to thank Antaiok" (so he called the Frenchman who had taken him prisoner) "that I am going to heaven ; I am very glad."

The murder of Jogues was the signal for another Indian war ; and for a time the French missionaries and laymen alike were absorbed in the primary duty of the defense of their own lives and of those dear to them. Through all the tumult and confusion which ensued, however, the geographical student may, by eager searching, trace the continuous opening up of new districts, and on the blank map which was spread out before us when we began our narrative, we may dot down the names of many a river and lake almost unconsciously discovered by the white men, in the very height of their struggle.

The storm broke first on the village of St. Joseph, now almost entirely Christianized. The able-bodied members of the community were away at the chase ; the women and children fell an easy prey to the Mohawk warriors. Father Daniel, the head of the mission, while administering the last rites of the church to the dying and the dead, fell at last beneath the poisoned arrows of the Iroquois, and was finally dispatched by a blow from a hatchet. Next St. Ignatius and then St. Louis were overpowered, and in the latter our old friend Brébœuf and his companion Sallemand met their death, the first after three, the second after seventeen hours of torture.

From St. Louis, the tide of invasion swept westward to Georgian Bay, where the Hurons had made a feeble effort to rally. Again they were defeated, and in their despair they sent a message by Father Dreuillette, a zealous missionary who had long been at work among the north-west tribes, to New England, with an entreaty for succor. But, as we shall presently see when we return to the colonies on the coast, the energies of the newly-formed federation were all required to meet the necessities of home defense, and no help came to the sufferers in the north. Dreuillette worked his way back by a new route to the St. Lawrence, that was all. Three years of almost constant massacres, in which many a noble death was met, alike by native converts and their teachers, were at last succeeded by a lull. The Iroquois were sated with bloodshed ; or, as some of the French authorities tell us, their hearts had been touched by the teaching of some of their prisoners. In any case, peace was made in 1650, and it was scarcely concluded, before a missionary was ready to risk his life by making a fresh effort to convert the men at whose hands his brethren had already suffered so much.

A certain Father Le Moyne, who had been the envoy intrusted by the Hurons with the ratifications of peace, pitched his tent on the Mohawk River, and a little later an Italian priest named Dablon, and a French missionary named Chaumonot, settled at Onondaga, chief village of the tribe of the same name dwelling on the banks of the Oswego, a river of the modern state of New York flowing into Lake Ontario. Wonderful to relate, they not only escaped death, but were received with eager welcome. A chapel sprang up as if by magic, and Chaumonot soon found himself in a position to visit the Senecas, the most powerful of the Five Nations, who lived far away in the west of the present State of New York, on a lake named after them, which is connected with Lake Ontario by the rivers Oswego and Seneca. Here, as at Onondaga, the natives seemed glad to receive the good tidings of the Gospel; but, as they declined to interpret "peace on earth" beyond the limits of their own tribe, and persecuted their neighbors the Eries with reckless cruelty, their missionary soon found himself at issue with them.

Disputes now arose, and of a little body of fifty Frenchmen who had settled on the Oswego, thinking the days of the old horrors were over, several were murdered. This, of course, aroused the terror and indignation of the survivors, who were compelled to make their escape as best they could, reluctantly accompanied by the missionaries. So ended the second attempt at converting the Iroquois; but not all the good seed sown was lost, and now and again, afterward, some fierce warrior of the Five Nations gave touching proof that he had not forgot the teaching of the good white men.

Meanwhile, the work of the missionaries in opening up the districts about the Great Lakes was being largely supplemented by energetic fur-traders, and in 1656 two young Frenchmen, accompanied by a number of Ottawas, appeared at St. Louis, astonishing their countrymen in that now flourishing settlement by the accounts they gave of yet other inland seas far away in the West, and yet other native tribes, differing in almost every respect, alike from the Hurons, Algonquins, and the Iroquois.

Here was a new field for missionary effort, and Dreuillette, the unsuccessful messenger to Maine, and Gareau, a Huron missionary, were chosen to lead the way in this fresh spiritual campaign. Accompanied by some of the Ottawas already mentioned, they were ascending the Ottawa, when they were attacked by the Mohawks, and Gareau was killed. Dreuillette, however, escaped, and advanced into the present Ontario, making his way thence to the banks of the Saguenay, long since discovered by Cartier, whence he undertook several short trips to the North-east, of which, however, few details have been preserved, though they greatly paved the way for the advance of the fur-trade.

While Dreuillette was laboring in the North, René Mesnard, who had been one of the missionaries to the Iroquois, excited by the accounts given by two fur-traders, who had spent a winter on the banks of Lake Superior, started to found a church among the fierce Sioux, or Dacotahs, dwelling in those remote districts. He reached the southern shores of Lake Superior in the autumn of 1660, and in the spring of the following year began his journey toward the modern state of Minnesota, which lies between the south-western extremity of the great lake and the Dakota territory. Letters describing his progress were occasionally received at Quebec, but they suddenly ceased ; and after much anxiety on his account, rumors were brought in by traders that he had become separated from his companions, and lost his way in the forests on the south of the Bay of Chagwamegan, and must have perished miserably. The event proved that they were right. Mesnard's body was found in the forest by a native, who long concealed the fact, lest he should be accused of the murder of the white man. The cassock and breviary of Mesnard having, however, been preserved as amulets by the Sioux, led to inquiries being made, and the truth was discovered.

In 1665, a fresh impulse was given to missionary effort in Canada by the transference of the country to a new West Indian Company, under the direct patronage of Louis XIV., who, recognizing the importance of the rich fur-yielding districts of New France, sent out a regiment to protect the traders. True, about this time New Netherland was conquered by the English, who thus became very formidable rivals to the French ; but the Iroquois still separated the two European nations, and yet a little longer the evil day of the loss of Canada was deferred.

The first hero to go forth under the new government was Father Allouez, who, following in the footsteps of Mesnard, arrived on the banks of Lake Superior early in September, 1666. Embarking on its waters in a native canoe, he reached the village of Chagwamegan, on the bay of the same name, where members of no less than ten different native races were assembled, discussing how best to prevent a threatened war between the Sioux and the Chippewas.

Scarcely pausing to rest after his long journey, Allouez advanced into the very midst of the dusky crowd, and, partly by promises of present help against the common enemy, partly by his eloquent description of the joys of eternity to the true believer, he quickly made many converts. He had, as it were, dropped down from the skies, straight from the home of the

Good Spirit. He was invited to remain; and accepting the hospitality tendered to him, he founded the mission of St. Esprit, to which, in an incredibly short space of time, flocked Hurons and Ottawas, with members of distant western tribes whose very names had never before been heard of; the Potawatomies, or worshipers of the sun, the Illinois, the Sacs, the Foxes, and many another race, sinking their differences for a time in their common eagerness to share the good tidings of great joy which the white man was said to have brought.

Now, for the first time, were heard whispers of the existence, not very far away from St. Esprit, of the great Father of Waters, the Mesipi, which flowed on and on forever to the south between vast prairies, where roamed the buffalo and the deer, where forests were almost unknown, and the wind swept unchecked over the tall whispering grasses.

Convinced that, from all he heard, the people on the Mesipi were ripe for the reception of the Gospel, and little dreaming of the identity of this great river with that of which the mouth had been discovered by De Soto so many years before, Allouez paid a visit to Quebec in 1668 to win recruits to go forth into the prairies. As usual, there were plenty of volunteers. Three short days after his arrival at the capital he was on his way back to Chagwamegan, accompanied by Louis Nicholas, and followed by Claude Dablon and James Marquette, who, as a preliminary step for the work before them, founded the mission of St. Mary's on the Falls, between Lakes Superior and Huron, close to the spot where the Chippewayans had had their first interview with a white man a few years previously.

From St. Mary's, which shortly became a rendezvous for young men anxious to help in the great movement, small parties went forth among the tribes dwelling on Lake Michigan, founding new missions on the site of the present Chicago, Milwaukee, etc.; and in 1669, Marquette, who to the zeal of a missionary added that of a geographical explorer, conceived the idea of navigating the great river. The Potawatomies assured him that the natives who dwelt on the Father of Waters would assuredly slay him, or, if he escaped their hands, he would be swallowed up by the monsters which haunted the deep places in the river. The French authorities were loth to consent to what seemed likely to end in a mere useless loss of life; but Marquette was resolute. He turned the long delay, before he could get permission to start, to account by learning something of the Illinois language, and in founding a kind of city of refuge for the scattered Hurons on the northern shores of Lake Michigan, which long formed a "key to the West, and rendezvous to the distant Algonquins under the protection of the French."

In 1670, leaving Allouez and Dablon to continue their explorations in Eastern Wisconsin and Northern Illinois, Marquette at last started for the South, accompanied by Joliet, a trader from Quebec, five young Frenchmen eager for adventure, and two Algonquin guides. Crossing Green Bay in birch-bark canoes, the little band of explorers ascended the Fox river, flowing into Lake Michigan on the west, for some little distance, and then crossed the country to the Wisconsin, on the banks of which they were very kindly received by a number of old men belonging to the Kickapoo, Mascoutin, and other tribes.

Here the guides, afraid to enter the Sioux territories and to face the horrors of the unknown South, returned to their homes, and the Europeans embarked alone upon the Wisconsin, down which they paddled for several days, eagerly scanning the prairies on either side for the first traces of the wild tribes of whom they had heard. Not a sign of human life was seen, however, until they came to the junction of the Wisconsin with the Mississippi itself. They found the great river without difficulty, and, to quote Marquette's own words, "they happily entered it with a joy that can not be expressed."

Down the glorious river, between the modern States of Iowa and Illinois, the two little canoes now floated, till, about sixty leagues below the mouth of the Wisconsin, our heroes noticed the trail of men on the western bank of the Mississippi. Determined at once to learn something of the people of the newly-discovered districts, Marquette and Joliet hastened to land, and, crossing one of the beautiful prairies of Iowa, they soon came to a group of three villages, one on the bank of a river, and two on a hill a little distance off. The river was the Moingona, now called Des Moines.

Four old men now advanced from the village on the stream, bearing with them the calumet of peace, a tobacco pipe, with a reed stem some two or three feet in length, ornamented with many colored feathers. Already familiar with this sign of amity, the white men knew they had now nothing to fear. The villagers were *Illinois*, which is the Indian word for "men;" and men they quickly proved themselves to be. Conducted to the wigwam of an aged chief, the French explorers were plied with eager questions; and when they told of the breaking of the power of the Iroquois by the "great

Captain of the French," the assembled "men" greeted the announcement with shouts of joy. Then followed the usual instruction in the broad truths of Christianity, and again the "men" rejoiced, doubtless connecting in their simple untutored minds the two items of good news. A grand feast was held in honor of those who had brought them, and when it was over, the visitors were escorted to their canoes by the chief and hundreds of his followers.

With a peace-pipe, the parting gift of the Illinois, hung round his neck as a charm against future dangers, Marquette continued his course, which now led him between the present States of Missouri and Illinois, among the weird perpendicular rocks forming so characteristic a feature of this part of the country, till he came to the junction of the Mississippi with its mighty and turbulent affluent, the Missouri, where the city of St. Louis now stands.

THE MISSISSIPPI AT ST. LOUIS. (1885.)

Overwhelmed with delight at the beauty of the scene before him, Marquette could hardly refrain from entering the Missouri then and there, to trace it to its source; but curbing his ardor—to be, as he vainly hoped, indulged at some future time—he continued his course down the now greatly augmented Mississippi, passing its junction with the Wabash or Ohio, and the homes of the peaceful Shawanees, till, with Tennessee on one hand and Arkansas on the other, he approached the most northerly limit reached by De Soto. There could be no doubt now of the identity of the Father of Waters with the Miche Sepe to which the Spanish hero had been led with the remnant of his forces by his Chickasaw guides ; and Marquette felt that his work was practically done. He determined, however, to enter the land of the Arkansas, and reached the village of the Mitchigamea (N. lat. 33°), where, for the first time on this wonderful trip, the natives came out against him with hostile intentions. Armed with bows and arrows, clubs, etc., the Arkansas warriors closed round the little birch-bark canoes in their own

larger vessels, and it seemed for a moment as if the fate of the intruders was sealed ; but, rising up among the gesticulating crowds, Marquette held his calumet aloft, and, as if by magic, the weapons sunk, and the yells of rage were converted into shouts of welcome.

On the following day, Marquette and his people were escorted, by the very men who had been so eager for their blood, to the village of Arkansea, and here, having learned that the Father of Waters pursued its

MOUTH OF THE OHIO RIVER.

course in a south-easterly direction to the Gulf of Mexico, our hero resolved to turn back. The return voyage up the Mississippi was little more than a repetition of the descent, till its junction with the Illinois was reached, when the canoes were embarked on the waters of the latter river, and a new land, consisting chiefly of extensive and fertile prairies, was entered. The men of Eastern Illinois showed themselves true brethren of the members of their tribe who had so hospitably received the French on the western side of the great river, and the explorers, after resisting all entreaties to take up their abode on the Illinois, were escorted in a north-easterly direction to Lake Michigan by way of Chicago, and arrived safely on the northern shores of Lake Michigan, after an absence of about two years.

A little later, Marquette went as a missionary to northern Illinois ; and after converting many of the Indians about Chicago to the faith, he started for north-eastern Michigan, intending to found a mission there. Having set up an altar on the little river bearing his name, he asked his guides to leave him alone for a short time, and when they returned to seek him, he was found dead. He was buried in the sand near the town called after him, and is still revered by the natives and settlers of the Lake districts, many of whom are said to invoke the aid of St. Marquette when in danger in their frail canoes.

While Marquette's career was thus cut short before he had even begun the realization of his dream of ascending the Missouri, the work he had commenced on the Mississippi was carried on by a man of a very different character. On his way back to Quebec, from his trip with Marquette, Joliet became acquainted with Robert Cavalier de la Salle, Governor of Frontenac, now Kingston, a French outpost on Lake Ontario, who had already made himself thoroughly acquainted with the immediate neighborhood. Fired by what he heard from Joliet, La Salle resolved to obtain permission from the King of France to go down the Mississippi, and open a trade in buffalo-hides with the Indians of the South. He hastened to France, and returned the same year, accompanied by an Italian soldier named Tonti, and provided with full powers from his sovereign.

The adventurers—with Father Hennepin, who accompanied them as missionary, and some sixty followers, including boatmen, hunters, and soldiers—began their journey, in the autumn of 1678, in a canoe built under La Salle's direction at Kingston, which carried them safely down the Niagara river and across Lake Erie to Fonawauta Creek, near the Falls at the southern extremity of the lake. Here some months were spent in cultivating the friendship of the Senecas and constructing a little sailing vessel of sixty tons, to which the name of the *Griffin* was given. The *Griffin* was successfully launched on Lake Erie on the 7th August, 1679, and entering the narrow strait called Detroit, on which the city of the same name now stands, she rapidly carried the expedition into Lake Huron, and thence through the Straits of Mackinaw to Lake Michigan, on the north-eastern shores of which a little colony was planted.

Lake Michigan was now traversed, and, landing on the shores of Green Bay, La Salle made what turned out to be the fatal mistake of sending the *Griffin* back to Niagara laden with furs, with orders for her captain to return with provisions with as little delay as possible. The *Griffin*, alas! went down with all on board before Niagara was reached ; and, ignorant of her fate, La Salle, Tonti, Hennepin, and a few followers went down Lake Michigan to St. Joseph, on the south-eastern shores, whence they made many interesting excursions into Illinois, discovering Lake Peoria, and winning many friends, alike among the Illinois and the Miamis of Michigan.

As time went on, however, and no tidings came of the ill-fated *Griffin*, which had been constructed at the cost of so much time and labor, the spirits of the party began to sink—a fact to which the name of Crevecœur, given to a fort built near Lake Peoria, bore striking witness. After many a consultation as to the best course to pursue, it was resolved that La Salle should return to Frontenac to obtain news and supplies, and that, during his absence, Tonti and Hennepin should remain at Crevecœur with the greater number of the followers.

Tonti, though deserted by most of his men as soon as their leader's back was turned, remained bravely at his post, until he was compelled to flee to Lake Michigan by an incursion of the Iroquois ; while Hennepin, with two companions, descended the Illinois to its junction with the Mississippi, which he ascended till he reached the beautiful fall in N. lat. 45°, between the modern states of Wisconsin and Minnesota, and to which he gave the name of St. Anthony, after his patron saint. From the Falls, Hennepin made several excursions among the Sioux, by whom he was for some little time held captive ; but, escaping from their hands unhurt, he returned to Green Bay by way of Wisconsin, and thence to Quebec.

Meanwhile, La Salle, on his arrival at Frontenac, found that he had been long supposed to be dead—that his creditors had seized his property—and that his good ship *Griffin* had never reached Niagara. Cast down, but not in despair, at this accumulation of troubles, he succeeded in again collecting men and stores and rigging for a new vessel, with which he hastened back to Crevecœur, to find it, as we know, deserted. He ascertained, however, that Tonti was living among the Potawatamies on Lake Michigan, and having erected a new fort some miles south of Crevecœur, which he called St. Louis, he rejoined his old comrade, and easily persuaded him to start on a fresh journey of discovery. Together the two heroes returned to the Illinois, and rapidly building a second vessel, they sailed in it, in 1682, on a voyage fruitful of the best results. Launched on the Illinois, the little bark floated without accident to its junction with the Father of Rivers, and thence on the broad waters of the parent stream, past the mouth of the Missouri, between Tennessee and Arkansas, and again between Arkansas and Mississippi, beyond the most southerly point reached by Marquette, past the spot where De Soto's body was committed to the deep, until at last the final home of the Mississippi and its many tributaries was reached, and Frenchmen stood once more on the northern shores of the Gulf of Mexico.

Having set up the arms of France in the low alluvial plains overlooking the gulf, and named the whole district Louisiana in honor of the French monarch, La Salle retraced his steps, and hastening to France with the good news of his successful trip, he was shortly placed in command of an important expedition for the colonization of newly-discovered districts.

Full of wild hopes of the great things he was now to achieve, La Salle sent a message to his old friend Tonti, begging him to meet him at the mouth of the Mississippi; but alas! the latter appeared alone at the rendezvous. Accompanied by twenty Canadians and thirty Indians, Tonti paddled down the now familiar Mississippi from Fort St. Louis with little difficulty, and awaited the coming of his old commander near the site of the present New Orleans. Day after day, week after week passed on, and no La Salle appeared. The four vessels bearing his little company of 280 persons, including two young relatives of the commander, named Cavalier and Moranget, were tossing about in the Gulf of Mexico, unable to make the land. La Salle, who believed he could have acted as pilot with the best results, was thwarted at every turn by Beaujeu, the admiral of the fleet, who, after passing between Florida and Cuba, insisted on maintaining a western course till he came to the Bay of Matagorda, in Texas.

Recognizing no landmarks, La Salle entreated Beaujeu not to disembark the forces without some further exploration of the coast; but he was unheeded. The boats were lowered, and the colonists were put on shore. The wrecking of the store-ship was the first disaster to overtake them; it was followed, as a necessary result, by famine and discontent, and in the midst of the confusion some Indians surprised the new-comers, and murdered two of them.

In this terrible crisis Beaujeu at last yielded to the superior experience of La Salle, who, restored to the command, had a fort constructed out of the wreck of the store-ship, and, leaving 230 persons in it, he started with sixteen picked men to try and find the Mississippi. His search was unsuccessful, and, fearing that the colony would suffer on the low lands by the bay,

La Salle returned to the fort and superintended its removal to a hill near by, to which he gave the name of St. Louis, claiming the whole of the surrounding country as the property of the King of France.

The fort strengthened by outposts, the colonists cheered by brighter prospects, La Salle now again ventured to go on a quest for the Mississippi and the faithful Tonti, only to return four months later in rags. Again and again the same thing was repeated. Far away from the alluvial coast region, to the cross-timbers or wooded lands and prairies of Eastern Texas, and into the mountain districts of New Mexico in the West, tenanted by the Navajoes, Apaches, Utahs, Comanches, and other wild predatory tribes, the unsuccessful explorer led his few faithful followers, until at last he was compelled to give up all hope of finding the great river connected with so many hopes. He returned for the last time to Fort St. Louis to find it almost in ruins, and of the 230 colonists only thirty-six still alive, dissensions among themselves and famine having been the chief causes of this terrible state of things.

It was evidently useless to remain longer on the coast, and La Salle now came to the desperate resolution of making his way back to Canada on foot. With sixteen companions, he started for the work, supporting himself and his party by hunting the wild animals of the prairie; and but for treachery. among his followers, he would probably have lived to tell the tale of a journey of which every stage was full of the most thrilling adventure. As it was, however, the wanderers had not proceeded very far before La Salle's nephew, Moranget, was murdered by two men named Dubaut and L'Archeveque, who had long cherished bitter feelings against the family, in whose enterprise they had embarked all their capital. La Salle, coming up soon after Moranget's death, and missing him from among the party, put the simple question, "Where is my nephew?" The only reply was a loud report from the gun of Dubaut, and La Salle fell dead at his feet. His body and Moranget's were stripped, and left on the prairie to be devoured by eagles and wild beasts, while the murderers calmly pursued their way. It is with little regret that we add that they were shortly afterward themselves slain by Indians, and that of the original party, seven only—fourteen long years after the starting of the original expedition—reached Arkansea, on the Mississippi, where they were kindly received by the Indians, who gave them a letter from Tonti to La Salle, which had been left with them when the former, having given up all hope of the arrival of his friend, had returned to the lakes of Canada.

While La Salle was vainly struggling to accomplish the end for which he had sailed to Louisiana, the French were not idle in the North. In the rich peltries of the far West the fur-traders found a source of wealth rivaling even the mines of the South, and a class of men—unique alike in their manners and their experiences—sprang up, as it were, in the heart of the wilderness, to whom the name of *coureurs des bois* was given. These rangers of

ASSASSINATION OF LA SALLE.

the woods seem to have left behind them the European prejudice against the natives, and in their wild expeditions in remote tracts, and among distant tribes, they adopted the Indian mode of dress, contracted marriages with "squaws," and brought up their half-caste children to lead a life differing but slightly, if at all, from that of their mothers' relations. The usual result followed : the natives copied the vices of their visitors without their virtues, and but for the missionaries, who settled wherever there seemed to be a hope of winning even a few souls to God, natives and settlers would have been involved in one common ruin, alike of body and soul.

Little by little the traders and missionaries penetrated as far north as Hudson's Bay, and as far west as the Saskatchewan, the shores of which were dotted with trading houses and chapels long before its very name was heard in Europe. Unfortunately, however, neither the seekers after souls nor the hunters of peltries were men to talk much of their exploits, and though fiction has drawn largely from life in the far West in these early days for thrilling situations, little is known of the facts of the first intercourse of the white man with the various races of the great western hyperborean group of nations. Not until the powerful rival of the French in the West, the Hudson's Bay Company—of the growth of which particulars are given elsewhere—had sent forth its heroes on expeditions which were something more than trading excursions, did the first volumes appear of that extensive and fascinating literature of western travel from which the latter part of our narrative will be culled.

To atone for the reticence of the fur-trader and missionary in the far North-west, traveler after traveler succeeded Marquette and La Salle in exploring the great lakes of Canada and the shores of the Mississippi. Of these, one of the chief was Baron La Hontan, who, starting from Lake Michigan, went down the Wisconsin to the Mississippi, and is supposed to have very nearly approached the settlements of the Spanish New Mexico. In any case, he heard from some Indians, whom he called the Guaczitares— a name we altogether fail to recognize as that of any known tribe—of the existence of white men in the South ; and, what was perhaps of more importance, he learned from some visitors to the Guaczitares that they came from a country beyond which lay high moutains, only to be crossed with great difficulty, but that those who had crossed them had reached a big salt lake 300 leagues round, and with a wide opening to the south. From the moutains one great river flowed into the lake, and another eastward to the Miche Sepe. The big salt lake was probably that part of the sea now known as Queen Charlotte's Sound, the river flowing into it the Columbia, and the mountain range the Rocky Mountains.

On his return journey, La Hontan descended a river supposed to have been the second alluded to by the Indians, which brought him in five weeks to the Mississippi, ascending which he came to the port of Crevecœur, then still under the command of Tonti, so that he may be said in some sense to have bridged over the gap between the two expeditions of La Salle. With his name must be associated, however, that of Father Charlevoix, the wellknown historian of New France, who made what may be called the grand tour of inland America, passing up the St. Lawrence, through the lakes, and then down the Mississippi to the Gulf of Mexico, meeting with few adventures on the way, but collecting vast stores of information respecting the manners and customs of the natives, and doing much to shake the narrow view hitherto entertained, alike of the extent and importance of the lands on the west of the Mississippi.

# CHAPTER VII.

HAVING traced the course of early discovery from the most southerly point of Florida to the mouths of the Mississippi on the west, and up the Atlantic coast to the 60th parallel of north latitude, from the Gulf of St. Lawrence to the central table-lands of North America in Minnesota and down the Father of Waters to the sea, we will complete our survey of the work done in the first two centuries after the discovery of Columbus by turning to the South-west, which from the first presented special difficulties to the explorers, on account of the rugged nature of its scenery and the persistent hostility of its inhabitants.

From Mexico went forth the first authenticated expeditions for the exploration of the districts now forming the south-western states of North America, and to the restless ambition of Cortes may be traced much of the hatred of the white man which still distinguishes the Apaches, Pueblos, Shoshones, and other aboriginal tribes of New Mexico, Arizona, and California.

As early as 1530, the conqueror of Mexico, anxious to retrieve his waning greatness by new discoveries to the northward, sent forth two brigantines, under Diego de Hurtado, to explore the coast above the 25th parallel of north latitude. These first vessels were wrecked, and their commander lost; but, nothing daunted, Cortes at once equipped two others to take their place, which put to sea in 1534, under two captains, named Grijalva and Mendoza. The former is supposed to have reached the northern portion of the Gulf of California, but the latter was murdered by his pilot, Ximenes, who afterward landed on the coast of California, where he and many of his men where killed by the natives. The survivors returned to Mexico with wonderful stories of their adventures and the wealth of the districts visited, which so inflamed the imagination of Cortes, that he soon afterward himself started for the North with three well-manned vessels,

A disastrous result ensued. Two of the ships were wrecked, and when about to prosecute his voyage in the third, Cortes was recalled to Mexico by a rebellion which had broken out in his absence. A little later, however, a certain Francisco de Ulloa, who had been throughout the companion of Cortes, spent a year in cruising about the Gulf of California, and discovered

FERDINAND CORTES.

it to terminate in N. lat. 32°, in a bay resembling the Adriatic, to which he gave the name of the Sea of Cortes.

In 1537, a new impulse was given to the flagging interest of the Spanish in the unknown districts to the north by the arrival at the Mexican capital of our old acquaintance, Alvaro Nunez, fresh from his wonderful experiences in Florida. His stories of his adventures, and, still more, his repetition of the rumors of gold in plenty somewhere on the north of the Gulf of Mexico, led to the sending forth in the following year of a monk named Fra

Marco da Nizza, with orders to find out "what there was in the extensive regions beyond Mexico."

Starting from Culiacan, then the most northern Spanish settlement in Mexico, Da Nizza, accompanied by several Spaniards and a few Indian guides, made his painful way, first through plains already desolated by the incursions of his fellow-countrymen, and thence into the territory now called Arizona, on the borders of which he was met by some natives of California, who told him falsely, as it turned out, that their home was on an island, and that its shores were washed by waters abounding in pearls.

Encouraged by this intelligence, Da Nizza passed on till he came to the encampment of a tribe of Indians who had never seen a white man, but who received him courteously, informing him that forty days' journey to the north, on the other side of lofty mountains, there existed a vast plain full of cities inhabited by a people whose wealth far exceeded their own. Passing on in search of this new El Dorado, the Father was presently met by some Indians from the plain in question, who confirmed all that he had already been told, and, pointing to some gold ornaments he carried with him, assured him that their land abounded in similar objects. Cevola, or Cibola, was the nearest and largest of their cities. It contained lofty stone houses, large places, etc.; in a word, it seemed likely to be a second Tenotchitlan; and, after a consultation with his companions, Da Nizza resolved to send one of them, Stefano Dorantes, on in advance, with an escort of three hundred Indians, to announce his own approach, hoping thus to enhance the *éclat* of his own entry with a view to obtaining a larger tribute for his employer.

The first part only of this programme was carried out. As Da Nizza was approaching the capital, a few days after his envoy had left him, he was met by an Indian, who told him that, on entering the city in all the pomp of ringing bells and waving plumes, Dorantes and his escort were seized by the people, stripped of all they possessed, and flung into prison. On their attempting to escape, they were shot down by arrows, and but few lived to tell the tale.

Resolved, in spite of the awful fate of Dorantes, not to return to Mexico without seeing Cibola, Da Nizza now disguised himself, and, accompanied by two attendants as brave as himself, he succeeded in approaching near enough to the scene of the massacre to be convinced that there had been no exaggeration in the reports of the wealth of the people of the plain.

CITY OF MEXICO

Secretly setting up a little cross as a witness of his visit, and a sign that the country henceforth belonged to Spain, Da Nizza now retraced his steps, narrowly escaping death at the hands of the Indians whose comrades had formed part of his unlucky escort, but finally arriving safely at Culiacan, there to arouse a perfect fever of enthusiasm by his account of all he had seen and heard.

Two years later, a costly expedition to Cibola, consisting of some two thousand adventurers, was fitted out by Mendoza, the Viceroy, who had superseded Cortes in the supreme command in Mexico. This expedition was divided into two parts, one of which, under Fernando di Alarchon, proceeded up the coast in well equipped vessels, while the other, under Vasquez de Coronado, proceeded overland by the same route as that taken by Da Nizza.

Sailing up the Vermilion Sea, or the Sea of Cortes, as the Gulf of California was then called, Alarchon presently came to the mouth of a large river, probably the Colorado, flowing into the head of the gulf in N. lat. 32° 10'. Entering the river, the Spanish were soon brought to a stand-still by the appearance on its banks of numbers of well-armed natives, who, with threatening gestures, forbade the intruders to advance further into their country.

Making conciliatory signs, however, Alarchon was able to open a parley, and an old man came forth from among the gesticulating crowds, stepped into the water, and presented Alarchon with a staff. This, it appeared, answered to the calumet of the inland tribes, and, accepting it with an embrace to the donor, Alarchon gave its bearer some rosaries, which were eagerly carried ashore, though their spiritual significance is scarcely likely to have been appreciated.

A good understanding having been thus established between the natives and their guests, the white men were allowed to proceed up the river. Some little distance from its mouth, the explorers met an Indian who knew the language of some of the native escort, and by this means intelligible communications were opened with the people. As their brethren had done in the South, the Spaniards gave out that they were the Children of the Sun, sent by the life-giving Deity to rule over the natives of Arizona. Asked how it was they had so long delayed their coming, and, having come, could not speak the language of their subjects, they replied in an evasive yet reassuring manner. In due course a second Indian joined the party, who not only knew all about Cibola, but had even heard of Da Nizza's expedition.

From him Alarchon learned that he was but ten days' journey from the great city, and he tried to persuade some of his companions to cross the country and communicate with Coronado, who must by this time have been within easy reach. No one could, however, be induced to make the venture, and Alarchon—somewhat rashly, as it seems to us—resolved to turn back. Sailing down the river, he returned to Mexico, having accomplished next to nothing.

Meanwhile, Coronado had bravely led his troops over the rugged mountainous districts of the north of Mexico, and in spite of much murmuring on their part on account of the hardships endured by the way, he had brought them safely to the plain of the Seven Cities. Here, on the very eve of success, he was met by a large force of armed Cibolans, who rejected all his efforts at conciliation. In the battle which ensued, the Spaniards were finally victorious, and the city of Cibola was taken; but Coronado was dangerously wounded in the assault, and the long hoped-for plunder was nowhere to be found. Cibola was but a large village, situated on a lofty and bleak plain, yielding plenty of grass, maize, and pebbles of rock crystal, but no gold, silver, or precious stones.

As soon as he could travel, Coronado, disguising his disappointment as best he could, took possession of Cibola in the name of his Catholic Majesty of Spain, and collected information on all sides as to the nature of the country beyond the plain of the cities. Learning that a great town called Quivira existed somewhere on the coast, he led his men to a distance of about 300 leagues through a level and somewhat barren country, finally arriving at the town in question, which turned out to be really large and wealthy, though its riches consisted in a fine breed of cattle, not in the precious metals and minerals for which the Spaniards had hoped.

Feeling that he had now accomplished something, Coronado then led his forces back to Mexico. As usual, very exaggerated reports were circulated by his followers as to what they had seen and done; and though its site has never yet been ascertained, Quivira was the goal of many a future expedition.

The next hero to attempt to penetrate to the North-west was Juan Rodriguez Cabrillo, a Portuguese mariner, sent out in 1542 by the indefatigable Mendoza. After rounding the modern Cape St. Lucas, Cabrillo sailed along the coast of California as far as N. lat. 40° 30′, where he saw two lofty snow-clad mountains, between which projected the now well-known modern headland to which he gave the name of Cape Mendocino, in honor of his employer. Sailing on beyond Cape Mendocino, Cabrillo was compelled, four degrees further north, to turn back, on account of the extreme cold. He arrived in Mexico in the spring of 1543, after ten months' absence, his voyage justly entitling him to be called the discoverer of Northern California, though that honor is usually claimed for our fellow-countryman, Sir Francis Drake, who, thirty-six years later, touched at Point de los Reyes, and, in ignorance of his predecessor's work, took possession of the country he thought he had discovered in the name of Queen Elizabeth, christening it New Albion.

In 1596, Mendoza's successor, Conde de Monterey, sent an expedition consisting of three vessels, under Sebastian Viscaino, to California, with a view to opening friendly relations with the natives. Crossing the lower portion of the Gulf of California, and rounding Cape St. Lucas, as Cabrillo had done before him, Viscaino soon came to a good harbor, which he named first St. Sebastian and then La Paz. After taking possession of the country for the King of Spain, by firing cannons and hoisting standards, the explorer allowed four Franciscan friars to admit such of the natives as were willing to the Holy Catholic Church, the simple people gazing with wondering admiration at the unintelligible ceremonies performed on their behalf. This double conquest made for the State and Church of his sovereign, Viscaino continued his voyage up the north-eastern coast; but a misunderstanding with the natives, and the failure of his provisions, compelled him shortly to return to Mexico. In 1602, however, he started again, this time at the head of a thoroughly well-organized expedition; and after a flying visit to the converts at La Paz, he sailed leisurely up the coast of California, discovering the harbor of San Diego (N. lat. 32° 47′) on the 10th November, and the Bay of Monterey (N. lat. 36° 33′), so named after the Viceroy, on the 16th December.

At Monterey, the expedition received an unfortunate check by the breaking out of scurvy among the crew of the fleet. The terrible symptoms of this disease, the cause and cure of which were then alike unknown, so appalled the Spaniards, that all but a few entreated to be taken back to Mexico. Their request was granted, one vessel alone, the *Capitana*, under Viscaino himself, prosecuting the voyage. A miserable remnant of those who had been stricken with the now only too familiar seamen's complaint were landed on the Mexican shores, and when for many months no tidings came of the *Capitana*, it was supposed that she was lost with all on board. Very different, however, had been her experience from that of her consorts. Viscaino took his vessel far away to the north, discovering in N. lat. 42° 51′ yet another great headland, to which he gave the name of Cape Blanco, and some miles beyond it again the mouth of a mighty river, supposed to have been the Columbia, and to have been identical with the fabulous Strait of Anian, by which, tradition says, the Dutch had penetrated from the northern to the southern sea.

Unable, from want of provisions, to penetrate further northward, or to ascend the newly-discovered river, the successful explorer now retraced his course, arriving at the island of Mazatlan, off the north-western coast of Mexico, with his men in good health, though much reduced by famine. Refreshed by the hospitality of the friendly people of Mazatlan, Viscaino and his men now hastened to report themselves to the Viceroy, and to beg for permission to make yet another trip at the leader's own expense.

Incredible as it may appear, this request was refused; and though, many years afterward, Viscaino was asked to lead another expedition, the delay proved fatal, for the gallant explorer died on the eve of setting sail.

With the death of Viscaino the first chapter of discovery in the southwest of North America may be said to have been closed. The next well-authenticated voyage up the western coast was that in which a Greek pilot named Juan de Fuca took part, and from whom Mr. Lok, an Englishman much interested in geographical discovery, obtained an account of his adventures many years after they took place. According to De Fuca, he made a voyage in 1592 through the long-sought Straits of Anian, situated between the 47th and 48th parallels of north latitude, beyond which his vessel entered the North Sea. That a voyage was made in this direction, though not with this result, seems proved by the exact correspondence of Queen Charlotte's Sound, between Vancouver Island and the mainland, with De Fuca's description of the channel turning, now west, now north-west. For the North Sea read the North Pacific, and the experience of many a future mariner is anticipated. The naming of the straits dividing the southern portion of Vancouver Island from what is now Washington Territory after De Fuca is a conclusive expression of the verdict of geographers on the matter.

Another voyage from the South was that of Admiral de Fonte, who is thought by some authorities to have penetrated as far north as the 53d degree, where his vessel was in great danger, owing to the multitude of islands impeding its progress. Captain Barnardo, the second in command to De Fonte, carefully explored the winding of this archipelago, while De Fonte entered a large river leading into a vast lake also dotted with islands, in a bay of which he found an English ship lying at anchor, the first, according to the Indians, ever seen in these high latitudes.

On the latter portion of this story great doubt has been thrown; but again we are almost compelled to accept the truth of a visit having been paid to the labyrinth of islands, channels, etc., now bearing the names of Graham, Moresby, and other modern explorers, from the correspondence between their appearance and the description of his archipelago given by De Fonte.

Leaving the work of Behring, Spangberg, Meares, Vancouver, Kotzebue, and other successors of De Fuca and De Fonte in the hyperborean regions, we return to the Spanish in the South, to find our next hero of discovery in an old Jesuit priest named Eusebius Francis Kino, who, in 1658, went forth alone from his Mexican monastery to try and win over the wild tribes of the North to the faith of which he was a minister. With no weapon but the cross, and no food but such as he was able to beg by the way, the father pressed on through the present province of Sonora till he came to a river supposed to have been the Santa Cruz. Following its course, he entered Arizona, and arrived at the junction of the Santa Cruz with the Gila, which in its turn joins the Colorado some miles above its mouth.

Crossing the Gila, Kino ascended its northern bank, and came to a country which he characterizes as the most wonderful ever seen by the eye of man. Its people, who were "kind, generous, and hospitable," dwelt in well-built villages clustering on the banks of streams, and employed their time in the manufacture of a kind of cotton cloth and of very beautiful feather-work. They were also skillful picture-writers, and on the walls of their public buildings was preserved a pictorial record of their history. Mines of gold and silver—which they understood how to work with considerable skill, though they set but small value on the ore when excavated—promised to yield a splendid return to the emigrant, while immense flocks of sheep and herds of cattle constituted another source of almost inexhaustible wealth.

Worshiping the sun as the one supreme God, these simple yet intelligent natives kept a fire ever burning on their altars in his honor. With its undying flame they connected their own prosperity, and they therefore showed little readiness to substitute for it any less material guarantee of well-being.

Father Kino made few converts to the belief in the spiritual God, whose altar is the heart, and whose chief purifying agent is adversity ; and, passing on among the fire-worshipers, he trod his weary way in a north-westerly direction till he came to the so-called Fire Mountain, supposed to have been the San Francisco Mountain. Here he altered his course for the East, and after a long tramp through the forest, he reached the head-waters of the Mimbres, the course of which he followed till its waters suddenly sunk away in the earth, a phenomenon often since commented upon by modern travelers.

Many months were spent by the missionary in the wild districts on either side of the eccentric Mimbres, with little or no result so far as his main object was concerned, the native tribes being then, as now, peculiarly averse to the reception of religious teaching. Finding it useless to remain longer among them, our hero therefore at last resolved to return to Mexico, and there obtain recruits for the further prosecution of missionary work in the more hospitable Arizona. After no less than seven years of fruitless effort, he at last accomplished his purpose, and toward the end of 1670 we find him starting with three other Jesuits for the Gila, on the banks of which he established a mission for the conversion of the Yaquis in 1672. Between that date and 1679, no less than five missions were founded among these and others of the New Mexican tribes, the Pueblos, Opotoes, etc., themselves aiding in erecting the beautiful buildings, the ruins of which, especially that of San Xavier del Bac, in the beautiful Santa Cruz valley, still bear witness to the religious zeal and architectural skill of these early teachers in the West.

Had the Jesuit Fathers been content with the gradual but sure growth of their influence in fair Arizona and New Mexico, the conclusion of our story might have been different. As it was, however, their eagerness to extend their spiritual influence, and—alas, that we should have to say it !—to appropriate for the use of their order the gold and silver abounding in the mountains on the north of their new homes, led to the sending out of expeditions beyond the limits occupied by the tribes friendly to their interests. The wrath of the terrible Apaches, dwelling in the now desolated plains and mountain fastnesses on the north-west, was aroused : and in 1680 they swept down upon the Spanish settlements in such numbers as to carry all before them, compelling the missionaries to flee for their lives into Mexico. Again and again they returned with the same result, until at last the missions were finally abandoned, having wrought nothing but evil to those for whose benefit they were primarily established.

After the expulsion of the Jesuits by the Apaches, the districts to the north-west of Mexico were for many years left unvisited by any Europeans, with the exception of a few venturesome miners, who, working at the risk of their lives in the north of the present province of Arizona, won for it its name, originally Arizuma, or the silver-bearing country. To atone for this pause in inland exploration, however, the coasts of both Upper and Lower California became thoroughly well known to Spanish pearl-fishers, who were followed, as the French *coureurs de bois* had been in the North, by Roman Catholic missionaries, eager to be the first Christian teachers to win the ears of the natives. In the course of about half a century, many missions had been established in Lower California ; and though, owing to the law forbidding priests to marry, no permanent root was taken in the country by them, and no homes gathered about their chapels, they paved the way for the advent of the settler, and exercised a refining influence, alike on the wild Spanish fishermen and the fierce and degraded Californian Indians.

The beginning of the 18th century witnessed the first chapter of the thrilling drama of the fall of the Jesuits from the lofty position they had held throughout the world for two centuries. Expelled from Portugal in 1759, and from France in 1764, they flocked to Spain, hoping to find a refuge in the first home of their order. They were disappointed. In 1767, the edict for their banishment, alike from the mother country and her colonies, was issued by Charles III. of Spain, and the Jesuits both at home and abroad found themselves involved in one common ruin.

Rallying as best they could from the blow which deprived them of all their property, and exiled them from the land of their adoption, those members of the disgraced order who had settled in Lower California resolved to begin a new crusade in the north of the same country.

Under the leadership of Father Junipero Serra, appointed president of all the missions to be established in Upper California, the Fathers went forth to set up the cross among the Ahwashtes, Altahmos, Romanans, Klamaths, Modoes, Shastas, Eurocs, and others of the almost countless tribes forming the two great families of the Central and Northern Californians.

Dividing into two parties, the first expedition started for Northern California by land in 1768. The first division, under Captain Rivera of Moncado, after a terrible journey across country, arrived at the site of the present San Diego

(N. lat. 32° 47 , W. long. 117° 8') on the 14th of May, 1768, and there founded the first settlement of white men in Upper California. The second party, under Father Junipero himself, arrived at the new colony on the 1st of July, and the first North Californian convert was baptized on the 16th of December of the same year.

Early in January, 1769, a second detachment of Jesuits started in three vessels—the *San Carlos*, the *San Antonio*, and the *San José*—to reach San Diego by sea. The first arrived on the 1st May, having lost all her crew,

THE GOLDEN GATE, SAN FRANCISCO.

except two or three officers, from scurvy and famine; the second put into port at San Diego on the 10th April, with eight men missing; and the third was never again heard of.

After a rest of a few weeks, the survivors of the unfortunate fleet, their numbers augmented by a party of emigrants from Sonora and an escort of Lower Californian Indians, started, under the command of Don Gaspar de Portala, who had been appointed military governor of the new country, for the North, intending to find the Bay of Monterey, and there found a second

branch of the mission.  The pioneers failed to find Monterey, but on the
25th October, 1769, they discovered the now famous harbor of San Francisco,
justly named the gem of the Pacific, its Golden Gate, the outlet connecting
it with the ocean, forming the entry to the finest seaport on the western seaboard of America.  Land-locked as it was, the noble bay had escaped the
notice of previous explorers, and even now its great importance seems
scarcely to have been recognized.  Naming it San Francisco, after the titu-
lar saint of the Jesuits, Portola led his party back to San Diego, and for
six long years the site of the present capital of California was left to the
undisturbed possession of the natives.

For sixty years after their first arrival at San Diego the Jesuits carried all
before them in
Upper Califor-
nia, and when
the overthrow of
the Spanish do-
minion in Mex-
ico — which has
been character-
ized as the death-
blow of the mis-
sion system —
took place in
1822, their settlements along the coast numbered as many as twenty-one.

CITY HALL, SAN FRANCISCO.  (1885.)

As in Lower California, however, the exclusiveness of the missionaries was
fatal to the growth of permanent settlements: the emigration of Europeans
to the districts belonging to them was discouraged ; no inland colonies
were founded ; and, after living for years in an almost patriarchal state,
more than 18,000 Indians owning no authority but theirs, the Fathers were
deprived, by act of the Mexican Congress, of their plantations, and forbidden to employ the Indians to work for them.  As a result, they were
compelled, one by one, to abandon the country for which they had done so
much.  During the latter years of their sway, many speculators and trappers
had, in spite of their opposition, penetrated into their territories, and the
first seeds had been sown of many a now thriving community ; but, before
we relate the adventures of those travelers whose exploits entitle them to
rank among our heroes, we must go back a couple of centuries to trace the
further course of exploration in the Eastern States,

# CHAPTER VIII.

WE left the New England colonies on the eve of the first great Indian war, which originated in the jealousy of the Pequods—a fierce race living between the Narragansetts and Mohegans of New England and the Iroquois of the East—at the sudden influx of foreigners into the fertile districts of Connecticut. Although, strictly speaking, it is scarcely within our province, we will give an outline of this terrible struggle, affording, as it does, a typical example of the general policy pursued toward each other by the natives and settlers in the New World.

As early as 1634, a Captain Stone had been murdered, with all his crew, off Fort Good Hope, a Dutch outpost of Connecticut; and in the two years which followed, aggressions and robberies on the part of the Pequods were of frequent occurrence. The crisis was not reached, however, until 1636, when our old friend, Captain Oldham, fell a victim to the fury of the Indians. The details of this second tragedy will never be known, and it is more than possible that the outrage may not have been altogether unprovoked, the captain having been a man of hasty temper, disposed to carry matters with the natives with a very high hand.

Oldham was last seen alive starting in a vessel of his own on a trading excursion up the Connecticut River, and a little later a fisherman named Gallop, at work on Block Island, caught sight of the boat drifting out to sea, crowded with Indians, who were evidently at a total loss how to manage their capture. In a moment Gallop, accompanied by one man and two boys, started in pursuit; the vessel was boarded, and, without pausing to inquire into the rights of the matter, the four newcomers laid about them right and left, till the Indians were driven off, leaving many of their number dead or dying on the deck.

This summary vengeance inflicted, Gallop looked about him for its justification, and found Oldham and his men lying in their own blood, covered with ghastly wounds. The news of their death spread like wildfire far and near; and though, to the calm judgment of lookers-on, reconciliation with the Pequods still seemed possible to those who were exposed to a fate such as that which had overtaken the Puritan captain, nothing short of the extermination of the whole tribe of the offenders appeared to meet the necessities of the case. The colonial leaders, however, observed the forms of civilized warfare, and, before a blow was struck, formally demanded the yielding up of the murderers of Stone and Oldham, with the restitution of all property stolen from the whites. As we know, those who had slain Oldham had most of them shared his fate. Evasive answers were returned as to the murderers of Stone and the stolen property, and it appeared evident that nothing could be accomplished by negotiation.

In August, 1636, hostilities commenced by the dispatch to Block Island of one hundred men, under the command of John Endicott of Salem, whose orders were that he should kill all the Pequod warriors he met with, but spare their women and children. A landing was effected on Block Island in the midst of a shower of arrows, and a fierce struggle ensued, in which only one Englishman was wounded. The Indians were hopelessly defeated, and fled into woods and fields of the island, where they were soon overtaken by the English, who put them to death without mercy. Not content with this wholesale slaughter, Endicott also burned two villages of sixty wigwams each, the stacks of maize in the course of being harvested, and all the standing corn, so that the unlucky Pequods who had escaped the sword would be compelled either to starve or to flee their country.

The massacre of Block Island over, Endicott repaired to the mainland, where dwelt the warriors who had murdered Stone. Halting at the mouth of the Pequod River, now the Thames, the English leader sent a message to the natives, demanding that Sassacus, their chief, should be sent to him immediately; and when no answer was returned, the attack was begun. As on Block Island, the natives fell an easy prey to the well-armed white men ; and having slain all he found, and burned their villages, Endicott set sail for Boston, where he arrived safely, after an absence of one month only.

Thanksgivings were held in all the churches, in gratitude for the "signal mercy" which had preserved the little band of avengers, of whom two only had been left behind, in their terrible work ; but that work had in reality only begun. The unhappy survivors of the "signal mercy," driven to bay, had joined the inland members of their tribe, and the tale of the two massacres at which Endicott had presided roused a deadly enmity against the whites throughout the length and breadth of Pequod land ; nay more, even the Narragansetts and the Mohegans, who had long since sworn allegiance to the English, and were the bitter foes of the Pequods, began to show signs of making common cause with the sufferers. Had they done so, the very existence of the colonies would have been in peril, and the history of the United States of America might never have begun.

It was our old friend, Roger Williams, who saved from extermination the brethren who had cast him out from among them. More familiar than any other emigrant with the ways of the Indian, he read the signs of the times truly, and determined, at whatever risk to himself, to prevent the coalition of the Pequods with the Mohegans and Narragansetts. To quote his own account of the matter—" The Lord helped me immediately to put my life into my hand, and, scarce acquainting my wife, to ship myself, all alone, in a poor canoe, and to cut through a stormy wind with great seas, every minute in hazard of life, to the sachem's (the Narragansett chief's) house. Three days and nights," he adds,

JOHN ENDICOTT.

" my business forced me to lodge and mix with the bloody Pequod ambassadors (come to agree on the terms of alliance against the whites), whose hands and arms, methought, reeked with the blood of my countrymen."

At the end of the three days Williams had effected his purpose, and, instead of an alliance with the Pequods, the Narragansetts had made a new treaty with the English. The Mohegans followed their example, and, their forces augmented by many a dusky warrior, the white men of Connecticut,

under Captain John Mason, shortly sallied forth once more against the common foe, their destination this time being the chief stronghold of the Pequods, a fort near the present town of Stringbow, on the Pawcatuk River. The fort was surprised at night, and though the Indians fought with desperate courage, and at one time seemed likely to be victorious, they were finally overwhelmed. Their wigwams were then set on fire, and six hundred men, women, and children perished in the flames. The morning broke on a scene of terrible misery ; yet the cup of Pequod disaster was not yet full. As the English, who had again lost but two men, were resting from their horrible night's work, six hundred native warriors were seen advancing proudly toward the ruins of their homes.

Arrived within sight of their desolate village, the unhappy Pequods are said to have paused for one moment in silent agony, and then, with a yell of rage and despair, to have swept down upon the invaders, many of whom were slain in the first onslaught, though the final result to the Pequods was but a repetition of previous struggles. All but a little remnant were slain without mercy, and, returning red-handed to Saybrook, at the mouth of the Connecticut, the victors were joined by a number of recruits from Massachusetts, whose arrival had been delayed by the excitement caused in the parent colony by the expulsion of Anne Hutchinson for heresy.

Thus reënforced, the Connecticut settlers hunted the survivors of the original owners of the soil down like beasts of prey. Their chief, Sassacus, fled in his despair to the Mohawks, who betrayed his trust by murdering him, and sending his scalp to the English ; and in July, 1637, five months after the beginning of the war, the last scene of the long tragedy took place in a swamp where stands the modern town of Fairfield. Three hundred Pequod warriors were there surrounded, and while many were slain and some few escaped, two hundred were taken prisoners alive. In spite of their eager entreaties for death, the unhappy men were sent, some of them to the Bermudas as slaves, and the remainder dispersed among the Mohegans and Narragansetts, to be to them " hewers of wood and drawers of water."

While the Pequod war was still in progress, a fresh colony arrived at Boston from England, including John Davenport and Theophilus Eaton, men of wealth and social station, whom the Massachusetts authorities would gladly have retained among them. There were, however, now no good lands to spare for new-comers near the old settlements, and it was absolutely necessary for them to seek some other home. At the close of the war, therefore, Eaton and Davenport led their little band into Connecticut, where a tract of land, south of the settlement of Saybrook, had been already purchased for them of the native chief for "twelve coats of English cloth, twelve alchemy spoons, twelve hatchets, twelve hoes, two dozen knives, twelve porringers, and four cases of French knives and scissors."

Originally called Quinniack, or Quinnepaca, the new settlement shortly received the name of New Haven, and grew with a rapidity hitherto unknown in colonial annals. From among its wealthy members, one after another went forth to found new towns in its neighborhood, until, in a very short time, Connecticut was colonized all along the shore and far inland. This great movement was further supplemented by the constant arrival of new recruits, alike from the mother country and the elder colonies of Massachusetts, and we soon find the English pushing their outposts as far south as the Hudson, gradually displacing the Dutch, and again driving the Indians to desperation. In 1643, the settlements in Massachusetts, New Hampshire and Connecticut formed that league, under the title of the United Colonies of New England, for mutual protection against the Dutch, French and Indians, which may be looked upon as the opening of the first chapter of the political history of the United States; but for the continuation of that history we must refer our readers to the many volumes on the subject already in existence. Our task being to trace the gradual opening up of new districts, we must leave the infant federation to fight out its battles, alike with its European neighbors, the schismatics within its own borders, and the true owners of the disputed territories, unwatched by us. We return once more to the South, to find the districts between Virginia and Florida occupied under the name of Carolina, so-called in honor of Charles IX. of France, by a few non-conformists from England and Virginia, who had gathered about the promontory aptly named Cape Fear (N. lat. 33° 48′) where they hoped to work out their own salvation, free from the temptation of the world they had renounced. Their expectations were, as a matter of course, disappointed. After the English Restoration, Charles II. re-asserted his claim to that part of America long known under the general name of South Virginia, and granted the fertile districts between Albemarle Sound (N. lat. 35° 59′), and the river St. John (N. lat. 30° 23′), to eight of his favorite noblemen, the terms of concession making them absolute sovereigns within the limits named.

The result of this arbitrary proceeding was a mighty influx of emigrants, from every part of Great Britain and its dependencies, to the fruitful lands which had long been claimed as their exclusive property by the Spaniards. The original proprietors were literally crowded out by "gay cavaliers" and rapacious planters, who soon made the very name of white man hateful in the ears of the unfortunate Indians. Under the governorship of the terrible Seth Sothel, a man whose name will live forever as that of the most infamous of many reckless rulers of Carolina, the natives were hunted down on every side, and sold as slaves to West Indian planters, while those among the emigrants who retained any reverence for the human or divine had their feelings outraged at every turn.

Not until the 18th century was considerably advanced did the Carolineans obtain any relief from this terrible state of things. Petition after petition was sent to the mother country by the unhappy sufferers, setting forth how the Indians were "assaulted, killed, destroyed, and taken" under the sanction of the law; how even the clergy openly led the most dissolute lives, etc., etc. The breaking out of an Indian war in 1715 seems to have been the first thing to arouse the home authorities to the dangers threatening their vast possessions in the West. The revolt was crushed with an iron hand, the survivors of the natives taking refuge in the swamps of Florida, and in 1721, George I. consented to take the government of Carolina into his own hands.

A few years later, the lands granted to the eight noblemen by Charles II. were bought up by the Crown for some £28,000; and from that time the colony grew rapidly in prosperity and importance, extending its settlements as far south as the Savannah river, across which went forth pioneers into the state afterward called Georgia, in honor of the English monarch, long before the first body of emigrants from the mother country landed on its shores. Thus, as New England and Virginia may be said to have been the parents of Carolina, the new-born colony became in its turn the founder of the infant community of Georgia. It was in 1732 that this, the youngest but one of the original thirteen states of the Union, was first settled by a colony from England, under the leadership of the now famous Oglethorpe, who, like John Eliot in the North, made it his chief object to conciliate the Indians.

Soon after the arrival of the emigrants from Europe, Oglethorpe succeeded in bringing about a congress between the so-called Creek Indians and the English, near the site of the modern Savannah, at which meeting peace was solemnly made between the dark warriors and their pale-faced guests. This treaty between the Creek Indians and the whites was succeeded by one with the Cherokees dwelling on the north of the new settlements, and as a policy of a similar kind was pursued with regard to religious refugees from other English settlements, Georgia shortly became a kind of harbor of refuge for all who were suffering in mind, body or estate. Its progress in worldly prosperity, though slow, was sure ; and, when the treaty of 1763 concluded a war of triumph for the English, it had extended its limits far away to the South, the West, and the North-west, in spite of many a bloody contest, now with the Spanish, and now with the various Indian tribes in the West.

We have now accounted for the first appearance of the white man in all the districts of North America bordering on the Atlantic seaboard, and are free to turn our steps inland, joining, as our first hero in this new field, the great Quaker, William Penn. He was the founder of the "Keystone State," which forms the connecting link between the first French settlements on the Great Lakes and those of the Dutch and English in the United States.

It was in 1681, after a stormy career in England, that Penn first turned his attention to the New World, and obtained from the English Crown, in lieu of a large sum of money due to him from it, a grant of an extensive tract of land, encroaching alike on the boundaries of New York, New Jersey, and Maryland. It was included between the 40th and 43d degrees of north latitude, and was bounded on the east by the Delaware, already connected with so many thrilling memories.

WILLIAM PENN.

Determined, with that rigid sense of honesty which characterized his sect, to appropriate nothing unfairly, Penn, before he started himself, sent out agents to purchase from the Indians the land upon which he proposed settling ; and all things being thus prepared for his advent, he set sail from England, arriving at Newcastle, on the Delaware, in October, 1682. Here

he was most enthusiastically received, his fame as a sufferer for righteousness' sake, and as an eager philanthropist, having preceded him.

A day of general rejoicing was succeeded by a solemn leave-taking of the
colonists, and then, embarking on the broad waters of the Delaware, Penn
made what resembled a royal progress from one station to another, till he
came, toward the end of November, to the borders of his own dominions.
His first act on landing in Pennsylvania, as the new districts had already
been christened, was to hold a solemn meeting with the Indian chiefs, and
make with them that treaty of peace which was followed by such excellent
results for his people. Beneath a large elm tree at Shackamaxon, on the
site of the modern Kensington, the sons of the forest, hitherto accustomed
to very different treatment from the white man, awaited the approach of
him whom they looked upon as a messenger from the Great Spirit in awe-
struck silence. As Penn approached, the oldest sachem rose and bade him
welcome, adding that the nations of the Delaware were ready to listen to
his words.

"We meet," replied Penn, as he stood a little in advance of the chief of
his colonists, "on the broad pathway of good works and good will; no advantage shall be taken on either side, but all shall be openness and love. I
will not call you children, for parents sometimes chide their children too
severely; nor brothers only, for brothers differ. The friendship between
you and me I will not compare to a chain, for that the rains might rust, or
a falling tree break. We are the same as if one man's body were divided
into two parts: we are all one flesh and blood."

This speech, which has become historical, and is proudly quoted in every
account of the founding of Philadelphia, appealed direct to the very hearts
of those to whom it was addressed. Here, at last, was one who owned true
fellowship with them, who would feel as they felt, who would protect them,
and, better still, whom they themselves could aid. Again their spokesman
stood forth, and, in the name of every tribe, from the Schuylkill and the
Delaware, the Susquehanna and the Juniatta, replied, "We will live in
love with Father Onas (the native name given to Penn) and his children, as
long as moon and sun shall endure." The treaty between the two parties
was then signed, the Indians adding the emblem of their tribes to the names
of the white men; presents were exchanged, and the solemn scene was at
an end. We may add, however, that the peace thus cemented was, unlike
most compacts with the sons of the soil, preserved inviolate as long as the

Quakers ruled in Pennsylvania, and to it was mainly due the unexampled rapidity of the growth of the new settlement.

Penn's next care, after his interview with the Indians, was to call together the emigrants—the greater number of whom were of his own religious persuasion—and present them with their constitution, framed so as to insure alike political and religious freedom ; a fact resulting in the flocking to his

PENN'S TREATY WITH THE INDIANS.

settlement of persecuted members of every sect from the New England and Virginia colonies. In January, 1683, the foundations were laid, on the west bank of the Delaware and at the mouth of the Schuylkill, of that fair town, now the second in importance in the Union, called Philadelphia, or the "City of Brotherly Love," the streets of which were named after the groves of chestnut, pine, and walnut trees through which they ran.

Before the end of its first year, the infant city contained eighty houses, and four years after its foundation it numbered 2,000 inhabitants. As the years rolled on, and the mineral and agricultural wealth of the western districts of Pennsylvania became more and more fully revealed, town after town sprang up within its boundaries. In the beginning of the 18th century, we find John Harris founding the beautiful Harrisburg, under a grant from Penn, in the midst of the magnificent scenery on the left bank of the Susquehanna, and though the French and Indian war which broke out in 1754 checked for a moment, as it were, the laying out of new cities, the now

THE TEA IN BOSTON HARBOR.

flourishing town of Pittsburg rose on the site of Fort Duquesne, at the junction of the Alleghany and Monongahela Rivers, as soon as the victory of Forbes in 1758 established the power of the British.

In 1774, the quarrels between the mother country and her now mighty American colonies—of which the most thrilling incidents were the Stamp Act riots of Boston in 1768, and the revolt against the payment of the tea dues in the same city in 1773, when the boys of Boston, disguised as Indians, flung the cargoes of tea into the sea to prevent the payment of the tax—resulted in the War of Independence, during which, strange to say, took place those first explorations of Kentucky, Tennessee, and Ohio which were to add so greatly to the power of the American Union about to be formed. But before we join the pioneers of the new era of discovery in the West, we must turn once more to the South, to bring our account of the work of the French down to the important date we have reached in the history of their English rivals in the East.

INDIAN ORNAMENTS.

# CHAPTER IX.

THE work begun by La Salle was taken up, after the peace of Ryswick (1697) had terminated the war between the French and English, by Lemoyne D'Iberville, a Canadian by birth, who, in 1698, sailed for the mouth of the Mississippi from San Domingo, accompanied by his two brothers, Sauville and Bienville, two hundred colonists, and a few women and children.

After a successful voyage, our hero cast anchor in the present Mobile Bay (N. lat. 30° 40', W. long. 80°), and on the 2d February, 1699, landed his people on Ship Island, where huts were at once erected for the temporary shelter of the emigrants. While this work was in progress, D'Iberville explored the neighboring Bay of Biloxi and the mouth of the Pensacola River—already, as we know, visited more than once by the Spanish—and at the end of the month made his way thence, with forty-eight picked followers, to the mouth of the Mississippi.

Entering the muddy waters, encumbered by the floating trunks of rotting trees, which formed the outlet of the great Father of Waters, the explorers sailed slowly on between the low alluvial banks till they came to a Bayagoula village, just below the junction of the Red River with the Mississippi, where all doubt as to their having found the mighty stream they sought was set at rest by the production of a letter, in their own language, left with the Indians by Tonti long years before.

Now completely satisfied as to his whereabouts, D'Iberville made his way back to Ship Island in a south-easterly direction, through the Manshac Pass and Lakes Maurepas and Pontchartrain, so named after two French ministers accompanying the expedition. Finding the colonists suffering from the unhealthiness of their situation, their leader sanctioned their removal to the Bay of Biloxi, where a fort was at once erected, which was to insure to the French the peaceful possession of the vast tracts allotted to them by their monarch, extending from the Rio Grande, or Rio Bravo del Norte, now forming the boundary between Texas and Mexico, to the 85th degree of west longitude.

Having thus laid the foundation of what he hoped would become a great French empire in the South, which should gradually extend until it met and coalesced with that of the North, D'Iberville returned to France to win new recruits for his enterprise, leaving his brothers in charge of the infant settlement.

Thus left for a time to its own resources, the little colony struggled on as best it could—the monotony of its life in the barren wastes on which it had been set down broken only by an occasional visit from some missionary, who would appear suddenly at the mouth of the Mississippi, after a wild trip from his distant station, in his birch-bark canoe—until its very existence was threatened by the sudden appearance of two well-armed English vessels, under the command of Coxe, a physician, who had bought up an old patent granting the territory occupied by the French to Robert Heath.

Coxe had come to claim the lands on either side of the Mississippi, and to explore his new possessions. Entering the great highway, he sailed up unmolested for about fifty miles, when he was met by Bienville, also engaged in explorations, who, seeing how powerless he would be to resist the intruder, solved the difficulty by assuring him that the river was not the Mississippi, but another stream belonging to the French.

Suspecting no treachery, Coxe turned back, and the spot which witnessed this somewhat ignominious retreat is still known as the English Turn. The emigrants—most of them Huguenot refugees, who had accompanied the unsuccessful Englishmen—settled in Carolina ; and though they subsequently begged to be allowed to join their fellow-countrymen in Louisiana, they were refused permission to do so by the French monarch.

The close of the year witnessed the return of D'Iberville with sixty emigrants from Canada, whom he settled at a spot about fifty miles from the mouth of the Mississippi. While engaged in erecting a fort for the protection of the new colony, he was visited by our old friend Tonti, the companion of La Salle's early explorations, and in company with him he ascended the river as far as the Natchez country, where a third settlement, first called Rosalie, and afterward Natchez, was founded.

A little later, the knowledge of this part of the country was further ex-

tended by a trip made by Bienville across the Red River, an important tributary of the Mississippi, to Natchitoches; and about the same time Le
Sœur, another adventurous Frenchman, ascended the great river as far as
the Falls of St. Anthony, penetrating into the prairies of Missouri, and
spending a whole winter among the Iowa Indians.

Unfortunately, these isolated efforts were not seconded by any well-
organized attempts to trace the courses of the affluents of the Mississippi, or
to gain information respecting the habits of the natives; and the vast tracts
on either side of the Father of Waters remained pathless wastes to the
European throughout the reign of the French in the Southern States. That
reign, however, was not of very long duration. Yellow fever and other terrible complaints, which still have their haunt in the low lands on the northern shores of the Gulf of Mexico, soon began to work havoc among the settlers at Mobile and the outlying homesteads; and in 1703, only one hundred
and fifty of the many emigrants who had settled from time to time in Louisiana survived. In 1719, a fresh impulse, and that of an extraordinary kind,
was given to emigration to the most southerly districts owned by France, by
that gigantic commercial bubble known as the "Mississippi Scheme,"
which, projected by John Law, Comptroller-General of the finances of
France in the minority of Louis XV., will long be remembered as having
brought about the ruin of thousands. The company to which the working
out of Law's scheme was intrusted was called the Company of the West,
and owned the exclusive privilege of trading to the Mississippi, farming the
taxes and coining the money of the states to be formed. Thousands of
whites and hundreds of negroes to serve as their slaves, were introduced to
Louisiana under the auspices of the new company; Bienville was appointed
governor in the room of his brother D'Iberville, who had fallen a victim to
yellow fever; a site was chosen for the capital of the empire, which was to
rise from the graves of so many Europeans, and the foundation stones were
laid of the modern city of New Orleans, so called in honor of the then Re-
gent of France.

Only one short year after this imposing beginning, the Mississippi bubble
burst; John Law became a bankrupt and an outcast; the lands on the Mississippi, assigned at enormous cost to those whom he had duped, remained
unoccupied, and emigration suddenly ceased. The seeds already sown bore
good fruit, however, in the gradual extension of the French outposts northward. The settlers who had come out to make their fortunes remained to

struggle for bare existence, and the middle of the 18th century found the northern half of Louisiana under the care of Jesuit missionaries, while the seaboard districts were watched over by Capuchin friars. The presence of these zealous teachers of Christianity could not, however, prevent many a terrible struggle with the natives, who again and again made a futile effort to rid themselves of the intruders, the justice of whose appropriation of their lands they naturally failed to see.

Into the terrible details of Indian massacres and French retaliations we

NEW ORLEANS.

need not enter here ; suffice it to say, that when, in 1754, an English grant of lands to the Ohio Company brought on the French war, the soil of the Mississippi valley had already received that baptism of native blood which seems to have been everywhere a preliminary sowing for the harvests of the white man. The struggle which gave to Great Britain the vast hyperborean regions of America, and to which we shall have presently to refer again, also shook the power of France in the South, and resulted, first, in the cession, in 1763, of the lands on the east of the Mississippi to England, while Spain acquired those in the West; and, in 1804, in the purchase by the American Government of the whole region between the Mississippi and the Rocky Mountains, a transaction doubling the area of the United States, and ushering in a new era of discovery. Before we accompany the heroes deputed to explore scientifically the newly-acquired districts, however, we must complete our story of the colonization of the so-called middle states by joining Daniel Boone, to whom is due the honor of having been the first to settle beyond the Alleghany Mountains, which had long formed the western limit alike of colonization and travel.

Boone, whose early life was passed in North Carolina, was first led to turn his attention to the "Far West," as Kentucky and Tennessee were called in the early days of which we are writing, by the glowing accounts given of the exuberant soil and vast quantity of game met with on either side of the Kentucky River by a hunter named John Finley. In 1767, Finley penetrated almost into the rich cane-brakes of Kentucky; and two years later, he and five other men of a similar stamp persuaded Boone to be their leader in an exploring expedition to the newly-discovered hunting-grounds.

On the 9th June, 1769, the little band started on their arduous trip from Boone's house on the Yadkin, and made their way on foot up a rugged mountain of the Alleghany range, the summit of which was reached as the sun was setting. Before them lay the fertile valley of Kentucky, with its rolling plains, tenanted by the buffalo, the deer, and other game, alternating with rugged hills, while beyond stretched vast forests haunted by the wild red men, members of the Chickasaw, Cherokee, and Shawanol tribes, who were as yet untamed by intercourse with the white man.

After a couple of months of successful hunting, the party divided for the more thorough exploration of the country. Boone and a man named Stewart, whose fortunes alone concern us now, reached the Red River north of the Kentucky, where, as they were preparing for the night, they were surprised by a party of Indians, who made them prisoners, and treated them, some say with reckless cruelty, others with rude hospitality. In any case, they were not very securely guarded, for, on the seventh night after their capture, they managed to get away, and while wandering about in the woods, they were met by Boone's brother, who had followed his track, and another adventurer from North Carolina, who had followed the track of the pioneers through the wilderness.

Cheered by good news from home, and by the companionship of the new-comers, Boone resumed his explorations with fresh courage ; but a little later he and Stewart again fell into the hands of Indians. This time Stewart was scalped, though Boone escaped and rejoined his brother, with whom, and the third white man, he decided to spend the winter in the wilderness, and collect furs with which to trade in the spring. The third white man, whose name does not transpire, shortly afterward got separated from his companions, and was never again seen alive. A skeleton and some pieces of clothing, found long years afterward near a swamp, are supposed to have been his, but no details of his fate were ever discovered.

BACKWOODSMEN.

In spite of this second tragedy, the brothers carried out their plan. Building a comfortable log hut to shelter them at night, they spent the days in hunting game, and when the spring of the ensuing year approached, they had collected a vast stock of the skins of wild beasts which had fallen beneath their unerring aim. It was now decided that the elder brother, Squire Boone, should return to North Carolina for supplies, while Daniel remained alone in his primitive habitation to protect the peltry and add to the stock. For three months Daniel wandered about alone, making a tour of observation to the South, and exploring the country on either side of the Silt and Green Rivers. On the 27th July, Squire Boone returned and the brothers together made their way to the important Cumberland River, a tributary of the Ohio, where they found traveling difficult on account of the number of so-called sink-holes, the depressions resulting from the sinking of the earth after heavy rains in a limestone country.

In March, 1771, we find the energetic explorers again on the Kentucky River, where they resolved to form a settlement, and whence they started in the ensuing month for the Yadkin of North Carolina to bring out their families. Two years elapsed before the necessary arrangements could be made, and meanwhile rumors reached the Eastern States of explorations made by other parties, who, without any preconcerted plans, were simultaneously wandering about on the banks of the Cumberland and Tennessee Rivers. In June, 1769, but one month after the first entry into Kentucky of Boone, some twenty men, from North Carolina and West Virginia, made their way over the Alleghanies, and through the Cumberland mountain pass to the river of the same name, into the south-west of Kentucky, the whole of which they thoroughly scoured, returning home in April, 1770, laden with the results of their hunting excursions.

In the same year, 1769, a second company of hunters built a boat and two trapping canoes, and in them paddled down the Cumberland River to the Ohio, and again down the Ohio to the Mississippi, embarking on which they made their way to Natchez, where they sold their furs to great advantage. This was of more importance to them than the fact that this trip of theirs connected the work of the English from the East with that of the French from the South, which alone entitles them to a place in our narrative.

In 1771, the Cumberland was again navigated, this time from the north, by Casper Mansso and some half a dozen companions, who penetrated into the so-called barrens of the south of Kentucky, where they met other hunters from the East. Thus, by the time of Boone's return in 1773, Kentucky, though still unsettled by any white man, was no longer the unknown district it had been on his first visit, and he appeared to have many rivals in the field.

The little caravan of settlers which included Boone's own family and that of five others, started on its arduous journey across the Alleghanies in September, 1773, and in the now well-known Powell's Valley its numbers were augmented by forty well-armed men, who had determined to throw in their lot with the emigrants. The transit of Powell's Gap or Pass was succeeded by that of Wallen's Ridge, and the augmented party were entering the last of the triple range of mountains by the way of Cumberland Gap, when they were suddenly attacked by Indians. Six white men, including Boone's eldest son James, were killed, and the cattle were dispersed, before the Indians were driven back. This tragedy so disheartened the emigrants that they declined to go further ; and though Boone, in spite of his intense grief at the loss of his boy, would have persevered, he was obliged to yield to the numbers against him.

Back again then the survivors tramped, and took refuge at an outpost in the south-west of Virginia, where Boone remained, eating his heart out in compulsory inaction, until June, 1774, when, to his intense delight, he received an appointment as agent to a North Carolina company for purchasing lands in Kentucky. At the head of a party of surveyors, Boone joyfully started once more for the land which he looked upon as his own, and after a long journey, of which unfortunately, no details have been preserved, he stood again upon the shores of the Kentucky River, which he thoroughly surveyed with the help of his comrades, returning in safety in the ensuing year to his family in southern Virginia. .

The reports given by Boone and others of the fertile lands in Kentucky resulted in the formation of a company, at the head of which was a man named Richard Henderson, for the purchase from the Cherokee Indians of a vast tract of land in Ohio and Kentucky, the natives having, by various hostile demonstrations, given proof of their intention not to permit the quiet appropriation of their soil. Daniel Boone, as having already had some intercourse, though not of the most encouraging kind, with the Cherokees, was chosen as the agent in the negotiation, and, after much speechifying, he obtained a hundred square miles of territory on the Kentucky and Ohio, an old warrior closing the final bargain with the words, "Brother, we give you fine land, but you will have trouble in settling it."

The shrewd sachem was right, for Virginia refused to recognize the purchase from the Indians as valid, and claimed all the lands between its western boundaries and the Mississippi for its own. Not until after a long and weary period of litigation was Boone able to realize the wish of his heart, and lay the foundations of the first settlement in Kentucky. His company had to be content, after all, with a very limited district to colonize ; and after he had built his first fort, to which the name of Boonesborough was given in his honor, on the south side of the Kentucky River, he was greatly harassed by the treacherous attacks of the Cherokees, who, although they had received the value of two thousand pounds sterling in goods for their lands, lost no opportunity of annoying the white intruders.

In spite of all these difficulties, Boonesborough was ready in 1774 for the reception of Mrs. Boone and her children, and in the ensuing year the infant settlement was reënforced by the arrival of three other families. The summer of 1775 also witnessed the establishment of many other stations, including that of Louisville, on the Ohio, which soon became a kind of rendezvous for hunters, and a harbor of refuge for emigrants seeking a suitable site for the building of their new homes in the wilderness. Gradually the forests of oak, maple, walnut, etc., of Ohio, the now well-cultivated agricultural districts of Kentucky, and the less fertile cretaceous regions of Tennessee, became dotted with the homes of settlers, each of which in time sent forth new pioneers yet further to the westward.

The conclusion of the war between Great Britain and her mighty colonies in 1783, which gave to English America a political constitution of its own, was succeeded by a tide of emigration across the Alleghanies, and all the best districts for settlement in Tennessee and Kentucky were rapidly filled. In 1788, the Ohio Company, from New England, formed a settlement of considerable size on the north-west of the river from which it took its name, and after a long, desultory struggle with the Wyandots, Delawares, Pottawatomies, Kickapoos, Piankashaws, Miamis, and other tribes occupying the surrounding districts, obtained a legal claim to their lands in 1795 by their purchase from the natives by the United States Government. The peaceable possession of these rich territories thus secured, they were soon portioned out into townships; city after city rose in the wilderness; and, to quote from a traveler who crossed the Alleghanies at the period of which we are writing, "Old America seemed to be breaking up and moving westward." Every state sent forth its bands of emigrants, and no traveler on the now well-worn tracts across the formidable mountain ridge, dividing the old homes from the new, could advance far without coming upon family groups pausing for the return of some father or brother who had seen his dear ones part of the way.

By the close of the 18th century, Ohio was also completely filled up by the settlements of the white men, while the natives, who had sold their birthright, slowly retreated before them into the present states of Illinois and Indiana. But yet again the same programme was gone through. The whites, to whom so much room had already been given, clamored for more;

again their Government listened to their demands. The level lands, watered by sluggish streams, between the Ohio and the Wabash, were bought as those of Ohio had been, and received, as if in irony of the unlucky Indians who had taken refuge there, the name of Indiana. In a similar manner was formed the State of Illinois, the Sack, Fox, and other more northerly tribes ceding their territories as readily as their southern neighbors had done.

Now and then some pioneer penetrated into the southern districts of Michigan, where, as we know, the French had long since established outposts, and in which were now situated Detroit and Mahimillinac, the two chief seats of the Canadian fur-trade. In 1803, the purchase by the Americans of five millions of acres between Lakes Michigan and Huron brought the emigrants from the States face to face with those from Canada. There were no more unoccupied districts to be bought in the neighborhood of the Great Lakes ; and it will be in company with the scientific explorers of modern times that we shall renew our acquaintance with the border lands between the American Republic and Canada.

Returning in the wake of emigration to the South, we find the cession of French territory to the Americans in 1763 resulting in the influx, into the districts between Georgia and the Mississippi, of a vast number of adventurers from the old states and the new. The general name of Louisiana, given by the first comers to the whole of the valley of the Mississippi, became restricted to the small state between the Father of Waters and the then Spanish Texas, while the new and important American settlements on the east of the great river were called Mississippi in its honor. A little later, the tract between the new state of Mississippi and Georgia was settled under the title of Alabama, and of all the eastern districts between the St. Lawrence and the sea there remained but Florida—still, in spite of a temporary change of ownership between 1763 and 1801, in the hands of the Spanish—to be acquired by the ambitious American Government. That its possession was eagerly coveted will be readily understood, and after a long series of negotiations, combined with the occasional use of force, it was annexed to the great republic in 1821.

As a matter of course, the Mississippi was not long allowed to present any barrier either to emigration or exploration, and the taking possession of the districts on the east was but a preliminary step toward the acquisition of the vast tracts stretching away to the Pacific on the west.

After a long and somewhat stormy series of negotiations, Texas, first visited by La Salle in his vain quest for the mouth of the Mississippi, and afterward colonized by the Spanish from Mexico, was ceded to the all-powerful American republic, and, being rapidly settled by enterprising emigrants from the East, it soon in its turn formed the starting-point for new expeditions westward. First California, and then Arizona and New Mexico, became the property of the United States, while the intervening districts between the first state on the Pacific seaboard to become the property of the American republic and the Mississippi were gradually filled up by an ever-increasing tide of emigration from the East and from the South, from the North and from the West. Step by step, little by little, the red men receded before the march of the whites, making every now and then a deeply pathetic, but ever futile attempt to stem the advance of their insidious destroyers. What was originally a vast population of some millions of aborigines—ranking among them, to quote the words of their great historian, Hubert Howe Bancroft, "every phase of primitive humanity, from the reptile-eating cave-dweller of the Great Basin to the Aztec and Maya-Quiché civilization of the southern table-land . . . vanished at the touch of European civilization, and their unwritten history, reaching back for thousands of ages, ended. . . . Their strange destinies fulfilled, in an instant they disappeared, and all we have of them besides their material relics is the glance caught in their hasty flight, which gives us a few customs and traditions, and a little mythological history."

Simultaneously with the advance of the Americans westward, the districts now collectively known as British America were being rapidly opened up by enterprising explorers of various nationalities ; but, to avoid any further break in the continuity of our narrative, we will reserve our account of the Hudson's Bay and other companies who took part in the great work in the North for a future chapter. We will follow first the fortunes of the earliest heroes sent forth by the United States Government to survey the regions west of the Mississippi, which, when purchased, were as little known as the heart of Africa before the journeys of Livingstone, Butler, Speke, Grant, Baker, Stanley, and others.

THE UPPER MISSOURI.

## CHAPTER X.

THUS far our heroes have, with few exceptions, been pioneers rather of
Christianity, emigration or commerce, than of discovery properly so
called. Early colonization in America was not, as in Africa, preceded by
scientific exploration. We have no trans-Atlantic Park or Bruce, no Lander
Oudney, or Clapperton; the white martyrs who baptized the soil of the New
World with their blood fell, not in the cause of geography, but in that of
their homes or their religion. Only in the extreme North have we any
romance in American travel which can at all compare with that so inseparably connected with the winning of each of the secrets of that sister continent
so aptly named the Dark.

The great lakes, rivers, and mountains of America, which we will in our turn call the "Fair Continent," were rather found than discovered. The emigrant, seeking water for his cattle, or timber for his log hut and his fire, pitched his tent by some vast inland sea or rushing stream, unconscious that he had done more than choose well for his immediate temporal needs. Other log huts rose beside his own ; the neighboring lake or river or forest received the name of the first person who turned its resources to account, or retained a corrupted form of its original Indian denomination. Peculiarities in the manners, customs, or appearance of the natives, which would have been full of significance to men such as Park or Bruce, Livingstone or Stanley, passed unnoticed by the lonely squatter of the woods, and whole chapters of discovery were left unwritten by the unconscious agents in the opening up of new tracks.

Not until the beginning of the present century can we be said to have possessed a literature of inland North American discovery, and our narrative has hitherto been culled little by little from piles of volumes dealing with other subjects than ours, and referring *en passant* only to geographical problems. The young states forming the infant republic had too much to do in welding into one whole the varied and often incongruous elements of which they were themselves composed, to be able to pay much attention to the enterprising spirits who went forth from among them to found new homes in the wilderness. But when the turbulent infancy was over, and what we may call the young manhood of America began under the enlightened guidance of the great Washington, first President of the United States, a new era of discovery was ushered in. The republic, no longer content with its ignorance of the course of its rivers, the height of its mountains, and the resources of its vast tracts of prairie and forest lands, began the organization of exploring expeditions. The first of these was that sent out, under Major Pike, in 1805, with instructions " to explore the Upper Mississippi, to inquire into the nature and extent of the fur-trade, with the residence and population of the several Indian nations, and to make every effort to conciliate their friendship."

Pike embarked on the Mississippi at Fort Louis, a little below the mouth of the Missouri, on the 9th August, 1805, in a keel-boat about seventy feet long, accompanied by an escort of twenty soldiers, and after successfully navigating the somewhat difficult current, then much impeded by sand-bars, he reached the mouth of the Missouri in safety. Above its junction with its chief affluent, the name of which signifies the Mud River, the course of the Father of Waters is comparatively smooth, and no incident of importance occurred till, on the 6th September, the mouth of the Wisconsin was reached, where the arduous portion of the young officer's work began.

Having obtained guides at the Indian village of Prairie des Chiens, then an important outpost of the French fur-trade, Pike continued the ascent of

SIOUX VILLAGE.

the great river till he came to the mouth of the Iowa. Here he was met by a party of Sioux or Dacotah Indians, whose chief gave him a hearty welcome, assuring him that the redskins had tried to keep themselves sober in his honor. In this, says Pike, they had not been very successful, and in their unsteady gait and wild salute of three rounds of ball fired at random,

to the great risk of their guests, the young leader noted some of the first
symptoms of the fatal effect of the influence of the whites on the once simple and manly natives. At a dinner of a semi-civilized description, the
Sioux chief gave Pike the pipe of peace, telling him that it would insure
his friendly reception among the "upper bands" of his tribes, and begging
him to try and bring about peace between his people and the Minnesota Indians of the East.

Thanking his host for the pipe of peace, the power of which had already
been proved by his French predecessors on the Mississippi, and promising
to do his best with the Minnesotas, Pike pursued his way, between hilly
country and prairies dotted with the encampments of the Sioux, till he came
to the mouth of the majestic Chippeway on the east, succeeded, a few miles
further up, by the yet more beautiful Minnesota, or St. Peter's River, on
the west.

The explorers were now approaching the summit of the central table land
of the North American continent, where, 1,680 feet above the sea-level, are
situated the sources alike of the St. Lawrence, the Mississippi, and the Red
River of the North, the three great arteries, bound, the first for the Atlantic
Ocean, the second for the Gulf of Mexico, and the third for Hudson's Bay.
As the common home of the infant streams was neared, the navigation of
the Mississippi became more difficult, the river between the mouth of the
Minnesota and the Falls of St. Anthony consisting of a series of rapids dashing over huge rocks encumbering the bed of the stream. Pike persevered,
however, in his work of navigation, his little bark experiencing many a narrow escape in its passage between the frowning precipices, until the Falls
themselves were reached, when he was compelled to leave his own boat and
take to small canoes.

For four miles above the Falls, in the grandeur of which Pike owned himself a little disappointed, all went well, but the remainder of the trip was
fraught with difficulties and dangers of every description. Again and again
the travelers were compelled to disembark, and wading through the water,
often not a foot above the rocks, drag their boats after them, while every
now and then some wild Sioux warrior would appear upon the beetling
heights shutting in the now restricted Father of Waters, and brandish his
spear above the heads of the defenseless whites.

On the 4th October the mouth of the Crow River was passed on the west,
and the first signs of dangers of a new description were noted in the wrecks,

lying here and there of bark canoes, cut to pieces with tomahawks, and with broken paddles and arrows lying near. Pike's interpreter told him that the canoes were of Sioux and the arrows of Minnesota construction, pointing to the conclusion that war was raging hotly close at hand. Further examination of the relics revealed marks on the paddles of the canoes signifying that Indian men and women had been killed, and the guide was eager in urging retreat, on the ground that their party would be taken for Sioux invaders, and be cut to pieces at the first Chippeway village before any explanation could be given. Only a little time before, three Frenchmen who had ventured up the river had been murdered by the Chippeways; surely the white man would not risk sharing their fate?

But the white man, true to his English blood, was not to be intimidated, and pressed on in spite of all difficulties, till, about two hundred and thirty miles above the Falls, in N. lat. 45°, his men began to drop from fatigue and the severity of the cold. It was evidently impossible to proceed further by water, and Pike realized, now that it was too late, how fatal a mistake had been made in starting so late in the season. After consultation with his party, it was resolved to leave a small detachment with the bulk of the provisions in a log fort, and proceed in sledges with the hardiest of the men to the sources of the Mississippi.

The fort was built with infinite difficulty, and it was not until mid-winter that the sledge journey was begun. Following the course of the Mississippi, now dwindled down to a small stream, scarcely three hundred yards wide, creeping sluggishly along through a flat, uninteresting country—its wide snow-clad stretches tenanted only by troops of elks, with here and there traces of recent conflict between the Indians of the North and the Sioux of the South—the pioneers reached the mouth of the Pine River, flowing from Leech Lake—the most southerly of the cluster of small reservoirs forming the sources of the great river—on the last day of the year.

Here a deserted Chippeway encampment of fifty wigwams—or lodges, as they are called in this part of the country—was found, the marks about it, as interpreted by the Sioux guide, signifying that fifty warriors had recently marched against their enemies and killed four men and four women. The quaint record of the conflict consisted of four painted poles, sharpened at the ends to represent the women, placed about four cedar puppets representing the men, the whole inclosed in a rough circle of poles, hung with deerskins, plumes, silk handkerchiefs, etc.

A little beyond this strange monument, Pike's party were overtaken by some Chippeways, accompanied by a Frenchman and an Englishman. They were at first about to discharge their arrows, but, recognizing the American flag, they desisted, and gave the explorers all the information in their power. On the following day, Grant, the Englishman, and a member of the North-west Company, took Pike to his house on Red Cedar Lake, one of the sources of the Mississippi, and the young American's wrath was greatly excited on seeing the English flag waving from the roof. Somewhat mollified on hearing that the flag was the property of the Indians, having been taken in some skirmish, Pike resumed his journey under the guidance of a Chippeway warrior named Curly Head, and arrived, on the 13th January, 1806, at another establishment of the North-west Company on Sandy Lake, where he was hospitably received.

A tour of the lake was successfully made, with the aid of some of the hardy agents of the North-west Company, and its latitude was determined to be 49° 9′ 20″ N. Leaving this, the second of the sources of the Mississippi, on the 21st January, our hero started for Leech Lake, with a young Indian as guide, and after a most arduous journey on foot in snow shoes, such as are worn by the Indians, on the 1st February he reached that important and central point, long supposed to be the main source of the Father of Waters. Here, as on Red Cedar and Sandy Lakes, he found agents of the great North-west Company established in a well-built fort, and learned from them that from what are called the Forks of the Mississippi the right branch bears north-west, entering Lake Winnipeg eight miles further north, and beyond that again running to Upper Red Cedar Lake, a distance of eight miles ; while the left branch, called that of Leech Lake, bears south-west, and runs through a chain of meadows to the De Corbean River, with which, and with the Red River of the North, it is connected by a series of portages.

Unable, owing to the lateness of the season, to test the accuracy of the information obtained, Pike was reluctantly compelled to turn back after making a survey of Leech Lake ; and it was not until many years afterward that the journeys of Cass and Schoolcraft corrected the mistaken assumption that Leech Lake was the main source of the Mississippi.

Before turning his back on Leech Lake, however, Pike obeyed the second clause of his instructions by summoning a council of Chippeway warriors, on whom he urged the conclusion of peace with the Sioux, inviting some of them to return with him to St. Louis. He succeeded in both these objects, though the latter was only brought about after much persuasion. As was natural, the Chippeways were not over-eager to trust themselves in the Sioux country; but when Pike exclaimed at the close of the interview, "What! are there no soldiers at Leech, Red, and Rainy Lakes who have the heart to carry the calumet of peace for their Father?" two celebrated young warriors, bearing the extraordinary names of the Buck and the Beau, sprang forward to offer their services. They were eagerly accepted, and adopted as Pike's children. We are happy to be able to add that their young "father" allowed them to have no reason to regret their decision, but that they arrived with him in safety at St. Louis, after a successful return voyage down the Mississippi.

Soon after his arrival at St. Louis, after this fairly successful trip, Pike was again sent out on an exploratory expedition; this time with orders to survey the regions south of the Missouri, and to trace the Arkansas and Red Rivers, already known as tributaries of the Mississippi, to their sources in the far West.

The exploring party, which consisted of twenty-three members, including a surgeon and an interpreter, started on this second journey on the 15th July, 1806, taking with them a number of Indians belonging to the Osage and Pawnee tribes, who had been redeemed from captivity among the Potawatomies, and were now to be restored to their friends. Ascending the Missouri in two boats, the mixed company reached, on the 26th July, the Osage River, which, flowing from the south, pours its vast bulk of waters into the Missouri. Here they were received with eager, though quiet enthusiasm by the natives, and a touching scene ensued between the relatives restored to each other through the mediation of the white men.

The Osage Indians, dwelling in the fair country on either side of the beautiful river named after them, seem to have attained to a rare degree of civilization, possessing a kind of republic, presided over by a small body of chiefs, whose resolutions required the ratification of a selected council of warriors. Pike and his white companions were feasted with grain, beans and pumpkins, the number of entertainments being rather embarrassing, as it was considered etiquette to taste of every thing offered.

Leaving the friendly Osage Indians still rejoicing over the return of the captives, Pike now struck across the country in a south-easterly direction for the Arkansas River, passing the mouth of the Platte and Kansas, both minor tributaries of the Missouri, on whose banks dwelt the Pawnee

Indians, a race differing but little, if at all, from the Osages. After an arduous march through a mountainous country, the dividing range between the Kansas and Arkansas Rivers was crossed on the 14th October, and late on the same day a branch of the latter river was reached.

On Sunday, the 19th October, the Arkansas itself was first sighted, and, crossing it in canoes, constructed on the spot under his own superintendence, the gallant young leader proceeded to carry out the instructions he had received, by tracing its course through all its devious windings, in what was then an untrodden wilderness, tenanted chiefly by buffalo, elk, deer, and wild horses.

Being totally unprepared for the great length of the river between its junction with the Mississippi in north latitude 34° 54' and west longitude 91° 10', or for the severity of the climate, as its birthplace in the Rocky Mountains on the borders of Utah was approached in mid-winter, the explorers endured very great hardships. The head of the Arkansas River was reached late in December, and was found to be no less than 192 miles west of its outlet from the mighty ridge dividing the rivers flowing into the Pacific from those which find their final home in the Arctic Ocean, Hudson's Bay, or the Gulf of Mexico.

Footsore, weary, and half-starved though he and his followers were, Pike paused but long enough to ascertain the exact position of the source of the Arkansas, before he struck across country to work out the second portion of the problem given to him to solve, namely, how and where did the most southerly of the western branches of the Mississippi rise, and what was its course before entering the now well-known lowlands of Louisiana?

Under the impression that the Red River must spring into being almost simultaneously with, and certainly at no very great distance from, its sister tributary the Arkansas, the young commander led his exhausted men in a southerly direction, and presently came upon a broad stream flowing in a south-easterly direction. Surely this must be what he was seeking; and, elated at the rapidity of his imaginary success, Pike erected a fort on the banks of the newly-found river, in token that it henceforth belonged to the United States. The next step was to embark on the stream, which, as the explorers hoped, would soon bring them down to the outpost of Natchitoches, near its junction with the Father of Waters.

All went well for several days. Visits from Spaniards from the South only served to strengthen the impression that the Red River was found, but on the 26th February a terrible revelation was made by the arrival of a party of Europeans from Santa Fé, one of the Spanish stations in New Mexico, who informed Pike that a party of Utah Indians, members of the great untamed Shoshone family, were about to attack him, and that he was infringing the laws of the Mexican Government by navigating the Rio Bravo del Norte without permission.

CAPTAIN LEWIS BEHOLDING THE MISSOURI.

The report of the intentions of the Utahs seems scarcely to have troubled Pike, but at the mention of the Rio Bravo del Norte, he exclaimed, "What! is not this the Red River?" "No, sir," replied the spokesman of the detachment from Santa Fé; "it is the Rio del Norte." "Immediately," adds Pike in his own account of this bitter disappointment, "I ordered my flag to be taken down and rolled up, feeling how sensibly I had committed myself."

He was right; the Spaniards had come out to make the intruders their prisoners, for New Mexico, Arizona, and Texas had not yet been ceded to the United States. In vain Pike pleaded that he had been acting in ignorance; he and his people were compelled to accompany the escort to Santa Fé, and though they were treated most courteously and hospitably, rather as guests than as captives, all hope of reaching the Red River had to be abandoned.

After a detention of some months at Santa Fé, already a fine city, situated among the Rocky Mountains on a plain 1,047 feet above the sea-level, the Americans were sent back to their own territory by a circuitous route through New Mexico and Texas, which, though then as now tenanted by the wild and predatory Navajoe, Apache, Utah, Comanche, and other tribes, they found to be traversed by fairly good roads made for the use of missionaries and miners, who had now for more than two centuries been at work in these western wilds.

Pike arrived at Natchitoches on the Red River on the 1st July, after an absence of one year from the United States, and we hear no more of him as an explorer. The work done by him was, however, but the prelude, or rather—as much of it was simultaneous with that of the heroes we are now about to join—the accompaniment of the more extensive expedition under Captains Lewis and Clarke, sent out by the American Government in May, 1804, with orders to explore the Missouri, the chief of all the affluents of the Mississippi, to its source, and then to make their way by the shortest route to the first navigable water on the western side, which they were to trace to the shores of the Pacific.

The new expedition, consisting of some forty-five members—sixteen only of whom were, however, to go the whole distance—and provided with one keel-boat and two open boats, started up the Missouri on the 16th May, 1804. The French outposts of St. Charles and La Charette, in the present state of Missouri, were passed, the exact positions of the mouths of the Osage, Kansas, and Platte tributaries were noted, and the unknown districts occupied by the Ottoe Indians were entered in July. Here the American explorers held a meeting with a number of Ottoe chiefs, who expressed themselves pleased that their land now belonged to the white men from the East instead of the French, and added the naïve hope that their father, President

Jefferson, would send them arms to defend themselves from their enemies, and hunt game for themselves and their little ones.

Beyond the mouth of the Platte, or Nebraska, the work of surveying the Missouri became extremely arduous, on account of its many and sudden windings. On one side lay the picturesque prairie and forest lands of Iowa, with its rugged ravines and striking bluffs ; on the other the vast plain of Nebraska, sloping gradually upward to the Rocky Mountains. Now in Iowa, now in Nebraska, the party steadfastly followed the course of the fickle river, and toward the close of August they came to the mouth of the Sioux River, on the borders of Dacotah, where they found themselves on comparatively familiar ground, the Dacotah or Sioux warriors having long been on friendly terms, alike with the Americans from the East and the French from the North.

A little above the mouth of the Sioux the Missouri makes a sudden and abrupt detour to the west, known as the Great Bend, following which our heroes were proceeding to traverse Dacotah, when, on the 25th September, a difficulty for the first time occurred with the natives, some of whom declared that the expedition should proceed no further. The large boat was waiting in the middle of the river for Captain Clarke, who had gone on shore with five of his men, when a party of Indians gathered about the small detachment with bent bows and threatening gestures. It was a critical moment, but, fortunately for the Americans, a signal given by Clarke to the soldiers in the boat was seen and understood. Twelve men jumped from it into one of the smaller boats, and, supported by this reënforcement, the Captain lowered his weapons, advanced to the leader of the Indians, and offered his hand. It was not accepted, but, surprised at this sudden movement, the Indians paused in the very act of drawing their bows to see what might be the meaning of the white man's strange behavior.

Finding his proffered hand rejected, perhaps because the red men had not yet learned the significance of its offer, Clarke turned his back on his assailants, and, surrounded by his men, walked quietly back to his boat. He was allowed to embark and put off unmolested, but before the large vessel was reached, the native warriors had decided that he was a man to be feared and courted. Four of the boldest, therefore, jumped into the Missouri, waded to the boat, and with many quaint and touching gestures offered their friendship to their white brother. It was accepted, as a matter of course ; the four representatives were allowed to go up the river for some little distance in the big boat, the like of which they had never seen before ; and the next day a grand meeting of the Sioux was held, at which the whites were most hospitably entertained, though most of the speeches in their honor wound up with petitions for presents.

After a thorough examination of the Great Bend, which has been justly characterized as one of the most remarkable features of the Missouri, forming, as it does, a circuit of some thirty miles, Lewis and Clarke led their men in a north-westerly direction to the mouth of the Cheyenne or Skyenne, just below the 45th parallel of north latitude, where they were met by a French trader, who informed them that the previous winter he had penetrated to the Black Mountains, three hundred leagues to the westward, proving our assertion at the beginning of this chapter, that the first exploration of America was accomplished, as it were, unconsciously.

Early in October the travelers entered the districts occupied by the Mandans, a native tribe holding some very peculiar notions with regard to the powers of the Great Spirit, whom they also called the Great Medicine, recognizing his agency in every cure of ill, whether physical, mental or temporal. Unfortunately, in spite of this strangely advanced creed, the Mandans were a degraded and dissolute race, ready to give and equally ready to take offense ; the tomahawk being the usual weapon resorted to for revenge.

In spite of the unpromising character of the people among whom they found themselves, the American leader resolved, as the season was now so far advanced, to build a fort in the Mandan country in which to spend the winter, and to resume their task with fresh ardor in the ensuing spring. The friendship of the Mandans and of the Minnetarees, dwelling in the highlands of Minnesota on the east, was conciliated by presents, etc., and a site chosen for the fort in N. lat. 47°. Aided by the advice and assistance of a number of the English Hudson's Bay Company, and of a Canadian Frenchman who had spent some time among the Cheyenne Indians, the soldiers quickly constructed, not only a fort for their protection, but a number of cabins for their comfort ; and the whole of the winter was passed in studying the ways of the natives, hunting, etc., the monotony of the residence in the spot being often relieved by visits from French or Canadian fur-traders, from whom much valuable information was obtained.

Early in April of the ensuing year, 1805, the camp at Fort Mandan, as the temporary settlement had been called, was broken up, and the party, now numbering thirty-two, and with their means of navigation increased to eight boats and canoes, once more embarked on the Missouri. To aid in intercourse with the Shoshone or Snake Indians of Montana, Idaho, and Oregon, two interpreters were secured, namely, George Drewyer and Toussaint Chabornæan, the latter of whom was accompanied by his wife, a young Snake woman who had been taken prisoner by his tribe some time before.

On the 13th April the mouth of the Little Missouri was passed, and on the 26th that of the rapid Yellowstone River, from Sublette's Lake in the Rocky Mountains. From this great landmark the course of the Missouri—and, as a result, of the explorers—was due west, and the character, alike of the scenery, the fauna, and the flora, changed perceptibly. In the journals from which our narrative is culled, we find notes on the strange appearance presented by banks and sandbars covered with salt, looking like frost; on the

YELLOWSTONE LAKE.

white and red "bluffs," probably rich in minerals, on either side of the stream ; and most interesting of all, on meetings of frequent occurrence with white or brown bears.  On more than one occasion, Captain Lewis almost lost his life in encounters with these formidable creatures.  His first escape was from a white bear, one of two which suddenly appeared in his path when he was on shore with only one hunter, and which, though badly wounded, pursued him for a long distance.

On another occasion Lewis went in pursuit of a brown bear, which had been wounded by some of his men, and found the poor creature lying in a kind of bed in the earth, two feet deep and five feet long, which he had scooped out for himself after receiving his death blow.  Lewis put an end to his agonies by firing through his skull, and in his account of the matter he speaks in terms of high admiration of the courage and intelligence displayed by all the brown bears he had opportunities of watching.

In the different journals kept by various members of this great expedition, our readers who love sporting adventures will find many another fascinating anecdote of a similar kind to the two we have selected ; but, with our heroes, we must press on for the West, pausing, as they did, on the 3d of June, 1805, at a spot some miles above the mouth of the Yellowstone, where the Missouri divides into two great channels, or forks, as they are called in America.  Thus far, all had been successful.  The course of the Missouri had been carefully traced, and something had been learned of that of every great tributary ; but now a mistake would be fatal.  From what the natives said, the leaders of the expedition were convinced that one of these two channels led to the sources, not only of the Missouri, but also of the Columbia, that great river of the West first, as we believe, discovered by Viscaino in 1602, though the honor due to him has been given to a certain Captain Gray, of Boston, who, in 1792, entered the mouth of the mighty stream when on a trading expedition, and gave it the name it still retains, after his own vessel.

The camp was pitched below the junction of the two forks, and an earnest consultation held as to which of the two channels should now be followed.  The one flowing from the north was narrower but deeper than that from the south, and its waters were of the brown, turbid character which had already earned for the Missouri its name of the Mud River.  Surely this northern branch must be the true Missouri !  So urged all the members of the expedition, except the two leaders, who, judging more scientifically than their men, were of opinion that, though broader, the southerly branch, with its clear and transparent current, was more likely to have come from the rocky home assigned by all the natives to the great tributary under survey.

The men, though unconvinced of the justice of their superiors' opinion,

VIEW IN THE ROCKY MOUNTAINS.

yielded at once ; and after a cursory examination of the northern branch. it was resolved to follow the more southerly. The natives of every district traversed, and the traders who had visited the western coast, had agreed in describing some very magnificent falls formed by the Missouri at no very great distance from its source. The finding of these falls would therefore be the final proof that the river was the true Missouri, and Captain Lewis now hurried forward with a few men, in the hope of solving all doubt before the main body started from the junction.

A march of a couple of days brought the pioneers to a lofty ridge, from which they had their first view of the Rocky Mountains—that grand continuation of the Cordilleras of Mexico, which forms a kind of backbone to North America, and is the common ancestral home of the rivers of the far West, and of many of those whose last resting-places are in the extreme North or the Gulf of Mexico. Twelve miles beyond the ridge, a short halt was made, on account of the illness of Captain Lewis, and on the ensuing day, June 13, as the party were leisurely proceeding on their way in a southerly direction, the leader heard a sound which made him forget his weakness, in the hope that the Falls were now within a short distance.

Hastening in the direction of the "roar," the explorers soon came in sight of what looked at first like a column of smoke, but which turned out to be spray driven by the wind; and seven miles from the spot where the sound of the falling had been first heard, they came upon the magnificent cataracts, second only in beauty to those of Niagara. Sending back a man with the joyful news of his discovery to Captain Clarke, Captain Lewis now proceeded to examine the Falls, and to his delighted surprise he found that the scene which had so impressed him on his first arrival was, as it were, but the opening chapter of a series of rapids and cascades extending over a distance of no less than sixteen miles and a-half. Above what our hero named the Crooked Falls, on account of the rugged and irregular nature of the rocks over which the water dashes, the river makes a sudden bend to the north, and as Lewis was following its course, he heard a roar as of a continuous discharge of musketry above his head.

Turning rapidly to ascertain its cause, the leader, after traversing a few hundred yards only, reached the culminating point in the panorama. A huge shelving rock, with a surface unbroken by any irregularity, rises up as if by magic from the bed of the river, which dashes over the obstacle in an uninterrupted sheet of water, and is received in a ravine of picturesque beauty, between the rugged sides of which it foams and rages, as if in despair at the result of the effort made in its stupendous leap.

In the very moment of this great and significant success, when the triumphant conclusion of the expedition had become almost a certainty, Captain Lewis had yet another narrow escape in an encounter with a brown bear. Absorbed in the examination of the beauties around him, he had forgotten that, though as yet unknown to civilization, the neighborhood was already tenanted by many a formidable foe to the explorer; and he had forgotten even to load his rifle, which was hanging useless in his hand,

GRIZZLY BEAR.

when he suddenly became aware that a large brown bear was advancing stealthily upon him. There was nothing for it but flight; for what could an unarmed man do against so terrible an antagonist? Captain Lewis therefore made for the nearest tree as fast as his legs would carry him, but, finding the bear gained rapidly upon him, it struck him that the river would be a safer refuge. Into the Missouri, therefore, he plunged, and, standing in it waist deep, he confronted the bear, holding before him the weapon known as an expontoon.

The bear duly arrived at the water's edge, and the Captain's fate seemed sealed ; but at that critical moment, for some reason never explained, the huge quadruped took alarm, turned tail, and ran up the bank with greater haste than dignity, turning about every now and then as if fearful of being pursued.

This terrible danger escaped, Lewis resumed his examination of the surrounding scenery, and when, a couple of days later, he was joined by Clarke and his men, it was resolved that no time should be lost in continuing the ascent of the Missouri. It being absolutely impossible, however, to take the boats over the Falls, a considerable delay occurred before any arrangement could be made for transporting the baggage. A skin-boat, the frame of which had been brought in readiness, was first put together, but it was found altogether inadequate to the purpose for which it was intended ; and under the direction of Clarke, eight strong canoes were finally constructed, in which such luggage as could not be dispensed with was packed. The remainder of the luggage was then concealed in a deep hole called a *cache*, or deposit, which was carefully closed to protect it from the Indians and white bears which haunted the neighborhood of the Falls, and which would certainly have made strange havoc among the valuable books, specimens of plants, drawings, etc., had they come upon them unexpectedly.

Before the end of June, all was ready. The canoes admirably answered the purpose for which they were intended, and the voyage was resumed in the highest spirits. Little progress had been made, however, when Captain Clarke missed some geographical notes he had taken, and turned back, accompanied by his servant York, the interpreter Chabornaean, and the latter's wife and child. To retrace his steps for the sake of making sure of a few facts seemed a simple enough proceeding, yet in so doing Clarke ran a risk of never completing his journey. On his arrival at the Falls, a terrible storm came on, and he took refuge with his party beneath some shelving rocks in a ravine hard by, thinking to resume his walk in an hour or so. As he waited, however, a torrent of rain and hail suddenly seemed to collect in a solid mass, and poured into the ravine in a strong current, bringing with it huge fragments of rocks, uprooted trees, and all manner of *debris*. There was not a moment to lose ; the Captain seized his gun, and, pushing before him the Indian woman, who had caught her child up from the net in which it lay at her feet, he sprang up the ravine, closely followed by Chabornæan. So sudden was the rise of the water, that it was up to Clarke's waist before he gained the bank ; and as he turned to look back on reaching that refuge, he saw the whole ravine filled, and the net from which the child had been rescued whirled rapidly out of sight. An instant's hesitation, and the whole party would have been swept down the Great Falls.

Returning in haste to his camp after this miraculous escape, Clarke found that his companions had suffered terribly in the storm. Many of the men were bleeding from wounds received from the hail ; and after the rain and wind had ceased, the heat had been so excessive that even strong soldiers had succumbed to it. Some men sent back next day to look for Clarke's gun, compass and umbrella, which he had left behind in his hasty retreat, found only the compass, covered with mud and sand, at the mouth of the ravine, and reported that huge rocks now choked up what had been an empty defile when the leader's party had taken refuge in it.

Beyond the Great Falls the navigation of the Missouri was extremely arduous. The channel was often narrow, and much obstructed by shallows, inlets, and impediments of every description. Here and there, some village perched on a bluff overlooking the stream broke the almost solemn loneliness of the scene ; but the quaint booths composing these villages were chiefly deserted, their owners, the Snakes or Shoshones, spending the greater part of their time in hunting. Onward, however, pressed the eight canoes, and about the middle of July the first spurs of the Rocky Mountains were reached, hemming in the river ever more and more, sometimes even almost shutting it in from light and air, so closely did the perpendicular cliffs on either side approach each other.

On the 19th July, the grand range of rocks from which the Missouri issues, forming one of the most magnificent mountain passes of the world, was reached, and the first part of the journey may be said to have been performed. Naming the pass the " Gates " of the Rocky Mountains, our heroes made their way through it in their canoes, each stroke of the paddle revealing fresh beauties and ever-increasing solemnity. " The convulsion of the passage," says Rees, alluding to the first breaking forth of the Missouri from its mountain cradle, " must have been terrible, since at its outlet there are vast columns of rock torn from the mountain, which are strewed on both sides of the river—the trophies, as it were, of the victory."

The Gates of the Rocky Mountains form a gorge of between five and six miles long, and beyond it the scenery is of very great beauty. Anxious now to reach the sources of the Missouri and the headwaters of the Columbia, Lewis and Clarke paused but to note the chief features of the neighborhood, and shortly reached a spot where the great river they had followed so far divides into three forks. To these they gave the names of Jefferson, Madison and Gallatin, after three great politicians of the young republic, and, after some hesitation between them, selected the first, flowing in a south-westerly direction, as the most likely to be the true Missouri. The event proved that they were right. The Jefferson led them through the very central recesses of the Rocky Mountains, and on the 12th August, 1805, a small gap between the lofty mountainous ridges was reached, from which issued the springhead of the mighty Missouri.

The exact position of the source of the river, the course of which they had followed for no less than 3,000 miles, was carefully noted by the explorers, and found to be N. lat. 45°, W. long. 112°; and, after congratulating each other on the great success achieved, the journey was resumed with fresh ardor and enthusiasm.

It was now of the utmost importance to obtain guides, as the expedition was totally at a loss as to the direction to be taken to reach the Columbia. Traces had again and again been seen of the encampments of Snake Indians, and a fairly good native road traversed the mountains ; but the red men had evidently heard rumors of the approach of the pale skins, those scourges from the South and East who had already driven so many tribes westward.

In the absence of guides, it was decided to follow the Indian road to the summit of the mountains ; and the same day which witnessed the discovery of the source of the Missouri, was also the date of the first visit of white men to the summit of the ridge forming the watershed between the Pacific and the central table-lands of North America. Pausing but a few minutes to gaze upon the wonderful panorama stretching away to the South Sea, for which so many previous explorers had sought in vain, the Americans began the descent of the Rocky Mountains, and at a distance of about three-quarters of a mile from their summit, they came to a small "creek of clear water running to the westward." Subsequent observations proved this to be the Columbia ; but, unable without assistance to be sure of its identity with the second river to be explored, the leaders of the party still followed the Indian road, and on the 13th July were rewarded for their patience by coming upon a small party of Indians, who fled at their approach.

Eagerly giving chase, Captain Lewis and several of his men succeeded—though the men escaped—in surprising a woman and a little girl, who, recognizing the hopelessness of getting away, sat down on the ground and bent their heads, ready for the death-blow which they thought they must expect from the strangers. Greatly touched by this pathetic action, Lewis laid down his weapons, and, taking the woman by the hand, made signs to her that she was to be unharmed. She appeared to understand him, and, giving her a few trifling presents, the leader persuaded her to go and fetch another woman who had been with her when he first came in sight of the party. In a few minutes the two returned, and, after painting the cheeks of his three captives with vermilion, a sign among the Snake Indians of peace, Lewis induced them to lead him to their camp, that he might confer with their chiefs.

After a march of two miles, with the Indians leading the way, a troop of some sixty warriors, mounted on good horses, was sighted. The mediators hastened to meet the chief, explaining who the white men were, and a scene of some absurdity ensued, the Indians embracing the Americans, and covering them with grease and paint. This wild welcome was succeeded by the smoking of a pipe of peace in common, Captain Lewis first taking a whiff and then passing it round to his hosts. The friendship between the Snakes and Americans thus ratified, the chiefs conducted their white brothers to their camp, where a grand consultation was held as to the best means of reaching the Columbia, and tracing its course to the Pacific.

The information given was not very satisfactory. The river, said the Indians, flowed through a country where timber for building canoes and food for filling the stomach were alike scarce. No one cared to undertake the task of guiding the explorers on their perilous journey, and, although, after a good deal of persuasion and bribery, ten men were induced to promise their assistance, it was in such a grudging fashion as to promise but little success.

At this juncture a touching incident occurred. The wife of Chabornean, the interpreter, who, it will be remembered, was a Snake by birth, entered the camp, and, recognizing her brother in the chief, she flung herself into his arms, and with many tears sobbed out her joy at finding him still alive. The accounts given by the restored captive of the kindness of the white men, their faithfulness and generosity to those who trusted them, and their power to avenge themselves on those who deceived them, were fruitful of

the best results. The chief of the Snakes consented to send help to the
main body of the expedition, which had not yet scaled the heights of the
Rocky Mountains, and while preparations were being made for the advance
of the whole party to the Pacific, Captain Clarke was provided with guides
for a trial trip to the Columbia.

Mounted on a fine horse, lent to him by an Indian, Clarke quickly reached
the river, though the mountains to be traversed were rugged and broken in
the extreme ; but here the difficulties in tracing the course of the Columbia
became so great, that it was evidently impossible to do so without spending
the whole of the remainder of the year in the neighborhood. So far as we
can make out from the various accounts of his expedition, Clarke did not
actually reach any of the headwaters of the Columbia, which are situated
between N. lat. 54° and 42°, but he made a sufficiently thorough survey of
the mountains from which the more northerly of its two branches proceeds,
to convince himself of the identity of that branch with the river of Viscaino
and Gray. A result of this trial trip of secondary importance was that the
leader recognized the hopelessness of attempting to descend the Columbia
in canoes, and on his return to the Indian camp, it was agreed that a detour
should be made in a northerly direction, so as to strike the river below the
mountain pass from which it flows on its way to join its sister stream in N.
lat. 46° 5 , W. long. 118° 55'.

On the 23d August the expedition was once more en route. The sources
of the Missouri had been discovered, the position of those of the Columbia
determined, and the country between the two traversed more than once.
All, therefore, that now remained to be done was to trace the great river of
the West to the Pacific. Accompanied by a number of Shoshone guides,
the Americans made their way toward the ocean by a rugged Indian path,
halting now at one, now at another Indian village ; and after much wandering to and fro, with terrible sufferings from cold and hunger, they entered
a district inhabited by a people calling themselves Ootlashoots, who turned
out to be members of one of the numerous inland Columbian tribes who inhabit the regions on the Pacific between N. lat. 52° 30' and 45°.

After leaving the Ootlashoots, the explorers endured the extremities of
famine, and were compelled first to kill and eat their horses, and then to
purchase for food the dogs of wandering Indians met with on their painful
way to the coast. At length, on the 13th September, the lower course of the
upper branch of the Columbia, to which the name of Lewis was given, was

reached, and from Twisted Hair, a chief of the Nez Percés, or Pierced-nosed Indians, another inland Columbian tribe, the joyful news was heard that the ocean was not far distant. Twisted Hair and his subjects, who received their peculiar appellation of Nez Percés on account of some of them wearing a white shell suspended from their noses, assisted their white visitors in building canoes, in which the explorers floated easily down the now wide and rapid Columbia to the home of the Sokulks, belonging to the same great family as the Ootlashoots and Nez Percés, a wild but peaceable peo-

BASALTIC PINNACLES ON THE COLUMBIA RIVER.

ple, living in well-built huts, and clothing themselves in the skins of elk, deer, and other trophies of the chase.

Below the Sokulks dwelt the Pishquitpaws, who had never seen a white man, and were proportionately astonished at the sudden appearance among them of the Americans. Except that they wore scarcely any clothing at all, the Pishquitpaws differed but little from the other inland Columbian tribes visited; and when their terror at the arrival of their strange guests— who they thought had fallen straight from the sky—was somewhat subsided, they were ready enough to give information and show hospitality.

As the canoes floated down the Columbia toward the Great Falls, the spirits of the party were cheered by the sight on the west of a lofty snow-tipped mountain, which they identified as that of St. Helen's, seen by Van couver from the mouth of the great river; and on the 22d October the Falls themselves were reached, where the Columbia, driven into a narrow channel some forty-five yards wide, with a huge black rock on one side and mighty hills on the other, whirls and boils in a terrific manner. The Indian guides voted this passage impassable for canoes; but, unwilling to undergo either the delay or fatigue necessary to transport the baggage by land, the leaders of the expedition determined to run the risk of shooting the Falls in their frail barks. To their own relief and the intense delight of the Indians the passage was successfully performed, and all dangers seemed now over, when the explorers discovered that the Falls were but the gateway, so to speak, of a yet more formidable impediment to navigation, known as the Great Narrows, where the river for three miles had literally to eat its way through a black rock varying in width from thirty to one hundred yards. Into this terrible passage, however, the canoes entered, and after a struggle, in which the skill and endurance of every member of the party were tried to the utmost, the smooth waters below were entered, and in the numerous seals disporting themselves on either side of the little vessels, the weary explorers read signs that the coast was now indeed near at hand.

The Columbia now gradually widened; on the first day of November the first appearance of tide water was noticed, and about the eighth of the same month the first view was obtained of the Pacific Ocean. A somewhat tempestuous trip of a few days followed this great era in American exploration; but the close of the month found the whole party in the mouth of the great Columbia. The American continent had been traversed for the first time by scientific observers, and the true extent of the American dominion could never again be doubted.

The first week in December was spent in beating about the Pacific coast in search of a suitable refuge in which to pass the winter, and on the 7th a small bay was selected, which was called Merryweather, after the Christian name of Captain Lewis. Here temporary tents were soon erected, and, in the long dreary months which followed, acquaintance was made with the Clatsops, Chinnooks, Killamucks, and other seaboard tribes of the great Columbia family, who, though differing in much, agreed in a remarkable fondness for artificial deformity, especially for the flattening of the forehead. Hence the designation of Flatheads applied to all the tribes dwelling west of the Rocky Mountains by their cousins of the East.

With the early spring the camp at Merryweather Bay was broken up, and the exploring party turned their faces homeward. A journey of a couple of months, over much the same route as that followed on the way to the Pacific, brought them once more to the navigable portion of the Missouri, and, sailing down, they arrived at Fort Louis, at its junction with the Father of Waters, on the 22d May, 1806.

THE GIANTESS GEYSER OF YELLOWSTONE.

# CHAPTER XI.

TO bring our account of the course of discovery between the 30th and 60th parallels of north latitude down to the date of the return of Lewis and Clarke from their great expedition, we must join for a moment some explorers of yet another nationality, who, from the North, continued the work begun by the Spanish from the South, opening the way for the completion by Englishmen of the examination of the Pacific shore of America.

Early in the eighteenth century, the Russians, though they had failed to round the most northern promontories of Asia, had penetrated to its eastern shores, and were thus brought nearer to America than any other European power. After the establishment of stations in Kamtschatka, the efforts of the Russian Government were directed to ascertaining whether the two great continents were or were not connected ; and when this question was partially set at rest in 1728 by Behring, who reached the Asiatic side of the straits bearing his name, an expedition was at once fitted out under his command for sailing direct to the northern shores of America, and discovering if possible, the long sought passage.

The story of the heroic struggle of Behring, and his melancholy death after his discovery of the Aleutian and other islands, with the adventures in the same latitudes of his comrade, Tchirikow, belongs to the history of Arctic exploration. We mention them here, however, as the openers of the north-western gate of the Pacific, their discoveries having greatly simplified the problems still to be solved between Cape Mendocino and the most southerly point reached by them.

The news of the existence of navigable straits between America and Asia resulted in the turning of the attention of scientific men of Europe to the North-west, and the relinquishment for a short time of the efforts of navigators to reach the extreme North by way of Davis Strait and Baffin's Bay.

The great navigator Cook was the first to avail himself of the new passage. Not content with the splendid results achieved in his first two voyages, he determined to make yet another, and in his famous old ship, the *Resolution*, accompanied by Captain Clarke in the *Discovery*, he sailed from Plymouth for the third and last time on the 12th July, 1776.

CAPTAIN JAMES COOK.

As is known to every schoolboy, Cook reached the Sandwich Islands in safety, and, steering from them across the Pacific, he arrived on the western coast of America, in about N. lat. 50°. Steering into the inlet now known as Nootka Sound, between the island of the same name and that now called

Vancouver's, the great explorer sailed up the coast, passing between the modern Queen Charlotte's Island and the mainland. Cook, however, made no minute examination of its many interesting phenomena, till he came to Cape Prince of Wales (N. lat. 65° 33', W. long. 167° 59 ), whence he made a flying visit to the opposite coast before entering on the passage through Behring Straits, which was the most noteworthy feature of this grand trip. Leaving him to pursue his work to the bitter end which closed his splendid career, we join, as the next hero to add any thing to our knowledge of that portion of the north-west coast now under notice, Captain John Meares, sent out in a vessel named the *Nootka* by the merchants of India, with orders to supplement Cook's discoveries by every means in his power.

The *Nootka* reached the coast of America, in N. lat. 60° 20', W. long. 146° 30', after a protracted voyage across the Atlantic. The winter had already set in, and it appeared impossible to do any thing in the way of exploration until the spring. Captain Meares, was, however, unwilling to return without achieving any definite result, and he therefore, in spite of the mutinous spirit of his men, resolved to land on the shores of Prince William's Sound, and at least gain information respecting the natives of these remote latitudes.

The people of Alaska, a strong, large-limbed, and tall race, with flat faces, high cheek-bones, and small, bead-like black eyes, who delighted in disfiguring their lips and noses with pendent ornaments, seem to have stood in considerable awe of their visitors, and supplied them with game and fish in abundance during the first few weeks of their stay. Early in November, however, all the terrors of the winter closed in upon the exiles ; food became scarce, and, in January, scurvy in its most awful forms broke out among them. When the hoped-for spring of the ensuing year, which was to effect so much, at last set in, half the men of the expedition had found their last resting-places beneath the snow, and the survivors were reduced to the greatest extremities.

At this critical juncture two English trading vessels hove in sight, and from their captains, Portlock and Dixon, relief was obtained, though it seems to have been very grudgingly given, Meares being looked upon as an intruder likely to interfere with the profits of the fisheries. Before food was given to his starving men, a promise was exacted from him that he would not trade on the coast, and he was therefore compelled to return to the Sandwich Islands just as he might have begun his work of exploration.

Nothing daunted by this first failure, we find Meares starting again for
the North in January, 1788, this time in command of two vessels, the *Felice*
and *Iphigenia*, and with a crew devoted to his service. After an interesting
voyage across the Pacific, and a short halt in King George's Sound, our hero
reached the Straits of Juan de Fuca, discovered, as we have seen, two centuries before by a Greek pilot of that name. Here the vessels were overtak-
en by a terrible storm, and, the rugged buttresses of Vancouver's Island
offering no shelter, their captains were compelled to steer for the south.
The rocky shores of the modern Territory of Washington, then dotted with
Indian villages, the mouth of the Columbia River, the pine-clad heights of
Oregon, were passed in rapid succession—the names of Shoalwater Bay, De-
ception Bay, Destruction Island, and Cape Disappointment, given by Meares
to the most noteworthy features of the scenery, still bearing witness to his
despondency when thus driven in the opposite direction to that in which he
judged his work to be awaiting him.

The early summer found the explorers off the coast of Northern California, then still known as New Albion, and after an unsuccessful, because
probably a not very hearty effort to examine its fertile bays, the vessels
were once more turned northward, with Nootka Sound as their goal. The
weather being now more propitious, Meares sent a number of his men in
one of the long-boats up the Straits of Juan de Fuca, with orders to examine them thoroughly. The sailors, weary of their long detention on ship-
board, started on this trip with eager delight; but when day after day
passed by, and there were no signs of their return, their master became un-
easy in their behalf. At last, after a long period of suspense, the boat was
seen issuing from the narrow inlet, and an eager shout of joy from the large
vessels hailed the fact that the numbers of the men were undiminished. But
why did they row so slowly, and what was the meaning of their air of exhaus-
tion and dejection? As they came nearer, their comrades saw that each one
of them was bleeding from terrible wounds, and when they had been helped
up the ship-ladders, they told how they had been attacked as they rowed
up the straits by two canoes full of armed warriors, and only escaped after
a terrible struggle, which would probably have ended in the massacre of
them all, had not the death of the native chief struck terror into his subjects' hearts. As the dusky leader fell with a ball lodged in his brain, his
warriors took to flight, and the English, bleeding from their wounds, made
the best of their way back to their vessels.

Back again at last at Nootka Sound, fresh difficulties arose. The men, so loyal at first, showed signs of mutiny, and the chief offenders were sent on shore, where, falling into the hands of native chiefs, they endured much hardship, from which they were finally rescued by Meares, who received them back into his service, after repeated professions of contrition.

As will be understood, so much time had been lost in the détour to the south, that little was effected in the way of actual discovery on this second trip. Forts were, however, erected at several points on the shores of Nootka Sound, and a cargo of great value was taken back by Meares to his employers—two facts which paved the way for the fitting out of an important expedition, consisting of several vessels, under the great Vancouver, who added more than any of his predecessors to our scientific knowledge of the north-western shores of America.

De Fuca, Meares, and others of lesser note, had, throughout their examination of the new districts discovered by them, divided their attention between trade and geographical exploration. Vancouver appears to us to have been a man of a different and more intellectual stamp ; and though he can scarcely be said to have been the first to *see* the important island named after him, as it can not have escaped the observation of any mariners anchoring in Nootka Sound, he undoubtedly revealed the fact of its complete separation from the mainland, and won recognition for its great natural resources and its commanding geographical position.

Between the return home of Meares and the starting of Vancouver, disputes had arisen between the English and Spanish, as to which were the true owners of the lands from whence came the treasures brought home by the now numerous traders and whalers who frequented the Northern Pacific waters. These disputes were finally adjusted by the acceptance by the Spanish Government of Cape Mendocino (N. lat. 40° 26') as the most northerly limit of its jurisdiction in the New World. As a result, Vancouver's work was limited to the examination of the coast above that boundary ; and with the understanding that he should not encroach below it, he started from England on his grand voyage on the 15th December, 1790, arriving off the coast of America, in N. lat. 37° 55', about the 15th April of the ensuing year.

True to his instructions, Vancouver attempted no exploration of New Albion until he had passed Cape Mendocino, beyond which, however, he kept as close as possible inshore, noting the position of every prominent feature of the coast, and seeking in vain for any harbor in which to anchor his vessels. Past Cape Blanco (N. lat. 42° 51'), to which the leader gave the name of Orford, in honor of the English nobleman bearing that title, Cape Disappointment (N. lat. 46° 19',) and many another now well-known promontory, the little fleet slowly sailed, until, on the last day of April, the Straits of De Fuca were entered, and those discoveries began which opened a new era in our geographical knowledge of North-west America.

Entering the straits once supposed to lead direct into the Arctic Ocean, and carefully observing every peculiarity, alike of the shores of the long narrow island on the left and of the mainland on the right, our hero successfully navigated the Gulf of Georgia, crossed the 50th parallel of north latitude, and early in the summer of 1792, discovered the open sea-way leading back into the Pacific, to which he gave the name of Queen Charlotte's Sound.

The erroneous opinion still held by many, that the Straits of De Fuca were identical with the long-sought Gulf of Anian, and led direct to the Arctic Ocean, was now finally dispelled; and, resuming his survey of the Pacific seaboard beyond the most northerly limit of Vancouver's Island, the explorer next turned his attention to the labyrinth of sounds, inlets, and islands known as Prince of Wales, Duke of York, Admiralty, etc., the intricate windings of which had so long baffled the captains of trading and fishing vessels.

Before the close of the summer, the mouth of the supposed river, known as Cook's, flowing from Alaska into the Pacific a little above the 60th parallel of north latitude, was reached, and, sailing up, Vancouver ascertained it to be a close sound, thus solving a second of the problems of this hyperborean region, and finally proving the non-existence of any passage but Behring Straits from the Pacific to the Arctic Oceans. Cook's River, henceforth known to be an inlet only, though it retains its first misleading title in many modern atlases, was the most northerly limit of this great voyage of discovery; and the autumn of 1792 found Vancouver's battered little fleet entering the mouth of the Columbia River, which had been so named a few months before, after his own vessel, by a certain Captain Gray of Boston, who has been erroneously supposed to have been the first to discover it.

A thorough examination of this fine harbor, the only one of real importance between that of San Francisco on the south and Port Discovery on the north, completed Vancouver's explorations on this last trip to the West. He returned to England before the winter set in; and though his account of his work was received with much hostile criticism, every point laid down by him has been verified by later travelers.

The important work done by Behring, Cook, Meares, and Vancouver was greatly supplemented by minor heroes of various nationalities, including Robert Gray of Boston ; the Spaniards, Etevan Martinez and Gonzalo Haro, sent from Mexico to look after the interests of their Government in the North-west, who explored Prince William Sound ; Joseph Billings, from England, who touched at the Aleutian Islands ; and numerous French, English, and Russian captains. Their accounts of their explorations were not, however, in any sense original revelations, and we pass from them to the men who took up the work of the early French *coureurs de bois* and missionaries, pushing their surveys westward from Hudson's Bay, until they spanned the hitherto unknown gulf between the last inland outposts of their predecessors and the Pacific seaboard.

It was the failure of Baffin, Davis, and other early heroes of Arctic discovery to find the clew to the long-coveted secret of the vast labyrinth of straits, inlets, etc., between Greenland and the north-eastern shores of America, which first directed the attention of the thinkers of Europe to Hudson's Bay as a possible passage to the Pacific. As in Canada and elsewhere in America, however, scientific exploration, for its own sake, soon retired before the pioneers of commerce and settlement, making it next to impossible for the geographical student to trace the thin line of discovery with any certainty.

Strictly speaking, the work of the travelers who paved the way for the foundation of the great Hudson's Bay Company, destined to be so formidable a rival to the French *coureurs de bois*, belongs to Arctic history ; but, in the early days of which we are now writing, those whose main object was the discovery of the North-west Passage, often turned aside from it either from necessity or curiosity, and in the parentheses, so to speak, of their voyages, penetrated below the 60th parallel, which we have taken as our most northerly limit. Notably was this the case with the bold mariner, Luke Fox, of London, who, in 1630, obtained from Charles I. the command of a pinnace of eighty tons, manned by twenty men, with permission to cruise about Hudson's Bay until he found a northern passage out of it.

Fox's pinnace entered Hudson's Straits early in June, 1631, and, eagerly steering his way among the numerous obstacles with which they are always encumbered, he entered the bay itself in safety, sailed across it in a north-westerly direction, and reached the narrow passage known as the Welcome between its eastern shores and Southampton Island. Here, for some unknown reason, he turned southward, and, after an exciting cruise along the coasts of the great bay, he came to the mouth of its greatest feeder, the Nelson, in N. lat. 56° 35′. Convinced that no passage to the northern ocean was to be found so far south, and ignorant how near he had been to it when he changed his course at the outlet of the Welcome, he now struck across the bay in a north-westerly direction, till he came to the most southerly point of Southampton Island, called Carey's Swan's Nest.

So much time had been wasted in the détour southward, which has won for Fox a mention in our present volume, that he could now only advance a short distance along the channel bearing his name, between the east of Southampton Island and the western boundaries of the bay. Compelled to return to England without having accomplished much, he learned a little later, somewhat to his disgust, that his discoveries in the south of the bay had been continued by his rival, Captain James. James had met him at the mouth of the Welcome, in a little vessel fitted out by the merchants of Bristol, with the same end in view as Fox had—the finding of a passage to the East by way of Hudson's Bay.

James, told by Fox that he was quite sure not to succeed in his quest, had been driven, after this far from cheering meeting, to steer for the south in consequence of his inability to cope with the huge masses of ice which were now beginning to fill the northern half of the bay, and arriving at what is now known as Charlton's Island, in N. lat. 52° 5′, W. long. 80° 15′, he determined to winter there.

Terrible sufferings were now endured, but through them all James and his men kept up their courage, preparing, in face of every difficulty, for starting on the return voyage early in the following year. The battered vessel was refitted ; the southern shores alike of the island and of the bay, were carefully examined ; and when home was at last reached by the survivors of the party, the reports given by them, though not exactly encouraging to the general public, were such as to embolden a few enterprising spirits to see what could be done in the same direction.

A few years after the return of James to England, a Frenchman named Grosseliez made a journey of discovery from Canada, and, after a successful cruise up the western shores of Hudson's Bay, landed in Nelson's River. Here, to his intense astonishment, he found a little settlement of white men, who had made their way thither from Boston, and were struggling, in spite of the rigorous climate, scarcity of food, etc., to gain a permanent footing in the country. Leaving these unexpected rivals to fight out their battles as best they could, Grosseliez completed his own survey of the surrounding districts, and hastened with it to France, hoping to gain the patronage of the French monarch for an emigration scheme of his own. He entirely failed in this purpose, but his pertinacity won for him the notice of Mr. Montague, at that time English ambassador at Paris, who gave him a letter of recommendation to Prince Rupert, then, after many vicissitudes, in the very zenith of his prosperity.

Though at this time engaged in the eager prosecution of the newly-discovered art of mezzotint engraving, which owed so much of its perfection to him, Prince Rupert at once turned his attention to the geographical problem laid before him by Grosseliez. The desirability of securing to England the monopoly of the fur-trade of the North, with the possibility of winning a new water highway to the North through the as yet unexplored ice-blocked channels of the Great Bay, or to the Pacific through some inland passage still to be discovered, was recognized at once. Prince Rupert obtained the consent of his cousin, Charles II., to the sending out of a pioneering expedition under Captains Zachariah Gillam and Grosseliez; and in the summer of 1668, their little vessel entered Hudson's Straits.

This time the eastern shores of the bay were explored, and a little river flowing into the south-eastern extremity from Lake Mistassinie was discovered, to which the name of Rupert was at once given. A fort was erected at its mouth, and the adventurers returned home with a report that lands rich in furs stretched away as far as the eye could reach, on the east as well as on the west of Hudson's Bay.

Encouraged by the result of this preliminary experiment, Prince Rupert now obtained from Charles a charter, conferring on himself and nine associates absolute proprietorship, subordinate sovereignty, and exclusive traffic in a territory of undefined extent, embracing, however, all the regions discovered or to be discovered within Hudson's Straits, and all lands from which rivers flowed into Hudson's Bay, saving only such as were already in the possession of any Christian State or prince.

Now, as we know, the French, who claimed all lands from Canada to the Pacific seaboard on the west, and to the Arctic circle on the north, had already penetrated to the shores of Hudson's Bay, and up the Saskatchewan to the Rocky Mountains. From the first, therefore, the new corporation, known as the Hudson's Bay Company, found itself face to face with a formidable rival, and, to the great disappointment of its founders, the men who were sent out to develop the resources of the newly-obtained territories showed themselves altogether unworthy of the trust reposed in them. A brisk trade was carried on with the Canadians in the ordinary necessaries of life, but there was a total absence alike of mercantile enterprise and geographical zeal.

Not until 1721, some years after the claims of France to Canada had been finally abandoned, in fulfillment of the conditions of the Treaty of Utrecht, was any real effort at exploration made. At that date, however, a certain John Knight, governor of one of the forts of the Company, heard from some natives of a rich copper-mine in the north, and begged his superiors to fit out an expedition, with him as its leader, for the discovery alike of the mine and the Straits of Anian. It was now the turn of the Company itself to show lukewarmness in the good cause. Prince Rupert, who had been the very mainspring of the corporation, had long been dead ; his successors did not care to risk their capital in any scheme of which the success was not fully secured.

"But," urged Knight, "the charter by virtue of which you exist made the search for a north-west passage, and one to the Pacific from the East, absolutely compulsory ; if you decline to allow me to make such search, I will appeal to the King, who will doubtless withdraw his letters patent if you neglect their conditions."

Unable to shake the position taken up by their importunate servant, the Hudson's Bay Company at last roused itself from its lethargy, and fitted out two vessels, which they placed under the naval direction of Captains Barlow and Vaughan, who were, however, to consult Knight as to their route.

Full of eager delight at this, as he thought, complete realization of his hopes, poor Knight started on his voyage ; but of that voyage no record has ever been obtained. A year passed by, and there came no message to his employers ; two years, and still not a word from him. Search expeditions were now sent out, but they were either unskillfully or negligently conducted, and not until forty long years had gone by was the sad truth revealed.

In 1767, two whaling vessels, cruising about the now well-known passage of the Welcome, came to the entrance of a harbor never before noticed, and, entering it, their captains and crews were astonished to find its shores strewn with guns, anchors, and other European relics.   When they landed to examine this phenomenon, further evidence of the place having been the scene of a great catastrophe was found in the ruins of a house, and a little later in the discovery of the remains of ships under water.   There could be little doubt now that Knight and all the members of his expedition had met their death at the very commencement of their journey ; and, two years later, the explorer Hearne met some natives near the Welcome, who told him how, long years before, some white men like himself had come in two ships, and, landing, put together a wonderful house, the pieces of which they had brought with them.   These white men, added the Esquimaux, soon became sick, and though they went on working all the same, most of them died.   In the winter, the survivors were glad to buy train-oil, blubber, and seal-flesh, as all their own provisions failed them ; and some of them, who had been a long time without food, died of eating too greedily of the strange diet supplied to them.   In the following spring, but five remained alive, and these died one by one, the last survivor falling over the last but one in a vain attempt to dig his grave.

As may be supposed, the news of this awful catastrophe, of which the worst horrors were probably even then unknown, did not encourage further efforts on the desolate northern shores of Hudson's Bay.   Before the sad fate of Knight and his comrades was discovered, however, several attempts were made at the navigation of the various rivers flowing from the west into the vast inland sea, with a view to ascertaining if any of them led to the Pacific Ocean.   In 1737, a Captain Middleton entered the mouth of Churchill River (N. lat 56°, W. long. 30°), spent the winter on its shores, and in the ensuing spring sailed through the Welcome, up the Wager Sound, opening on to it on the west, and thence by way of the northern inlet of the Welcome, into Fox's Channel, thus completing the circuit of the bay all but accomplished by his predecessors, Fox and James.

Convinced that no passage from Hudson's Bay existed on the west, Middleton returned to England to announce that conviction, but all his assertions were met with scorn ; and, a few years later, yet another fleet, this time under the command of Captains Moore and Smith, started in the vain quest.   Hudson's Straits were entered in July, 1746, and the northern half of the bay being found impassable from ice, it was resolved to winter at the mouth of Nelson's River (N. lat. 56° 35', W. long 95°), and start on the exploring expedition early in the ensuing year.

This programme was carried out, and in spite of the intense cold, the party escaped many of the horrors usually attendant upon it to Europeans, by following the advice of some friendly Esquimaux, who gave them many hints as to the best way to avoid them. The summer of the following year found the expedition moving up the bay, and a thorough examination of the Wager Sound, proving it to be a close one, was made; but, alas! this

SLEDGE-DRIVING.

was the only result of what had appeared likely to be one of the most successful expeditions yet fitted out. Having discovered that no passage to the Pacific was to be found by way of the Nelson or the Wager, Moore and Smith came to the conclusion that no passage existed at all, and returned to England to announce that their work was done. That they were received with what we may really call a yell of execration is a matter of little surprise, but that expression of public scorn was followed by no renewed attempt in the same direction.

Knight, as we know, had disappeared, and the secret of his fate, anticipated by us, was still unknown. Middleton, Moore, and Smith had accomplished nothing. Surely it was time to make a change of tactics, and with
some such feeling the heads of the Company resolved to give up the question
of a water passage to the West for a time, and see what could be accomplished by land. Not until 1769, however, two years after the discovery of
the relics of Knight's expedition, was any thing definite attempted, and by
that date the Hudson's Bay Company had been to some degree supplanted
by that known as the North-west, which consisted of a number of British
merchants who, without charter, privileges, or public support, had been
quietly, though energetically, making good their footing in the great North-
west.

Our readers will remember all that we have told them of the French
*coureurs des bois*, and of their rapid advance westward, accompanied by
the Jesuit missionaries, who did so much to check their abuses. This advance at one time seemed likely to prevent that of any other Europeans ;
but the cession of Canada to England in 1763, a cession fraught with political consequences of such vital importance to the whole civilized world, shook
the power of the French to its foundation.

A royal proclamation was issued, organizing Canada under English laws ;
and no longer could the lawless proceedings of the *coureurs des bois* be tol-
erated. Henceforth the lakes and rivers would miss the skin-laden canoes
of the half-savage traders ; no more should the remote forests echo with
their shouts of joy as they brought down their prey, or the solemn wastes of
snow-clad plains be desecrated by their wild revels.

The change—as all great changes generally are—was gradual. The pioneers of the new order of things often surprised some little group of dusky
half-caste children, with eager eyes and vivacious ways of their French
fathers contrasting strangely with the shrinking timidity inherited from
their savage mothers. Now and then, too, bloody struggles took place between the hunters of the rival nations ; and the natives, delighted to see the
white men devouring each other, began those treacherous assaults, in which
they have ever proved themselves adepts, which culminated in the massacres
of Detroit and Michilimackinac.

This terrible transition stage, where such numerous rivals were contending
for the monopoly of the fur-trade of the great North-west, produced, as
transition stages so often do, many a bold spirit eager to win honor by facing

the exceptional difficulties of the time. First one and then another hero came forward to offer his services to the Hudson's Bay Company for new expeditions ; first one and then another member of its infant rival accomplished some traveling-feat hitherto looked upon as impossible. Some few among these, such as Hearne of the Hudson's Bay Company, and Mackenzie of the

AN ESQUIMAUX DWELLING.

North-west Company, worked below as well as above the 60th parallel of north latitude, and must therefore be noticed here.

Hearne, the first of this brilliant pair of adventurers to start, left the western shores of Hudson's Bay in November, 1769, and accompanied by two Europeans and a number of Indian guides, struck across country in a northerly direction, with the head-waters of the Coppermine River, so named after the mine supposed to exist in its vicinity, as his goal. Again and again compelled to retrace his steps to the advanced forts of his employers, on account of the scarcity of provisions and the extreme cold, our hero did not enter the great northern plain until December, 1770. Across it he was now, however, conducted in safety by an Indian guide, named Matonnabbe, who was accompanied by his eight squaws, on whom the chief burden of providing for the comfort of the party was thrown.

So well did these poor women fulfill their mission, turning to account every scrap of food which came in their way, that Hearne reached in safety the most southerly of the great hyperborean series of frozen lakes. Naming the smaller ones Cossed, Snow-bird, Pike, Peshew, and Cagead, he came in due course to the more important Athabasca, just below the boundary line of the 60th parallel of north latitude, and beyond that again to the Great Slave Lake, situated between N. lat. 60° and 63°, and surrounded on every side by rugged wooded heights, presenting a pleasing contrast to the white stretches of snow and ice extending on every side beyond.

These heights, which at first appeared inaccessible, were yet traversed by a rough and winding path used by the Indians in their wild hunting expeditions, and, following his dusky guides, Hearne succeeded in scaling them and gaining the plain beyond. Another march of short duration brought him to the source of the Coppermine River, which rises near the Great Bear Lake, a tributary of the Mackenzie, the discovery of which was reserved to Hearne's rival and successor, whose name it bears.

Instead of the wide river navigable for large vessels in the summer, and with mines hiding vast stores of mineral wealth within easy reach, Hearne found the Coppermine to be an unimportant stream flowing through a barren and desolate country. Disappointed and disgusted, he yet resolved to follow it to its mouth, and was proceeding on his journey with dogged resolution, when the monotony of the daily struggle with the difficulties presented by nature was broken by a struggle between his Indian guides and some Esquimaux, resulting in the massacre of the latter. In vain did our hero plead for mercy for the inoffensive dwellers on the coast. The inland races of North America entertain for their Arctic neighbors a hatred and contempt which must be witnessed to be realized; and face to face with Esquimaux, all private quarrels are merged in an eager desire for the blood of the common enemy.

Disgusted at having burdened himself with companions who of course rendered impossible any attempt at studying the ways of the new type of

IN THE ARCTIC SEAS.

human nature with which he was now brought in contact, Hearne pursued his way northward, and before the close of the summer he was rewarded for

his perseverance by reaching the mouth of the Coppermine River, and standing on the shores of the Arctic Ocean.  For the first time the eyes of a European rested upon that portion of the universal sea surrounding the North Pole
which washes the northern coast of America ;  for the first time the white man
realized the existence of yet another ocean—an ocean which must henceforth replace the fabulous unbroken masses of land figuring on all maps between the most northerly limit reached by explorers and the North Pole.

Before this great and unexpected revelation, throwing a flood of new light
on the geography of North America, and with it of the whole world, all
minor details sank into insignificance.  Hearne had proved beyond a doubt
that the Strait of Anian, if such a strait there were, had its eastern outlet,
if any, in the Icy Sea ; he had ascertained that the American continent
stretched away hundreds of miles beyond what had hitherto been accepted
as its western limits ; he had seen that the extreme North was inhabited by
a race differing essentially from all their southern neighbors ; he had noticed
the trace of the existence of thousands of whales, seals, and other valuable
denizens of the deep ; but what was all this, in Hearne's estimation, com-
pared to the unvarnished fact of the existence of a new ocean !

Hastening back to Hudson's Bay with the great news, Hearne saw the
copper-mine of which Indian tradition had told so much.  It was a poor,
exhausted mine, not likely to yield the smallest profit to the Company ; but
what of that ?  The Arctic Ocean lay beyond it !  Following a somewhat
more westerly course than on his northern journey, Hearne entered level
districts abounding in game ; but what of that ?  The Arctic Ocean washed
the desolate shores above the fur-yielding plains !  A fair young Indian
woman, who had escaped from some Athapescow warriors after the murder
of her whole family, was found dwelling alone in a little hut, supporting
herself by hunting deer and snaring rabbits.  Hearne's followers wrestled
for the possession of the young exile as a wife, and she was carried off by
the victor ; but this strange and significant scene could scarcely interest our
hero now.  The Arctic Ocean was awaiting its explorers—alas ! also its victims—and the ways of the natives, who had so little valued the great fact
of its existence, were of small account.

Roused from its lethargy at last by the report brought home by its gallant
employé, the Hudson's Bay Company now did all in its power to encourage
further research, and to its efforts were due the sending forth of Franklin
on his first great voyage, which ushered in a new era of Arctic exploration.

Before either Franklin, of Arctic renown, or Mackenzie, second only in fame as an inland explorer to Hearne, was ready to start, however, much good work was done by private adventurers, especially by Finlay, Currie, Frobisher, and Pond, who, between 1763 and 1778, penetrated to the banks of the Saskatchewan and Churchill Rivers, and to the shores of Athabasca Lake, making intimate acquaintance with the Hare and other Indian tribes, and paving the way for the voyages on the Mackenzie, Peace, and Slave Rivers, which were among the most noteworthy feats of the new claimant for the possession of the fur-yielding districts of the extreme North-west.

Alexander Mackenzie, the hero of these important trips, was bred a clerk in the service of the North-west Company, and, before starting on his voyage as a geographical explorer, properly so called, had served a long apprenticeship at the advanced station of Fort Chipewyan, on the Athapescow Lake, whence he made several overland excursions in different directions.

On the 3d June, 1789, our hero embarked in a native canoe on the Slave River, and following its course, then unimpeded by ice, in a northerly direction, he arrived on the 9th of the same month at the Slave Lake. Skirting along its shores in a westerly direction, he presently discovered the important river bearing his name, which has since been found to be identical with the Athabasca, rising in the Rocky Mountains near Mount Brown, and also with the Slave, the combined waters of the two streams flowing, after their junction, to the Arctic Ocean in Mackenzie Bay, N. lat. 70°, W. long. 136°.

Anxious to trace the course of the Mackenzie, the explorer was about to proceed along it in his canoe, when he was told by some wandering Indians that certain death would be the result, for the bed of the stream was haunted by huge monsters, who would devour all who came in their way. Moreover, it would take many years to reach the salt water. The white man had better return the way he came. In any case, he could hope for no help from the redskins.

Though these terrible prophecies did not affect Mackenzie himself, they paralyzed his guides, who declared they would go no further ; and after trying alike persuasion and force, the Europeans determined to do the best they could alone. They appear to have penetrated as far north as the Great Bear Lake, but here, for some reason of which we find no explanation in Mackenzie's journal, the canoe was turned southward, and the voyage back to the Slave Lake resumed. "My people," says Mackenzie, "could not refrain from some expressions of real concern that they were obliged to return without reaching the sea;" but he apparently made no great effort to gratify them.

Back again to Fort Chipewyan, Mackenzie lost no time in preparing for a

MACKENZIE'S FIRST VIEW OF THE PACIFIC OCEAN.

second journey of discovery. Embarking on the Peace River, a tributary of the Slave or Athabasca, he followed its course in a south-westerly direction, till he reached the first spurs of the snow-clad Rocky Mountains, whence issued the river under examination. Here the canoe was, of necessity, abandoned, and an arduous climb began, resulting, however, in the successful scaling of the rugged ridge, and the safe arrival at a village on its western side, where the weary travelers were regaled with salmon, a fish never before met with on their travels in North America.

The inhabitants of this remote home in the wilderness were of a far more civilized appearance than the Indians of the East ; and as the sea was approached by the explorers, they passed through settlements numbering hundreds of well-built houses, peopled by various tribes belonging to the southern branches of the great hyperborean group. Members of the Sicannis and other Rocky Mountain families were met with, who, one and all, showed courtesy to the white strangers, though they were jealous of any interference with their fishing or hunting ; and as the western coast was approached, the active and intelligent Thinkleets, chiefly of the Stikeen and Tungass tribes, excited the admiration of their visitors by their ingenuity in the construction of domestic and other implements, and their skill in painting and carving.

The shores of the North Pacific Ocean were finally reached in north latitude 52° 20′ 48″. The whole of the continent of British America had for the first time been traversed ; its vast breadth had been proved beyond a doubt ; and the connecting link between the discoveries on the western coast and those from the East, whether from Hudson's Bay, New England, or the Southern States, was added at last. Yet in Mackenzie's account of his work he scarcely notes the first sight of the sea ; we have searched in vain for any details of his sojourn on its shores. Having done what he came to do, he turned back, and retraced his steps, winding up the narative of his adventures with this simple and unostentatious sentence :—"Afte an absence of eleven months I arrived at Fort Chipewyan, where I remained for the purposes of trade during the succeeding winter."

# CHAPTER XII.

BY the beginning of the 19th century, or, to be more strictly accurate, before the year 1810, a general notion had been obtained of the extent, form, and main physical features of North America. The journeys of Pike, Lewis and Clarke in the southern half of the vast continent, with those of Hearne and Mackenzie from Hudson's Bay, were now followed up by a series of expeditions, working either under the orders or with the sanction of the American Government, by which the regions south of the Missouri, those bordering on the Upper Mississippi, and the fertile provinces now known as British Columbia, Washington, and Oregon, were thoroughly explored.

The first man to take up the work begun by the heroes we have been noticing was John Jacob Astor, who, after long negotiations with the various companies struggling for the monopoly of the fur-trade of the North, succeeded in founding yet another association, under the name of the Pacific Fur Company. This new confederation, having won the co-operation of many of the best agents of its rivals, found itself in a position to compete with them on more than equal terms, and, as early as 1810, a thoroughly well-organized expedition, divided into two parts—one going by land, the other by sea—started for the mouth of the Columbia, where it was proposed to erect a fort as the head-quarters of the new trade to be opened.

After a successful voyage from Montreal *via* the Sandwich Islands, the *Tonquin*, bearing the advanced guard of traders and emigrants, including Mr. M'Dougal, who represented Mr. Astor, cast anchor off the mouth of the Columbia. Here a landing was at once effected, and M'Dougal and his chief assistant, a man named Stuart, were hospitably entertained by the Chinooks, whose chief aided them in selecting a suitable place for the foundation of their fort, and showed no jealousy of their wish to settle near him.

The town now known as Astoria (N. lat. 46° 11′, W. long. 123° 42′) was quickly built ; a factory soon rose beside it ; the natives came in with their furs for sale ; and all seemed likely to go so well, that the *Tonquin* was allowed to start on a trading trip up the coast, leaving but a few settlers to await the arrival of the land party.  No sooner was the vessel out of reach, however, than rumors began to be circulated of a conspiracy among the neighboring tribes to massacre all the white men ; and while preparations were being made to meet this unexpected danger, some wandering Indians from the Straits of Juan de Fuca brought tidings that the *Tonquin* had been lost with all on board.  The truth of this melancholy event was soon confirmed by members of yet another tribe, and gradually the whole story leaked out.

The *Tonquin* had fallen a victim, not to the usual perils of the deep, but to a quarrel between Thorn, its captain, and some natives of Vancouver's Island.   Steering to the north, with an Indian named Samazee as interpreter in his proposed dealings with the natives, Thorn reached Vancouver's Island in safety, and cast anchor in the harbor of Neweetee, though Samazee warned him that the people about there were not to be trusted.   On the following day the ship was boarded by a number of natives, including two sons of Wicanainsh, the chief of the country round Neweetee, and an old chief named Nookamis, who had long been accustomed to drive bargains with the English.

Suspecting no evil, Captain Thorn prepared for a good day's business, and made what seemed to him fair offers for the finest of the sea-otter peltries brought by the redskins.  Nookamis shook his head ; he must have double the prices quoted.  His companions followed suit ; not a skin could poor Captain Thorn obtain.

Surprised and disgusted at the turn affairs had taken, the English now tried new tactics.  They took no further notice of the Indians, but paced up and down the deck with their hands in their pockets.  Nookamis, however, looking upon all this as a mere manœuver to try his patience, continued to ply the captain with offers of otter-skins ; and finding that nothing he said had any effect, he began to jeer the white man for a stingy fellow.  Thorn now lost his temper, and, turning upon his persecutor, he snatched the otter-skins from him, flung them in his face, and kicked him down the ship's ladder.

The rest of the natives were furious, and hurried after their spokesman, leaving the deck strewn with peltries.  A little later, some of the whites who had gone on shore returned to the vessel, and urged the captain to weigh anchor, as they feared a general attack from the natives. In this advice they were seconded by Samazee, who declared that the vengeance for the insult offered to a chief would be terrible. But Thorn's blood was up. He declined to leave the coast; and when further urged, replied by pointing to his guns, as protection enough against savages.

Early the next morning, when the crew of the *Tonquin* were still in their hammocks, a canoe full of Indians came alongside. Were these the prophesied avengers? Surely not! They were unarmed, and held up otter-skins in token of friendly intentions. They were allowed to climb on board, and so were a second party of twenty, who arrived immediately afterward.

A brisk trade was now begun; but as the officers turned over the skins offered to them, other canoes put off from the shore. The *Tonquin* was soon surrounded by them; its single ladder was quickly crowded with dusky warriors, who, pouring upon the deck in a steady stream, also produced skins, offering to trade with the captain on his own terms now, and implying, though not expressing, regret at the obstinacy of their representatives the day before. The chief things the natives wanted instead of their costly peltries were knives; and with an almost foolhardy recklessness, Thorn allowed them to appropriate a large number, in spite of the repeated warnings of his officers and the interpreter that treachery was intended. The only precaution taken was the telling-off of sailors to weigh anchor and make sail, the captain imagining that this would not be noticed, and that, having obtained his cargo of peltries, he could escape before the Indians had time to carry out any evil designs.

Never was a more terrible mistake made. The signal from the captain for the deck to be cleared was also that for the onslaught to be given. The knives just obtained, and the war-clubs already provided, were brandished on every side, and before they could defend themselves, many of the white men fell beneath the well-aimed blows.

The ship's clerk was one of the first to fall, and among the next victims was a man named M'Kay, who was flung backward into one of the waiting canoes, and there hacked to pieces by the squaws, who were watching the affray with eager delight. Very brave was the defense made by Thorn himself, and at one time he seemed likely to escape. He had fought his way nearly to the cabin, where he had left his firearms, when loss of blood compelled him to lean for support upon the tiller wheel. He was instantly surrounded, flung upon the deck, and stabbed to death with his own knives.

All but four of the crew shared the fate of the officers. These four, who had been aloft making sail when the conflict began, succeeded in reaching the cabin, where they made a hasty defense. The firearms, which now came into play, soon cleared the deck, and an hour after the fatal admission of the redskins on board, not a sign of them was to be seen.

The interpreter, to whom we owe this narrative, had wisely taken no part in the struggle, and retired with the natives. He tells further how the night was passed on shore among them, and how, though they were still eager for further revenge, they were deterred from approaching the vessel by their dread of the firearms. Early the next morning, a canoe, bearing the interpreter among others, ventured cautiously to paddle within hail. A man presently appeared on deck, and made signs to the redskins to come on board. They hesitated, but, curiosity prevailing over fear, several of them climbed up the ladder. They were allowed to wander about unmolested. The white man they had seen had disappeared; and one by one other canoes crept from the shore, till, as on the day before, the sea was covered with them.

The savages who had first arrived called to their comrades to come on, for there was no danger and plenty of plunder. They were obeyed by all, even by the hitherto cautious interpreter. Eagerly were the bales of merchandise now plundered; wild were the gestures of delight at the strange articles found among them—But what was that? Was the ship moving, or what? An instant's pause of expectation, and then the vessel blew up with a loud noise; the air was darkened with the bodies of the unhappy savages which fell in every direction, torn to a thousand fragments.

The interpreter again escaped as by a miracle. He was clinging to the main chains when the explosion took place, fell into the water, and swam to one of the canoes, in which he made his way back to the land, where crowds had already assembled, and met him with eager inquiries as to the cause of the terrible scene. He was still the center of an eager group when four white men were brought as prisoners into the village, who told how they had escaped from the *Tonquin* when Lewis, the man who had decoyed the natives on board, decided to blow up the ship. They had hoped to find their way to their comrades at Astoria, but they had been unable to get out of the bay; their boat was cast on shore, and they were soon seized by natives.

They were put to death with all the refinements of cruelty in which the Indians have ever been adepts; and not, as we have seen, until the interpreter managed to pay a visit to Astoria was the whole melancholy story known.

If the position of the Astorians was painful when it was supposed that the absence of the *Tonquin* would not be long protracted, we can imagine what it became now. The savage tribes around them, encouraged by the first success of their brothers of the North, and enraged at the terrible vengeance taken upon them, were more determined than ever to root out the hated white men from their land, and it appeared likely that they would accomplish their purpose, when M'Dougal hit upon a stratagem.

A few years previously, smallpox had ravaged the coast north and south of the Columbia; whole tribes had succumbed to it, and the mere mention of it was enough to cow the spirit of the most dauntless brave. None knew whence it came, but it was supposed to be sent by the Great Spirit to correct his children for their sins, and many connected it with the first coming of the white man.

M'Dougal, reminded by some trifling incident of the latter superstition, invited the leaders of the conspiracy against the infant colony to come and take council with him. They obeyed, wondering, doubtless, in their simple minds whether their designs had been discovered. When all were seated, and expectant silence reigned on every side, the white man stood in the midst and began his harangue.

"Your countrymen have destroyed our vessel," he said, "and I am resolved on vengeance. The white men among you are few in number, it is true, but they are mighty in medicine. See here," he went on, producing a small bottle; "in this bottle I hold the smallpox safely corked up. I have but to draw the cork and let loose the pestilence, to sweep man, woman and child from the face of the earth."

Great was the horror and alarm at this announcement. The chiefs, forgetting their dignity, gathered round the white man, imploring him to stay his hand; and after affecting to be unmoved for some little time, M'Dougal at last declared that, so long as the white people were unmolested, the phial of wrath should be unopened, but——

The remainder of the scene may be imagined. Eternal amity was finally sworn, and M'Dougal, henceforth to be known as the Great Smallpox Chief, was able to attend without interruption to the internal affairs of the colony.

While the Astorians were thus struggling with their difficulties, the land party were working their way across the country to their assistance. At the head of this second expedition was William Hunt, with whom was associated Donald Mackenzie, both men of tact and experience in dealing with the Indians.

The start was made early in July, 1810, from Montreal, which we have visited under so many different auspices, and, on the 22d, Mackinaw, on the junction of Lakes Huron and Michigan, was reached. This town, first an Indian village and then a French trading post, was now the center of a numerous and mixed population. Here traders bound for Lake Superior, for the Mississippi, the Missouri, the Arkansas, or other rivers, met on their way to their several outlying posts. Here they returned laden with the spoils of the far West.

A long halt was made at Mackinaw to collect recruits, who were not easily met with. It was no joke, urged the redskins, to travel with these white men ; they wanted you to go through wildernesses full of savage tribes, with whom they would have to fight, and if any of them escaped death at the hands of their fellow-countrymen, it would only be to starve in those desolate tracts on the other side of the Rocky Mountains. Why should our white man be so anxious to reach the Salt Lake (the sea)? or why, if his anxiety was so very great, would he not give his poor brothers their pay in advance, that the squaws and little ones at home might not pine away in hunger?

Not until the 12th August was the actual start made, and even then, instead of being able to strike across country at once for the mouth of the Columbia, the expedition had to make a voyage down the Mississippi to St. Louis, in order to settle certain difficulties, into which we need not enter here, with the numerous rival companies already alluded to. The starting point of so many expeditions was reached in September, and on the 21st November three canoes, bearing the new body of adventurers, embarked on the Missouri. Even now, progress was extremely slow.. Hunt was more than once compelled to return to St. Louis to settle disputes with his rivals ; and, as the boats crept cautiously along, rumors of a very discouraging character again and again reached the navigators. There was war among the native tribes, and a party of Sioux Indians were awaiting the arrival of the white men in the wilds of Nebraska, intending to massacre them all.

At the mouth of the Nebraska, signs appeared that the rumors of danger from savages were founded on facts. A frame of a skin canoe was found,

in which the warriors had evidently crossed the river, and at night the sky
was red with the reflection of huge fires, showing that the prairies had been
set on fire by the combatants.    Ignoring as much as possible all these terrible omens, Hunt, fresh from his last run back to St. Louis, carefully examined the face of the country on either side of the Nebraska ; the naturalists
of the party made their notes on the flora and fauna of the new districts ;
and on the 10th May, the village of Omaha, about eight hundred and thirty
miles above the mouth of the Missouri, was reached in safety.

Hospitably received by the little remnant of the once powerful Omaha
tribe, who had been in the habit of considering themselves superior to all
other created beings till the smallpox had swept half of them away, Hunt
rested here awhile before commencing his great journey westward, which
rivals in its terrors, and the courage with which they were met, some of the
more famous African expeditions.

At Omaha, the fame of the great chief Blackbird, who has figured in so
many romances, still lived, and Hunt and his party were among the last
white men to look upon the sacred mound beneath which his body reposes,
with its ghastly trophies of scalps still displayed on its summit, suspended
upon the staff of the hero's banner.    The mound itself is still pointed out to
the modern traveler, but the scalps, with so many other relics of the olden
time, are gone.

A little below the Great Bend of the Missouri, the first encounter took
place with the Indians.    A scout was seen galloping wildly to and fro on
the opposite bank as the traders were at breakfast, and at once divining the
meaning of his appearance, the canoes were brought out, and ready for all
contingencies, the white men pulled boldly up the stream.    Their suspense
did not last long.    An hour's row brought them suddenly face to face with
the enemy.    An island intervening had at first hidden them from sight, but,
as the canoes shot past it, the banks beyond were revealed, crowded with
warriors painted and decorated for battle.

To advance appeared certain death, to retreat scarcely less perilous, as the
savages could easily have followed the canoes down the river.    To pull into
mid-stream appeared at first a feasible compromise, but it was found that
the current was too strong.    A momentary pause, a few hurried questions
of each other, and the white men resolved to fight.    The boats were pulled to
the shore opposite the Sioux ; the guns were examined, and fire was opened
on the enemy.

The effect was marvelous. As the reports rang out, the dusky warriors faltered. It was something new in Indian warfare for those for whom the ambush had been prepared to take the initiative! The guns were now reloaded, and the Canadians prepared to row across the Missouri, intending to fire again when within easy range of their adversaries. As the white men rose to take aim, however, there was a cry of "Stop!" from their interpreter. The savages were holding their buffalo robes above their heads; it was their signal of a desire for peace, and a bloody struggle might yet be averted.

The guns were lowered; the Canadians resumed their seats. A dozen of the Sioux approached the banks, lighted a fire, seated themselves about it, and, holding up the calumet made signs to the white men to land. Seeing that no alternative was left them between trusting to these friendly overtures and fighting against terrible odds, Hunt and the other leaders of the party accepted the invitation, and were soon seated in the circle, smoking the pipe of peace in silence, as the inevitable preliminary of a treaty to be made.

This opening ceremony over, Hunt now explained the real object of his journey to be trade, only trade which was to bring about great results for the natives; and, as an earnest of his good intentions, he ordered a quantity of tobacco and corn to be brought from the boats and presented to the chiefs as a free gift.

Hunt's ready tact was rewarded as it deserved. The chief of the chiefs responded in his turn, saying that he had thought his white brothers were carrying arms to his enemies the Minatarees and Mandans, hence his hostility. Convinced that no supplies of weapons were among the stores on the way to the fastnesses of the hostile tribes, he would offer no further opposition to the expedition, which had better, however, keep to the other side of the river, as some hot-headed young fellows among his followers were not to be trusted.

So ended an incident that had threatened the very existence of the whole party. Hands were shaken all round—to shake hands was one of the first things taught by the white men to the red—and the traders re-embarked, taking care to follow the hint given by the now friendly chief.

The next day, June 1st, the Great Bend of the Missouri, first visited by Lewis and Clarke, was reached, a little beyond which the explorers met a large party of Mandan and Minataree warriors, by whom they were, very much to their surprise, received with great enthusiasm, and carried off to the camp in the wilderness for the night.

Glad to have won friends on both sides among the hostile Indians, Hunt now pushed rapidly on up the Missouri, halting here and there to trade with the natives, and on the 18th July reached the most northerly point on his voyage, an Aricara village, from which he proposed striking across country to the Black Mountains on the west.

Now began the most arduous part of this great journey. The vast prairies to be crossed were practically unknown to the white man, though they had probably been scoured by many an adventurous hunter, of whose experience no record exists. On one side dwelt the Cheyenne, on the other the Blackfeet Indians—at war with each other, as most Indian tribes appear to have been at this time. It was doubtful whether either or both would care for the white men to pass through their territory.

On the second day's march, some of the leader's anxieties were allayed by his cordial reception in a Cheyenne camp, the owners—cleanly, civil, decorous fellows—placing all they had at his disposal, and eagerly purchasing the trinkets offered to them for sale. On the 6th August, the friendly Cheyennes were left behind and the Crow country entered, where a subtle danger awaited the travelers, of which Hunt received warning just in time.

A short time previously, a man named Edward Rose had been engaged as interpreter for the passage of the Crow districts, he having been known to have spent many years among its wild inhabitants. That he had married a Crow woman, and identified himself with the interests of her tribe, was not known until afterward ; but on the eve of the entry into his adopted country, Rose was overheard proposing to some of Hunt's followers that they should desert to the Crow camp with all the horses they could carry off, where he (Rose) would join them, and show them how to entice other unsuspecting travelers from the right way to the coast.

Sending for Rose to his own tent, Hunt, showing no knowledge of his nefarious schemes, informed him that he should not require his services beyond the Crow country, but that, in consideration of his faithfulness, he should have a horse, three beaver traps and other valuable accessories to a hunter's equipment, when the Canadians were safely through the passes of the Black Mountains.

Surprised at this liberality, which made it really scarcely worth his while to play traitor, Rose resolved to undo what he had begun. A message was conveyed to his allies, the Crows, instructing them to treat his white friends courteously ; it was resolved in council by the chieftains that no harm should be done to the pale faces ; and Hunt, still showing no sign of knowledge of the by-play, entered the mountain fastnesses without fear.

The Black Hills, forming the dividing line between the waters of the Missouri and those of the Arkansas and Mississippi, were soon reached, and unappalled by the wild tales told of the genii, or thunder spirits, who would resent their intrusion, the Canadians endeavored to cross them. They failed in doing so, and their guide attributed their failure to the obstacles thrown in their way by the invisible " Lords of the Mountain." Of their interference, however, Hunt has given no record, his account being simply that he had to turn back because of the physical peculiarities of the mountains, their wild ravines and terrible precipices being simply impassable to all but the black-tailed deer, and the strange ahsata or big horns haunting its lonely defiles.

A considerable détour southward had to be made, and a path was finally found along a ridge dividing the tributary waters of the Yellowstone and Missouri Rivers, and on the 22nd August they met the first Crow warrior, who proved to belong to a large band returning from their annual trading trip to the Mandan country.

Rose was now sent on in advance, to hold a parley with his friends, and invite some of them to come to the Canadian camp. This many readily consented to do, and Hunt was agreeably surprised at the manly bearing of some of the young horsemen among his visitors, proving that, but for the timely warning received, it might have gone hardly with his party among them. Old and young, rich and poor among this mountain tribe were mounted on steeds of some description, and managed their horses with unrivaled skill ; the very babies, too young to speak, were tied on small colts or ponies, and wielded their whips as if by instinct.

Escorted by some two hundred equestrians, the dreaded passage of the Crow country was made, and the hunting-grounds of the Shoshones reached in safety. Rose and his dusky comrades were dismissed, and their places supplied by Shoshone trappers, who allowed the white men to share in their hunting expeditions, and led them to a commanding height, from which they pointed out three snow-clad mountain peaks, beneath which, they said, rose the Columbia.

Overjoyed at the thought of being almost within sight of the river at the mouth of which their comrades were awaiting them, the little band pressed on with renewed vigor, and on the 24th September they reached the banks

of a wide and rapid river—known as the Mad among the natives, on account
of its wild and turbulent course—where a consultation was held as to
whether it should or should not be followed. It was wide and deep enough
to admit the passage of canoes, and it might possibly flow into the Columbia. The Canadians one and all preferred traveling by water to "scrambling
over the backs of mountains," their trips up and down the St. Lawrence
and across the Great Lakes having rendered them the most expert of oars-
men. Already they saw themselves shooting from the Mad River into the
Columbia, and thence to Astoria.

Embarkation was almost unanimously decided on—although one or two
of the older members of the party hinted at the difficulty of return, if, after
all, the Mad River did not flow into the Columbia—and a fatal mistake
would probably have been made, had not two Snake Indians from the West
arrived in the nick of time, with the glad tidings that a trading post,
situated on the upper branch of the Columbia, was not far off, and that
from it the passage down to the sea was easy.

The programme was changed at once. The encampment was broken up,
the Mad River crossed, and a little later the post alluded to was reached.
It was deserted, but its log huts afforded an admirable shelter during the
construction of canoes for the voyage down the river; and on the 18th of
October all was ready for the last stage of the long journey. Fifteen canoes
were launched on the Henry River, so called after the owner of the trading
post, and a day's paddle brought the Canadians to its junction with their
old friend the Mad River.

The united streams now took the name of the Snake, and turned out, on
examination, to be identical with the Lewis fork of the Columbia—a fact
which greatly cheered the travelers, though their troubles were by no means
yet at an end. The Snake was encumbered with rocks, its bed was seldom
level, and again and again the canoes were nearly upset in the rapids. Not
a human creature was to be seen on the banks; and as prairie succeeded
prairie, and one wilderness of deserted mountains after another was passed,
the spirits of the adventurers flagged.

On the 28th October the climax of the difficulties was reached. The Snake
River entered a "terrific strait," its whole volume being compressed into a
space less than thirty feet in width, beyond which it flung itself down a
precipice, and continued its course, raging and roaring in such a manner
that Hunt named the cataract the Lion Caldron, a title which it still bears.

In attempting to navigate this awful passage, one of the canoes was completely destroyed, and one man drowned, while his comrades barely escaped with their lives. Further progress by water was evidently impossible. The hope of shooting rapidly down to the sea had again to be abandoned ; and, thoroughly disheartened, the travelers prepared to strike across country again, with a view to reaching the banks of the Columbia lower down.

Exploring parties were sent out in different directions to ascertain the best route ; all of the baggage which could possibly be spared was buried in *caches ;* and early in October the march was begun across a dry and trackless wilderness, tenanted only by a few wretched Shoshones, who fled at the approach of the white men.

Toward the end of November a large encampment of Snakes was reached, where provisions and some really trustworthy information as to the route to the coast were obtained ; but it was bitterly cold, and the sufferings of the party between the Indian camp and the Columbia were extreme. Not until the 21st January did the long-sought waters of the great stream of the West come in sight, and the transport of the weary travelers at this happy conclusion of their long wanderings may be imagined.

The spot at which the Columbia had at last been struck was a little below the junction of its two great branches, the Lewis and Clarke, in about N. lat. 46° 8', W. long. 118° 50'. Its banks were dotted with the miserable huts of a wretched horde of Indians called Akai-chies, who wore nothing but the undressed skins of animals, and lived by fishing, scudding up and down the Columbia in rude canoes of pine logs hollowed out by fire.

From these Akai-chies Hunt received the first tidings of his comrades of the sea expedition ; but fortunately, perhaps, for him, the simple savages only knew of the presence of white men at the mouth of their river, and could tell nothing of the disasters which had overtaken them. Eager to join their friends, the traders now pushed on along the Columbia as rapidly as possible ; and at a little village somewhat further down, they heard not only of the massacre on board the *Tonquin,* but of a plot for their own destruction. A party of braves said some wandering savages had arranged to attack the camp at night and carry off all the horses. With Hunt, to be forewarned was to be forearmed, and the precautions taken prevented any second tragedy ; but it was with a sinking heart that he led his men in the last stage of his awful journey. If the rumor of the massacre on the *Tonquin* were true, there was of course little hope that the few survivors of

Astoria had been able to hold their own against the natives, and the great expedition across the continent might perhaps end in the death of all concerned.

Early in February, after great sufferings from hunger and fatigue, canoes were at last obtained from some Indians, and, embarking on the Lewis fork of the Columbia, the Canadians rapidly shot down the river of so many memories to Astoria, where they arrived in safety, haggard, half-starved, and in rags, after a journey which occupied nearly eighteen months.

That the establishment at Astoria never flourished, as its founder hoped, is a well-known fact; but the heroic efforts made by the members of the two expeditions to carry out their instructions did much to pave the way for the colonization and civilization of the beautiful states of Oregon and Washington; and the numerous journeys, undertaken by Hunt, Mackenzie, and others among the various chains of the Rocky Mountains, though their main object was trade, justly entitle them to rank as pioneers of geographical discovery. To them, too, the United States Government, though scarcely our own, owes a debt of gratitude, their early occupation of Astoria having been a main point in the American claim to the Oregon territory, which at one time seemed likely to have become the property of Great Britain.

# CHAPTER XIII.

WHILE the expeditions lately described were in progress, efforts were being made by private individuals to supplement the work of Lewis, Clarke, and Pike. The lower course of the Red River was explored from Natchez by Mr. Dunbar and Dr. Hunter, and its upper waters were navigated by Dr. Sibley from Natchitoches, but nothing further was done toward determining the true sources of the Mississippi itself, until 1820, when Governor Cass, then in charge of Michigan territory, obtained permission to visit the highlands of Minnesota, and the great expedition under Long and James was sent by the United States Government to trace the course of its mightiest affluent, the Missouri.

Cass and his companions, accompanied by an escort of thirty-eight men, left Detroit, the capital of Michigan, in the spring of 1820, and made their way along the coasts of Lakes Huron and Superior to the borders of Minnesota, where they struck comparatively new ground, crossing the lovely basin of the St. Lawrence in a north-westerly direction, and reaching the shores of Sandy Lake in the middle of July. On the 17th of the same month, the canoes brought for the purpose were launched on the waters of the Mississippi, and the actual voyage of exploration began.

The strong current of the mighty Father of Waters rendered the ascent extremely arduous, and after a struggle, extending over one hundred and fifty miles, a series of impassable cataracts were reached, necessitating the carrying of the canoes and baggage for a considerable distance overland.

Beyond these cataracts, the Mississippi wound through extensive and beautiful plains, haunted by deer, buffaloes, and other large game, till the junction of the Leech Lake branch was reached, where the scenery became more mountainous. Another forty-five miles brought the explorers to the vast expanse of clear water known as Lake Winnipeg, where the river takes a sudden bend of fifty miles to the west, expanding beyond into a lake larger than any that had yet been traversed. To this the name of Cass was given, in honor of the leader of the expedition ; and, provisions now running short, it was resolved to turn back. To us who have access only to the official reports of the work done, the result obtained on this trip seems to have been very inadequate to the preparations made ; but, as we have more than once had occasion to feel, it is in the byways rather than the highways of our present subject that our pulse is stirred in sympathy with heroic deeds. The history of American exploration, properly so called, is almost entirely wanting in that element of romance, springing from the conquering of apparently insurmountable difficulties, which lends so subtle a charm to the record of the solving of the problems of African geography.

Long and James, leaders of the second of the two expeditions we have alluded to, embarked at St. Louis in a steam packet named the *Western Engineer*, the first to be launched on the inland waters of the Republic, in July, 1819 ; but a little above the mouth of the Kansas, they were robbed of all they possessed by Pawnee Indians, and compelled to return and refit.

Early in September a second start was made ; but the season was now so far advanced that it was necessary to winter near the mouth of the Platte, or Nebraska, so that it was not until the summer of 1820 that the actual journey of discovery can be said to have commenced. The first purpose of the expedition was now, in obedience to orders from headquarters, laid aside for a time, while a trip was made up the Nebraska, which was followed through the extensive level tracts—traversed by vast hordes of bisons and antelopes of various kinds, and rich in quarries of sandstone and limestone—forming the Platte valley, until the point at which the Nebraska divides into two forks was reached.

Here a halt was made, and it was resolved to follow the southern branch to its source in the Rocky Mountains. On the 30th June, the first buttresses of that now well known chain came in sight ; and on the 6th of the ensuing month, the camp was pitched opposite the chasm from which the Platte issues from its mountain home on its way to its junction, first with its northern branch, and then with the Missouri.

At this point, situated in N. lat. 39°, W. long. 105°, the Rocky Mountains presented an almost impassable barrier, a perpendicular wall of sandstone, some 200 feet high, running along on either side as far as the eye could reach, with granite masses towering beyond it to the sky. Several attempts were made to scale this wall, and from one height gained a view was obtained of both branches of the Platte, one coming from the north-west and the other from the south, but it was found impossible to reach the actual source of either.

A different route was now attempted, and, advancing in single file, the explorers had succeeded in reaching a great height, when their progress was again arrested by huge frowning precipices, along which no foothold could be obtained. With the aid of ropes, brought in readiness for some such emergency, several of the bravest of the party were lowered down a ravine, and reached the southern side of the wall, where they halted and refreshed themselves with what they took to be some bunches of wild currants. They had better have continued to endure the thirst from which they had been suffering, as this simple refreshment brought on violent headaches; and a little later, when one of the men paused to drink at what looked like a pure mountain spring, sickness immediately succeeded. The poor fellow had to be sent back, and only recovered after much suffering.

These two incidents determined the leader of the party to make no further halt until the descent of the western slope of the mountain was achieved, and his men were pressing on as best they could, when they were again stopped, this time by meeting a large bear in a narrow defile. In a moment a dozen rifles were pointed at the intruder, but before a shot could be fired, the huge brute turned aside, and climbed an almost perpendicular precipice some thirty feet high, leaving his enemies to gaze after him with almost envious wonder.

On the morning of the 13th July, the courage and perseverance of the advanced guard were amply rewarded by their coming in sight of the loftiest peak yet noticed, which, on examination, turned out to be the one already marked in Major Pike's map, bearing his name, and situated in N. lat. 38° 53′, W. long. 105° 52′.

The main object of the expedition was now accomplished, the almost precise situation of the sources of the Nebraska having been determined. Pike's Peak was ascended by a few adventurous spirits, and from its summit a magnificent view was obtained of masses of snow and ice, succeeded by fertile valleys and vast plains stretching away to the east. Careful notes having been taken of the main features of the scene, the explorers returned to camp, where they were in due course joined by their comrades, and an earnest consultation was held as to the next steps to be taken.

It was finally resolved that the head-waters of the Arkansas, the largest affluent of the Mississippi after the Missouri, and of several of its minor tributaries, should now be sought; and, with this end in view, a south-westerly course was pursued along the eastern base of the Rocky Mountain Chain. A weary march across the low, bare, sandy plains of the present state of Wyoming, strewn with broken sandstone, brought our heroes to the brink of the precipice dividing these lofty table-lands from the valley of the Arkansas, where they were alike cheered and tantalized by the sight of the river they were seeking, flowing through a rich and fertile country.

It was now decided to divide forces; Captain Long and most of the men, with all the heavy baggage, to go down the Arkansas to the Mississippi and await the rest of the party at Fort Smith, while Captain James and a few picked men should continue the explorations among the mountains. The first part of the programme was duly carried out, the chief discovery made being the existence of a number of chalybeate springs; but much disappointment and delay attended Captain James and his party in their wanderings among the then unknown tracts inhabited by the Yutas and other wild tribes bordering on the Salt Lake territory, a region about which a weird mystery clings even now.

Provisions and water alike ran short; the beds of streams, to which the travelers hastened to quench their thirst, turned out to be full of nothing but salt, and all efforts to find the source of the Arkansas failed. At last a broad tributary, supposed to be the Red River of the South, was discovered and followed, but it turned out to be the Canadian, which joins the Arkansas before the confluence of the latter with the Mississippi. The second half of the journey of exploration may therefore be said to have practically failed, though the way was paved by it for the colonists who, a few years later, migrated to the districts traversed.

The whole party met again at Fort Smith on the Mississippi, and made their way thence to the western coast by what had now become quite a well-known track. Disgusted with the poor results obtained, however, Major Long shortly afterward accepted the command of yet another expedition, the aim of which was to explore the vast tracts watered by the northern tributaries of the Mississippi, and which, though the property of the United States, were as yet practically unknown.

The explorers this time started from a village on the Ohio, from which they made their way across the province of the same name and part of Indiana to Lake Michigan, witnessing in their wanderings many terrible scenes of cruelty. The Potawatomies, inhabiting the high table-lands of this fertile district, are said to have tortured their captives and devoured their flesh with a savage cruelty quite equal to any thing ever witnessed elsewhere by European travelers; and it was with a feeling of intense relief that the white men turned aside, after entering the marshy districts bordering on Lake Michigan, to visit the mission station founded long ago by their fellow-countryman, Carey, the great Apostle of the Indians, who did for the neglected redskins of the present century what the good old Jesuit priests had done for their ancestors.

At this little oasis in the wilderness, fifty acres had already been cleared and six log-huts built, in one of which some fifty or sixty Indian children were being educated, their parents and chiefs encouraging their teachers in every possible way, though not themselves converts either to the civilization or to the religion of the white men. From the mission station the expedition proceeded through forests and across a rich fertile country of oak-openings and prairies, succeeded by swampy plains, till they found themselves on the southern shores of Lake Michigan, which presented the appearance of a vast ocean stretching away in an unbroken expanse as far as the eye could reach.

Huge broken bowlders of granite, piles of sand and pebbles, rolling waves and white-crested breakers, added to the impression first received, and it was difficult to believe that this troubled sea was but one of that long series of fresh water lakes from which issues the mightiest artery of North America, the St. Lawrence of many memories.

Reluctantly turning his back on the grand scene just described, Long now led his party in a south-westerly direction toward the Mississippi, passing near the site of the present Chicago, and crossing the fertile prairies of Illinois, where not a tree breaks the solemn monotony of the wilderness. As the Father of Waters was approached, however, the whole character of the country changed; hill and vale, forest and clearing, alternating with wildly picturesque rocks and mountains, between which the majestic volume of the river rolls in irresistible majesty.

Embarking on the broad basin of the now well-known river, the travelers commenced their actual explorations by struggling upward till they came to its junction with the Minnesota, or St. Peter's River, its largest tributary north of the Missouri, and which joins it near the Falls of St. Anthony. The Minnesota had never yet been followed to its source; and, entering it, Long slowly ascended it to its head-waters, now in a south-westerly, now in a westerly direction, on the borders of the Dakota territory, where he altered his course to due north, and quickly reached the small group of lakes from which issues the mighty Red River of the North, and which may be said to be set in an ever-shifting framework of swamps and flooded streams. Here are interlocked the head-waters of the northern tributaries of the Mississippi, of the St. Lawrence, and of many a minor stream ; and —strange phenomenon even in this land of physical wonders—no lofty ridge marks the watershed behind them. The heads of all the rivers are connected by canals, and canoes can shoot from one great artery to another with no change of level to mark the transition.

After a good deal of intercourse with our old friends the Sioux, the explorers launched their canoes on the Red River, and ascended it to the great Lake Winnipeg, or the Lake of the Assiniboins, connected by a number of small lakes and rivers with Hudson's Bay, and considered the largest, though scarcely the most important of the inland seas belonging to British North America.

From Lake Winnipeg the explorers descended the river of the same name, passing through scenery wilder and grander than any yet visited by them, and going through many a peril among the constant succession of cascades and cataracts, but arriving in safety at the Lake of the Woods, that small sheet of water destined to become so famous in the controversy relating to the boundary between the United States and the Hudson's Bay territories.

The Lake of the Woods, then surrounded by a deserted wilderness of rock and forest, was carefully examined, and from it the party made their way in a north-easterly direction to Lake Superior, the whole route consisting of little more than a series of lakes, streams, and swamps, broken by an occasional portage or bar of land, over which the canoes had to be dragged. All difficulties were, however, successfully overcome ; the existence of more than one continuous water-passage from west to east was proved beyond a doubt, and little more in the way of actual discovery was left to be done by future expeditions.

In 1830, however, it was found desirable to send an expedition to the North-west, with a view to restoring peace between the Chippeways and Sioux ; and the leader selected—the Schoolcraft who had been mainly instrumental in organizing the trip made a few years previously by Cass— received instructions to combine with his negotiations an exhaustive survey of the upper waters of the Mississippi. He reached Lake Superior in safety in 1830, but the waters of the rivers above it were so low at that time that nothing definite could be accomplished.

Two years later, Schoolcraft started again, and, after a successful voyage up the great river, he arrived at Cass Lake, the most northerly point reached by the predecessor who had given his name to that now famous sheet of water. Here the real difficulties of the expedition began. The Mississippi branched out into two forks, one of which—the eastern—was followed to its source in Lake Ussawa, whence an arduous tramp, or rather paddle, across country brought the party, first to the lofty ridge known as the Hauteur des Ferres, separating the tributaries of the River de Corbeau from those of the Red River, and then in sight of the western and main branch of the Father of Waters.

A number of sandy elevations had still to be scaled before the explorers once more stood upon the shores of the Mississippi, but on issuing from "a thicket into a small weedy opening," the goal of the journey suddenly burst upon them. Itasca Lake, the primal home of the western branch of the mighty river, lay stretched before them, and the last link in the chain of discovery connected with the longest water highway in the world was found.

Itasca Lake, the Lac la Biche of the early French explorers, is a beautiful sheet of water some seven or eight miles in circumference, with an outlet about twelve feet wide, whence the Mississippi expands into a broad and copious stream. Its volume appeared strangely out of proportion to the size of its source, till the presence of invisible subterranean springs, such as those near the African Lake Tanganyika, was ascertained.

A thorough exploration of Lake Itasca was succeeded by a perilous voyage down a series of rapids forming the first stage of the Mississippi's journey to the ocean ; but, after many a narrow escape, the canoes floated into the broad stream, flanked on either side by prairies, into which the river widens above Lake Cass, whence the trip to Lake Superior lay through districts already well known.

# CHAPTER XIV.

DURING the first years of the present century, the tide alike of emigration and exploration had set toward the northern territories of the United States. The discovery of the sources of the Mississippi and of those of its chief affluents, however, left little more to be done in that direction, and, in 1838, a new chapter in the history of modern American geography was ushered in by the sending out of a naval exploring expedition, under Captain Wilkes, with orders to make surveys along the western coast, especially of the bay now known as that of San Francisco.

On the arrival of Wilkes at Yerba Buena, as what has since become the gate of the Pacific was then called, the town consisted merely of a large frame building occupied by an agent of the Hudson's Bay Company, a store kept by an American, a billiard room and bar, a poop cabin of a ship used as a residence by a captain, a blacksmith's shop, and a few sheds, all of which had sprung up at intervals since California, deserted, as related above, by its early colonists, had become the prey of trappers, miners, and other adventurers of various nationalities.

The most prominent man then in California was a Swiss named Sutter, who had bought of the Mexican Government a tract of land thirty leagues square, and was now employed in laying it out under the imposing name of New Helvetia. He had already built a fort near the junction of the Sacramento and American rivers to which he had given his own name, little dreaming that the discovery of gold close at hand would shortly make that name world-famous, as the most powerful emigration magnet of the day.

Equally unconscious of the approaching, almost miraculous change in the aspect of affairs on the south-western coast of North America, Wilkes completed his survey, and returned home to report the harbor of Yerba Buena to be one of the finest, if not the very best in the world; and, a little later, the Government sent out an expedition, under Lieutenant John C. Fremont, to explore the southern half of the Rocky Mountain Range, with a view to the discovery of a good route to California.

Fremont left the mouth of the Kansas, at the head of a party of about

JOHN C. FREMONT.

twenty, about the 2d of May, and followed its course across the state of the same name, till he reached the barren banks of the Platte, or Nebraska. Here he decided to follow the southern fork of that important tributary of the Mississippi, and a march of a few miles brought the party into the districts occupied by the Arapaho and Cheyenne Indians, the former of whom at first appeared disposed to dispute the passage of the white men.

One encounter, which threatened to be serious, took place on the 8th July. The excitement of watching a fight between some eighteen or twenty buffaloes, which the explorers had at the last moment decided in favor of the weaker party by a few well-directed shots, had but just subsided, when some dark objects appeared on the horizon among the hills. More buffaloes, of course, thought every one ; but, presently, Maxwell, a trader who knew the neighborhood and its people well, happened to look behind him, and saw crowds of mounted natives furiously urging on their horses.

At first there seemed to be no more than twenty warriors, but behind them came others, and soon the hills and plains were darkened by the dusky figures. The explorers halted, drew together, and determined to sell their lives as dearly as they could, prepared to meet the onslaught with a volley of bullets. Another moment, and many of the Indians would have been rolling in the dust, when Maxwell suddenly recognized their leader as a man with whom he had often traded. "Don't you know me?" he shouted in the Arapaho language ; and, astonished at the sound of his own tongue, the chief wheeled his horse round. Then, dashing forward, he extended his hand to Fremont with the one word "Arapaho," meaning that, as a member of that nation, he was the friend of Maxwell's friend.

Escorted by the now courteous savages, the expedition pressed on, and, without further adventures of consequence, followed the south fork of the Platte to St. Vram's Fort, a trading outpost, situated just under the most easterly buttresses of the Rocky Mountain Range, about seventeen miles from Long's Peak. Pike's Peak could also be seen about one hundred miles to the south, and but little of actual exploration remained to be done in the immediate neighborhood. Fremont resolved, therefore, to alter his course, and follow the north fork of the Platte to Fort Laramie, a second remote outpost in the wilderness, whence he hoped to make his way to the head of the Sweet Water River, an affluent of the Nebraska issuing from the South Pass of the Rocky Mountains.

Crossing the fertile, garden-like valley of the Platte, with the low line of the frowning Black Hills on the left, the expedition reached Fort Laramie in safety on the 13th July, and were there detained a few days on account of difficulties between the white settlers and the Gros-Ventre, Cheyenne,

Sioux, and other tribes, who were scouring the country between the Platte and the Rocky Mountains, rendering it unsafe for travelers.

Imagining the dangers to have been overrated, however, Fremont and his colleagues resolved not to allow them to prevent the completion of their task. On the 18th, therefore, when the men had had time to recover from the fatigues of their long march, they were called together, and Fremont told them of his intention to proceed, adding that he was willing to release any one of them from his engagement who was desirous to retire from the service. Only one man availed himself of this privilege, and when he had been dismissed, amidst the ridicule of his comrades, active preparations were made for the continuation of the journey.

The tents were struck, the horses saddled, and the "stirrup-cup" was being enjoyed, when four chiefs made their way into the midst of the white men, and one of them having handed a letter to Fremont, they seated themselves in silence to watch him read it. The letter, which was in French, ran as follows :—

"Fort Platte, July 1st, 1842.

"Mr. Fremont,—The chiefs, having assembled in council, have just told me to warn you not to set out before the party of young men which is now out shall have returned. Furthermore, they tell me that they are very sure to fire upon you as soon as they meet you. They are expected back in seven or eight days. Excuse me for making these observations, but it seems my duty to warn you of danger. Moreover, the chiefs who prohibit your setting out before the return of the warriors are the bearers of this note.

"I am your obedient servant,

"JOSEPH BISSOUETTE."

This Joseph Bissouette was the interpreter engaged for the passage of the country between Fort Laramie and the Rocky Mountains, and the warning was therefore not to be neglected. The chiefs, whose names were given as Otter Hat, Breaker of Arrows, Black Night, and Bull's Tail, maintained silence while Fremont read and explained the letter to his men. Then one of them advanced, and, having shaken hands—a ceremony all Indians who have had any thing to do with white men are careful not to neglect—he made a speech to the effect that he and his people were glad to see their white brothers . . . they looked upon their coming as the light which goes before the sun, for they would tell their great father (so they called the President of the United States) that they had seen them, and that they were naked and poor. But these dear white brothers had come at a bad time. Some of the Indians had been killed by emigrants from the great father's lands far away in the East, and the young warriors in the mountains would avenge the blood of their relations, etc., etc.

To this harangue, which from the point of view of the poor dispossessed owners of the soil was really very moderate, Fremont, after a few general remarks, made answer—" We have thrown away our bodies, and will not turn back. When you told us that your young men would kill us, you did not know that our hearts were strong, and you did not see the rifles which my young men carry in their hands. We are few, and you are many, and may kill us all; but there will be much crying in your villages, for many of your young men will stay behind, and forget to return with your warriors from the mountains. Do you think that our great chief will let his soldiers die, and forget to cover their graves? Before the snows melt again, his warriors will sweep away your villages, as the fire does the prairie in the autumn. See! I have pulled down my white houses, and my people are ready; when the sun is ten paces higher, we shall be on the march. If you have any thing to tell us, you will say it soon."

The chiefs withdrew in sullen silence, the preparations for the march were resumed, and the expedition was again just starting, when Bull's Tail came back with a message that a young man should be sent as guide to the first stopping place. This apparently slight concession meant every thing. The presence of one warrior would, as all knew, protect the whole of the whites from the savages out on the hills; and, naming the place for the pitching of the camp that evening, Fremont cordially thanked the emissary, who returned at once to his comrades.

Following the north fork of the Platte, the explorers soon entered a desolate country, laid waste by the combined evils of drought and war. The interpreter urged Fremont to turn back, assuring him that death from starvation was all but inevitable. Again calling his men together, the leader once more gave them their choice of pushing on or returning, and all but six decided for the latter course. These six cried with one voice, " We'll eat the mules if buffalo are not to be had; " and, shaking hands with their comrades, the brave little remnant pressed on.

On the 31st July the Platte was left behind, and a short march brought the expedition to the banks of its affluent, the Sweet Water River, which flows in a gentle descent from the most picturesque gorge of the Rocky Mountains, now called the South Pass, but then practically unknown to the white man. Now climbing some rugged height, now pausing to rest on the banks of the river, the gigantic ridge called the Devil's Gate was left behind, and on the 7th August the South Pass itself was entered.

Instead of the arduous climb associated as a matter of course with the scaling of the Rocky Mountains, Fremont now found himself ascending a sandy plain, which brought him, imperceptibly as it were, to the primal home of many a river flowing into the Pacific. The watershed—as unique in its character as the swamps which nurse the infancy of the Mississippi and the St. Lawrence—left behind, Fremont led his little band up a long and beautiful ravine, discovering, a few miles further on, a lake "set like a gem in the mountains."

The newly-found sheet of water, which was ascertained to be the source of one branch of the Colorado of the West, was named Mountain Lake; and the instructions of the Government having now been fully carried out, it was resolved to return eastward. Before sounding the retreat, however, Fremont noticed a lofty mountain peak in the vicinity of the South Pass, and resolved to ascend it. This turned out to be a matter of considerable difficulty. First the mules were left behind, then boots and stockings were discarded, the use of the toes being absolutely necessary to the advance of the climbers.

Fremont himself was the first to reach the summit. Availing himself of a kind of comb of the mountain, he gained a point with an overhanging buttress, round which he crept, putting hands and feet in the crevices between the blocks, and often hanging over a vertical precipice several hundred feet deep), where a moment's giddiness would have been fatal. At last he stood, to quote his own words, "on a narrow crest about three feet in width, with an inclination of about 20° N., 51° E.;" and though he did not know it then, he had reached the highest point of the great Rocky Mountain Range, 13,590 feet above the sea-level—a point still known, in honor of its discoverer, as Fremont's Peak.

As he paused to rest, and gazed down upon the lovely view at his feet, stretching away to the shores of the Pacific, Fremont relates that a solitary bee came flying up from the eastern valley, and settled on the knee of one of the men. "A moment's thought," he adds, "would have made us let

this solitary pioneer of the advance of civilization continue his way unharmed ; but we carried out the law of this country, where all animated
nature seems at war." The bee was caught, killed, and placed among the
flowers collected on the way up ; and in this slight incident we read a melancholy prophecy of the fate awaiting the human inhabitants of the lands
now for the first time brought within the limits of that civilization which
has never yet proved itself wide enough to contain the red man and the
white.

From the summit of Fremont's Peak the explorers could see on the one
side the innumerable lakes and streams among which sprang the Colorado
of the Gulf of California, while on the other lay the romantic Wind River
Valley, whence flows the Yellowstone branch of the Missouri ; while far
away on the north rose the snow-crowned heads of the Trois Tetons, the
first homes of the Missouri and Columbia, with the less lofty peaks at the
southern extremity of the range which witnessed the birth of the Nebraska.
Of the whole scene, the most remarkable characteristic was, and is, the
traces of terrible convulsions of nature. The chain is split from end to end
into ridges and chasms, alternated with thin walls of rock, broken at their
terminations into natural minarets and columns, producing an effect of
weird, unearthly beauty peculiarly striking.

Noting, however, but the main features of a district now associated with
so many scenes of adventure in the great rush of emigration westward so
soon to follow, Fremont hastened back to his camp in the South Pass, and
thence returned to Fort Laramie, which he reached in safety without the
loss of a single man, all the prophecies as to the dangers awaiting him being
unfulfilled. A few weeks later, his report was in the hands of his Government, who marked their sense of their services by at once appointing him to
the command of a second expedition ; this time with orders to connect the
work he had already done with that of Wilkes, by examining the country
between the southern half of the Rocky Mountains and the shores of the
Pacific. With this end in view, Fremont, accompanied by some thirty-nine
men—Canadians, Creoles, and Americans—started from Kansas, near the
junction of that river with the Missouri, early in June, 1843.

Following the now well-beaten emigrant tracks for the West, the expedition reached the Rocky Mountains considerably to the south of the pass
discovered on the previous trip, and near the connecting ridge between the
Utah or Bear River Mountains and the Wind River chain. This ridge

separated the waters flowing to the Gulf of California on the east, and those on the west which run more directly to the Pacific, from that vast inland basin of lakes with no outlet to the ocean.

Crossing the Rocky Mountains, the party entered the fertile and picturesque valley of the Bear or Utah River, the chief tributary of the Great Salt Lake, first alluded to by Baron La Hontan in 1689, but never before visited by any white man except wandering trappers, whose eyes had been blind to the wonderful nature of the phenomenon now to be examined.

Slowly descending the lovely valley, tenanted only by a few Shoshone Indians, Fremont reached the now famous Beer Springs, situated in a mountain-locked basin of mineral waters, on the 25th August. These springs burst from openings in the rocks, and give off an effervescing gas, which produces an effect of great beauty, the water rising in trembling column to a considerable height, accompanied by a subterranean noise, accounted for by the natives in many a weird legend.

Beyond the Beer Springs the cavalcade pressed on to the wild western region between them and Salt Lake inhabited by the scattered Root Indians, who live almost entirely on roots and seeds, and on the 1st September reached the junction of the Bear and Roseaux Rivers, where an india-rubber boat provided for river navigation was inflated and launched on the waters of the united streams. A little further on, however, the river, which Fremont had hoped would carry him down to the lake, itself suddenly divided into a number of shallow branches, and the land journey had to be resumed.

Through low flats, across salt marshes, or the salt incrusted beds of dried-up lakes, the weary travelers plodded. On the 6th September their perseverance was at last rewarded by reaching the summit of a kind of ridge, from which they beheld, immediately at their feet, the waters of the long-sought inland sea, stretching in silent grandeur far beyond their range of vision, and receiving in its cold and lifeless bosom all the rivers of the vast basin of Utah, except the head branches of the Colorado and Humboldt.

From the center of the lake rose several islands, some of them 3,250 feet above its level, but no sign of animal or vegetable life could be detected on any of them. Equally lonely and deserted were the wild, weird heights and dreary stretches of briny wastes shutting in the shores of the "still innocent Dead Sea" itself, and it was with a feeling almost akin to shrinking that Fremont made preparations for launching his boat upon its waters.

After a somewhat perilous voyage, during which the clothes of the explorers became incrusted with salt, the boat was brought within wading distance of one of the smaller islands, and, landing, Fremont carefully examined its strange cliffs and masses, finding them also covered with the apparently omnipresent salt. A few temporary tents were then constructed of the driftwood scattered on the shores, and after kindling large fires to excite the wonder of any straggling savage on the lake shore, the successful explorers—the first of their race to spend a night near the site of the now world-famous Salt Lake City—lay down to sleep. .

In the morning, to the surprise of all, the noise of huge waves breaking on the rocks was the first sound to greet their ears, and no time was lost in making their way back to the mainland. The "still and lifeless bosom" of the lake had changed its character, and, though powerless to give or nourish vitality, proved its capacity to destroy. The fragile india-rubber bark was more than once nearly swallowed up in its treacherous waters, but late in the day all landed from it in safety, and on the 12th September the journey was resumed.

Following much the same route as that taken on the way to the lake, our hero now led his men back to the Bear River, and thence through the great basin bearing his name, and inclosing the vast system of rivers and creeks belonging to the newly discovered Dead Sea, to a ravine commanding a pass in the dividing ridge between the waters of the Bear River and the Snake or Lewis fork of the Columbia ; thus, so to speak, throwing a bridge of connection across from his own work to that of his predecessors.

On the 19th September the expedition arrived in safety at Fort Hall, a trading post situated in a low and fertile valley, some twenty miles long, formed by the confluence of the Portneuf and Snake Rivers. The winter was now rapidly approaching, yet Fremont resolved to push on first to the Columbia River, and from thence home by a new route, making what he characterizes as a "great circuit to the south and south-east," with a view to the exploration of the Great Basin between the Rocky Mountains and the Sierra Nevada. No persuasions could induce him to alter this determination, although the task he had set himself was pronounced absolutely impracticable. He arrived in safety at Fort Vancouver, about ninety miles from the mouth of the Columbia, on the 16th November, and almost immediately commenced the return journey ; but he had not proceeded far, when he found himself in a pathless wilderness haunted by bands of wandering Indians, from whom scarcely any guidance and no food could be obtained.

On the 10th December, a lake, to which the name of Tlamath was given, was discovered ; and on the 14th a stream was struck, which Fremont, from astronomical observations taken, concluded to be the principal branch of the Sacramento. He now hoped to find an opening in the mountains through which he could reach the districts explored in the early part of his trip ; but in this he was unsuccessful. Three weeks of exhausting wandering brought the weary travelers to another remarkable mountain lake, to which, on account of a tapering rock rising from its center, the name of Pyramid was given.

While the indefatigable hero was ascertaining the exact position of the

TEMPLE BLOCK, SALT LAKE CITY.

newly-found sheet of water, a few half-naked Indians, speaking a dialect of the Snake language, made their appearance, and said they lived in the rocks hard by, and that there was a river at the end of the lake. Cheered by being again in a country where human beings could live, Fremont led his party round the lake to the so-called river, and found it to be merely a fresh-water stream flowing into, not out of, the Pyramid. This at once convinced him that he had discovered, not the head-waters of any river, but a vast interior lake without outlet.

The last of the cattle brought for provisions for the party had been killed a day or two previously, and it was now a question of the utmost moment whether an attempt should be made to pierce the mountains on the east or go down through those on the west to the sea, when a number of Indians came out of a neighboring thicket who said their water was full of fish. The camp was at once pitched, and a little later the hungry explorers were enjoying a hearty meal of salmon trout. The natives, however, could give but little information about their country. They made a drawing of their river on the ground, representing it as issuing from another lake in the mountains three or four days distant, beyond which was a single mountain, and further away still were two rivers, on one of which white people like their guests traveled.

Whether these white people were settlers on the Sacramento, or travelers from the United States, there was no evidence to show; and after a long and eager discussion with his followers, Fremont resolved finally to abandon all idea of returning to the United States for the present, and to cross the Sierra Nevada into the valley of the Sacramento. This decision was greeted with eager acclamation by all concerned; and although the Indians assured him that the mountains were altogether impassable in the winter, not a moment was lost in preparing for the arduous undertaking.

The first peak of the most easterly range of the mighty rocky barrier was scaled on the 20th January; but a violent snowstorm coming on compelled the travelers to turn southward, and encamp on the eastern side of the mountains. A little further on a large stream was discovered, which was followed to its outlet from the mountains, where the ascent of the ridge was again commenced. A wild and narrow pass, through which ran an Indian trail, with mountains on either side cased in snow and ice, led up to a lofty height, looking down from which, several natives were seen skimming and circling about on snow-shoes.

The shouts of the whites, who were eager to obtain guides, only frightened the natives, who scudded rapidly away; but the next day a number of Indians were surprised in a little valley, and the travelers succeeded in re-assuring them by signs of friendship. With great difficulty—the language spoken by these children of the desert being quite unintelligible—Fremont made out that the waters along which he had been traveling belonged to the system of the Great Basin, on the edge of which he had been since early in December, and that the great ridge on the left must still be crossed before the Pacific Ocean could be reached.

Explaining to the Indians that he was endeavoring to find a passage through the mountains into the country of the whites, which he was going to see, Fremont begged them to find him a guide, to whom presents of scarlet cloth and other articles should be given. The redskins looked at the rewards offered, consulted together, and then, first pointing to the snow on the mountains, drew their hands across their necks to show how deep it was. It was impossible, they implied by their gestures, to go through this barrier of solid water; the white men must turn southward to begin with, and not westward, until after a long tramp in that direction.

To this compromise Fremont was obliged to consent, and, escorted by a young Indian guide, he led his weary followers ten miles in a south-easterly

SAN FRANCISCO IN 1849.

direction, reaching, on the 31st January, a gap in the Sierra Nevada, through which he hoped to penetrate to the fertile plains beyond. Again he was disappointed; the pass scaled, he still had before him a great continuous range, which he felt satisfied was the central ridge of the Sierra Nevada, the great Californian Mountain. He now knew, however, that the Bay of San Francisco, or Yerba Buena, as it was still called, lay on the other side of this great mass, and resolved, at whatever cost, to traverse it without delay.

The camp was pitched in the eastern side, and the fires had scarcely been lighted, when crowds of almost naked Indians rushed in, bringing with them long nets and bows greatly resembling those in use on the Sacramento

River, which, as Fremont knew, drains the great central valley of California. Here was an incidental proof of the approaching end of the long and terrible journey, for in nothing are local influences in America more distinctly reflected than in the arms and utensils of the natives.

Very eager were the questions put to the new-comers, who were, so to speak, links between the east and the west of the mighty barrier to be crossed, and having heard all that they could tell, Fremont informed his men of the resolution he had already long before come to himself, of crossing the Californian Mountain. Again a young man was induced by a large present to act as guide, and on the 1st February the great enterprise was begun.

Silently—for they knew how hazardous was the task before them—the explorers commenced the ascent of the mountain, along the valley of a tributary stream of the Salmon-trout River. Deeper and deeper became the snow, and it was soon necessary to break a road. Ten men were told off for this service, mounted on the strongest surviving horses, each man in succession opening a path until he and his steed became exhausted, when he drew aside and let his comrade pass him. Sixteen miles were thus traversed ; a height of 6,750 feet above the sea-level was attained, and still the icy peaks reared their heads with no sensible diminution in their lofty inaccessibility.

On the 4th February, two Indians joined the party, and one of them, an old man, made a harangue, much of which was understood by Fremont, who had now learned something of the language of the mountaineers. " Rock upon rock, rock upon rock, snow upon snow, snow upon snow lies before you," said the speaker, "and even if you get over the snow, you will not be able to get down from the mountains." The guide, on whom no word was lost, was so overcome by the apparent hopelessness of the situation, that he covered his face with his blanket and wept bitterly. "I wanted to see the whites," he moaned ; "I came away from my own people to see the whites, and I wouldn't care to die among them, but here  .  .  ." Sobs checked his voice ; "and," as Fremont adds with the quaint humor which runs throughout much of his narrative, "seated round the tree, the fire illuminating the rocks and the tall boles of the pines round about, and the old Indian haranguing, we presented a group of very serious faces."

The next morning, the guide, overcome by the horror awakened by the Indian's prophecy of disaster, ran away, and Fremont, rallying his men about him, offered to go forward on snow-shoes, with one companion, a Mr.

Fitzpatrick, and make a reconnaissance. The result won by this prompt measure imbued the whole party with fresh energy. From the summit of a peak ten miles from the camp, a view was obtained of a low range of mountains, which could be none other than those of the coast of California. Between the explorers, then, and this sea-board chain lay the valley of the Sacramento, and, when they eagerly scanned the intervening space with glasses, the course of a river could be made out, with dots of prairie land on either side.

Another six days of struggle with ice and snow, and the camp was pitched on the summit of the pass, 2,000 feet higher than that of the South Pass of the Rocky Mountains, in the dividing ridge of the Sierra Nevada, and in N. lat. 38° 44′, W. long. 120° 28′. Thus, for the first time, was revealed to the white man of modern days the phenomenon of a range of mountains at the extremity of the continent higher than the great Rocky Mountains themselves. The existence of the Great Basin was accounted for, and it was evident that here too there must be a system of small, land-locked lakes and rivers which the Sierra Nevada forever prevents from escaping to the Pacific Ocean.

The mountain barrier was conquered at last, and, descending the western slopes, with hearts beating high with hope and triumph, the heroes soon struck the waters of a river which turned out to be the American fork of the Sacramento. Following it through a beautiful and fertile country, they came, on the 6th March, to Sutter's Fort, outside which they were met by its owner and founder, who, as will readily be imagined, gave them an enthusiastic welcome.

Thus ended one of the most romantic and perilous journeys ever made in the United States. For the first time, the Sierra Nevada had been crossed by white men, and for the first time, the existence of an overland route between the East and the West had been proved.

The remainder of the trip to the sea, through the beautiful valley of the San Joaquin, though interesting, was tame in comparison with the transit of the mountains. After approaching the now well known Bay of San Francisco, Fremont made his way back by a more southerly and less difficult route than in his westward journey to the Great Basin, again visiting the Salt Lake of Utah, and making acquaintance with many a fine specimen of the southern branch of the great Shoshone family.

Toward the close of May, the Great Salt Lake was left behind, and a fort-

night's journey, through the comparatively familiar districts overlooked by
the mountains dividing the Pacific from the Mississippi rivers, brought the
party once more to the South Pass of the Rocky Mountains, first scaled by
Fremont three years before.   A slight detour southward, to examine three
peaks well known to the hunter and trapper, but hitherto unnamed, was
succeeded by a journey across the Rocky Mountains, rendered somewhat
exciting by a struggle going on between the Arapahoes and the Utahs, but
on the 18th June the summit of the ridge, 11,200 feet above the sea-level,
overlooking the head-waters of the Arkansas, was reached in safety.   The
Arkansas was now followed to its junction with the Mississippi, on the
broad waters of which the explorers embarked on the 18th July, arriving
at St. Louis on the 6th August.

In 1848, the indefatigable Fremont made another journey to California,
this time at his own expense ; but in attempting to cross the mountains between the Rio Grande and the Colorado in the depth of winter, his guide
lost his way, and nearly all the men and animals died a miserable death.
Fremont himself escaped, but we have been unable to obtain any record of
his adventures, or of the geographical discoveries made on this last trip,
which, however, took place after the discovery of gold near Sutter's Fort
and the admission of California to the Union had completely revolutionized
the aspect of affairs.

CAMPED IN THE DESERT.

# CHAPTER XV.

## TWO GREAT EMIGRATIONS.

SHORTLY after the discovery of the Great Salt Lake by Fremont, took place that remarkable event in Illinois which led to the peopling of the Great Basin with the Mormons, or Latter-day Saints, followers of the so-called martyr, Joe Smith, who, thrown into prison for the crimes he had committed in the name of religion, was murdered by a band of roughs on the 29th June, 1844. The State of Illinois had granted the Mormons lands, and they had lived long enough on them to found the city of Nauvoo, in which they had built a huge and imposing temple of polished marble.

After the murder of Smith, the original inhabitants of Illinois, disgusted at the immoral practices of the Mormons, compelled them to sell their property and leave the state. The Saints now resolved to emigrate far away from all civilized communities, and to found a new republic among the vast solitudes of the Rocky Mountains. Explorers were sent out in different directions to choose the best locality for the purpose, and their reports led to the selection of the Great Salt Lake Valley. Westward then the emigrants, headed by their new prophet Brigham Young, began to move, their exodus resembling that of the Israelites from Egypt more than any of modern times.

In February, 1846, the Mississippi, then frozen over, was crossed, and a journey of fifteen hundred miles, through a country without roads, bridges, rivers, or wells, and peopled by wild bands of Pawnee and Shoshone Indians, was commenced. Bravely, however, the multitudes pushed on, and however we may condemn their peculiar tenets, we can not withhold from them our admiration for the faith which braced them up in what they looked upon as suffering for righteousness' sake. Still more must we honor the moral courage which, when the war broke out between the United States and Mexico, led Young to send five hundred of his sturdiest men to help their country in her hour of need, the ranks of his followers closing up, when they were gone, to face the now double dangers of the way, with no perceptible weakening of resolution.

The Missouri was safely forded, and the great wilderness beyond was traversed without any great loss of life. Then came the ascent of the Rocky Mountains, already associated with the memory of so much heroism, and, early in the year 1847, the western slopes resounded to the clang of trumpets and the tramp of thousands going down at last to take possession of their desolate inheritance on the shores of the "still innocent Dead Sea."

Without a day's, with scarcely an hour's delay, work was commenced, and, as if by magic, the dreary wilderness began to blossom as a rose. The rivers of the hills were diverted from their courses to irrigate the fields; homestead after homestead rose from the salt-encumbered plains; patches of orchards broke the dull monotony of the sands; the Utahs and Shoshones were won over by gifts and kindness to act as hunters and trappers for the new-comers, and before a year was over, Salt Lake City rose from the banks of a river aptly named Jordan, between Lake Utah and the Great Salt Lake. A tabernacle—not so imposing as the last marble temple, but still a grand edifice to rise from such a spot—soon enabled the Mormons to worship once more according to their peculiar rites; emigrants poured in from every side, and in less than twenty years from the founding of Salt Lake City its population numbered 8,218.

As a matter of course, this great movement was attended by the opening up of the surrounding country. Numerous expeditions were sent out from the United States to inquire into the position of the infant community, and to explore new routes from the Great Basin to the Pacific. In the years 1849 and 1850 an exhaustive survey of the river systems, mountain ranges, etc., of the whole district was made by Captain Stansbury of the American army; and in his report the student will find much valuable information supplementary to that won by our heroes of actual discovery. But his work sinks into insignificance before the thrilling interest of the second great migration of our own day, that which succeeded the close of the war with Mexico in 1848 by a treaty consigning California to the United States, and the discovery, one month later, of gold on the lands of that Captain Sutter, who has already figured twice in our narrative.

From end to end of the earth spread the news of the existence of vast seams of ore on the hitherto deserted shores of the Bay of San Francisco. The name of Sacramento, the infant settlement founded by Sutter, was in every mouth; and from the north and from the south, from the east and from the west, a stream of adventurers began to struggle toward it. In 1849 took place the overland emigration of no less than thirty thousand souls, men, women and children—half of them entering California by the old Gila route, associated with the Franciscan fathers of the earlier portion of our narrative ; the other half literally forcing their way, step by step, across the rugged passes of the Rocky Mountains.

The Pawnees, the Sioux, and the Arapahoes, amazed and awe-struck at their numbers, fled at their approach, but the less easily cowed enemies of famine and pestilence thinned their ranks. Still undaunted, the survivors, leaving the dead bodies of their comrades a prey to the wild beasts of the wilderness, pressed on, and, the Rocky Mountains left behind, they swarmed into the valley of Humboldt's River, watering the western half of the newly-formed State of Utah. Many were here obliged to halt for want of fodder for their cattle or food for themselves ; and it is related that some of the adventurers, in their eager lust to be the first to arrive in the new El Dorado, set fire to the meadows of dry grass to hinder the progress of those behind them.

On the shores of the Humboldt River a separation took place in the ranks of those still able to proceed, some making for the head of the Sacramento Valley, others choosing the better route to the American fork of the Sacramento River. Of the former, nearly all perished before reaching their destination ; of the latter, many were rescued by the noble heroism of parties sent out from California to their relief. Enough of the original thirty thousand survived to fill the hitherto desolate valley of the new south-western state with life. Every ensuing spring brought new comers ; the little settlement of Yerba Buena became the port of San Francisco, which, from "a scattering town of tent and canvas houses," grew in four short months to a populous city, "displaying," to quote the words of Bayard Taylor, "street after street of well-built edifices, filled with an active and enterprising people, and exhibiting every mark of permanent commercial prosperity ;" while on every stream clustered the huts of miners, and from every sheltered nook rose the smoke of the settler's cabin.

# CHAPTER XVI.

SHORTLY after the great tide of emigration had swept into California, yet another vast tract of country, that now known under the several titles of Texas, New Mexico, and Arizona, was annexed to the United States. We have already visited these districts in the company of various early heroes, chiefly missionary; but in the adventures of Cozens, as related in his *Marvelous Country*, we find so many vivid pictures of the life of the wild inhabitants at the present day, that we propose supplementing our record of discovery by a short abstract of his travels.

Cozens left Merilla, a town of Mexico, in company with three other gentlemen and a few servants, in June, 1858, with the intention of visiting first the copper mines of Santa Rita del Cobre, on the Rio Mimbres, and thence making his way into Arizona. Simple as this programme appears, its execution was fraught with great difficulty, owing to the hostility of the Apaches, a wild native race inhabiting the mountain fastnesses of the north of Spanish America.

The party were riding happily along, after a careful examination of the mines, when the mule ridden by Mr. Laws showed signs of uneasiness. "There are evidently Indians near," said Cozens; to which Dr. Steck, a second of his companions, replied, "If there are, they know better than to attack their Great Father," the name by which he was himself called by the savages, among whom he had long been working. He was wrong! A few minutes later, a small cañon, or pass, was entered, with lofty rugged rocks on either side; and when retreat was impossible, the war-whoop of the Apaches suddenly rang out from above, and, echoing from side to side, filled every heart with horror.

A moment's pause, and then, spurring on their mules, the travelers endeavored to reach the mouth of the cañon, but, alas! even as they gained it, an arrow struck Laws in the back. He fell from the saddle dead, and the mule which had first given warning of the approaching catastrophe galloped riderless away.

The survivors hastily retreated to a neighboring height, determined to sell their lives as dearly as they could ; but though they waited an hour, revolvers in hand, for the arrival of the Indians, they were left unmolested. When the evening shadows lessened the risk, they returned to the spot where Laws had fallen, and, placing his corpse before them on their saddles, carried it with them to the summit of the highest hill within reach. There, by the light of the moon, a grave was dug, and poor Laws was buried. No stone or other memorial marked his resting-place, as it would but have served to provoked the desecration of his remains.

The next day the march was resumed, and, during an interesting trip among the lovely passes of the Mexican range, known as Los Organos, an adventure was met with, scarcely less exciting, though less tragical in its ending, than the encounter with the Apaches. The guide, who was a little in advance of the party he was escorting, suddenly pointed to a spot far up on the mountain, and observed laconically, "Yonder is the hole of a cinnamon bear." It was at once resolved that the owner of the lofty cave should be compelled to show himself, and pay for that privilege with his life.

The guide leading the way, all but Cozens, who was in no humor for the sport, proceede to climb up to the mouth of the hole, it being agreed that each should fire as he saw the bear emerge from his retreat. When all were in position, the guide commenced operations by dropping a large handful of pebbles in front of the mouth of the cave. The effect was almost immediate. But a minute or two elapsed before the hunted animal put his head out and calmly surveyed his tormentors. Rogers, one of the men farthest from the actual scene of action, now fired ; the bullet struck the bear on the nose, and, furious with pain, he rushed at one of the party named Parker, who, flinging down his weapon, fled to a fir-tree hard by. As the doctor scrambled up the tree, the bear gazing ruefully after him, two well-directed shots brought the latter down dead, and, after a hearty laugh at Parker's expense, the carcass was cut into strips, and packed among the stores for the journey.

A little later, a *détour* was made to visit the ruins of Le Gran Quivera, situated on a plain some ten miles distant from the mountains, and supposed to be identical with one of the seven cities of Cibola, visited by Father Kino. The ruins were found to be still in excellent preservation ; the remains of a large temple and of a skillfully-constructed aqueduct for bringing water from the heights above the town were distinctly made out, and the Indians told many interesting traditions of the days when "Le Gran Quivera had been a mighty Aztec metropolis."

In 1680, according to the redskins, when vast quantities of precious metal had been extracted from the mines, and they were about to be taken to the South, the Apaches came down from their rocky homes and attacked the miners. The latter, warned too late of the impending danger, had but time to bury their treasure when the savages were upon them. All but two were massacred, and these two, on their arrival in Mexico, gave such a terrible account of the cruelties inflicted upon their brethren by the Apaches, that no bribes could induce any one to attempt to recover the gold and silver left behind.

Of the near presence of the descendants of these dreaded warriors, our travelers received proof, before leaving Le Gran Quivera, in the loss of two valuable pack-mules and Dr. Parker's horse ; but, knowing the uselessness of attempting to recover the stolen property, the camp was struck, and the march resumed at once. A north-easterly course was now pursued, and, after passing through the remains of the strange petrified forest—the origin and history of which has been so much discussed—the banks of the Rio Grande, forming the boundary between Mexico and the United States, were reached, whence a pleasant ride brought the whole party back to La Merilla.

The little that Cozens had seen of the Apaches on this trip, combined with the wonderful stories told of them by their neighbors, and by those who had escaped from captivity among them, rendered him anxious to learn more of their ways. In spite, therefore, of the earnest entreaties of his friends not to risk his life needlessly, he determined to start alone for the encampments—or *rancheria*, as they were called—of the Pinal and Tonto Apaches, two of the most noted bands of this savage race dwelling near the banks of the Gila.

For this new and venturesome journey, Cozens was fortunate enough to secure the services, as guide, of an Apache war-chief named Cochise, of the Pinal tribe, who assured him that in his company no danger was to be apprehended from his brethren.

It was a lovely morning in June when the two strangely-assorted companions left the Chiricahui Mountains behind them, and, striking across country in a north-westerly direction, entered an Indian trail leading to the

Apache encampment, over a vast plain with nothing to relieve its monotony but an occasional glimpse of what looked like the gleaming waters of a vast inland sea, though it turned out to be the great mirage known as Green-horn's Lake.

Beyond the plains the travelers came to a mass of "cañons, ravines, ridges, gullies, chasms, and mountains," some of them presenting the appearance of exquisitely constructed Gothic cathedrals, while one so exactly resembled an organ, with pipes of green, white, blue, brown, and pink sandstone, that Cozens could scarcely believe it to be merely a natural phenomenon.

The Indian trail led into the very midst of this chaos of rocks, and, breathlessly following his guide, our hero presently found himself upon the edge of a pass, looking down a precipice two thousand feet in depth, with per-pendicular walls of a blood-red color, relieved at their summits with patches of grayish white alka-li. Cochise now made signs to his employer—master Cozens could scarcely be called—to dismount and leave his mule to find its own way down. Then with one word, *"Adelante!"* (Forward!), he led the way down the pass.

COCHISE.

Descending into the gloom beneath the overhanging rock-masses, and feeling their way step by step in the darkness, with the mules so close be-hind them that a moment's hesitation would have been certain death—for the animals would assuredly have pushed their masters over the abyss—the adventurers at last reached in safety the bed of the river, which had eaten out the pass of which they had availed themselves. Here a halt was made for the night, and on the ensuing day the descent of the ravine was com-pleted, under difficulties even greater than those already conquered.

Late in the afternoon, however, Cochise pointed out four or five black specks in the distance, perched on the strange truncated mounds so common in Arizona, and which have excited so much curiosity among scientific men. "They are Apaches," was the guide's laconic remark; and though Cozens pressed him with eager questions as to the next experiences to be anticipated, he could get no replies.

Silently the two plodded on for another two hours till they came to the summit of a bare bluff, when Cochise again paused, and, pointing to the valley beneath, exclaimed, "Look! Apache home!" Cozens obeyed, and, gazing down upon a lovely valley, watered by a copious stream, and surrounded on all sides by bluffs some hundred feet high, their surfaces worn by wind and weather into all manner of strange forms, he obtained his first glimpse of the goal of his journey.

The Apache huts, with yellow thatched, dome-shaped roofs, nestled here and there against the crags, or in little groups by the stream; from before each door rose the smoke of a little camp-fire; and beyond, on the slopes of the upper end of the valley, grazed thousands of cattle, ponies and mules.

As the two gazed motionless upon this scene of peace and plenty in the wilderness, they were suddenly perceived by the Indians. A loud yell notified the fact, and in a moment the village was astir; children running together, dogs barking, warriors hastily seizing their weapons. But Cochise, the wandering war-chief, raised his hand and gave utterance to a peculiar cry. He was recognized at once, the arms were thrown aside, and, quickly descending the bluff, the two travelers were received by a set of men whom Cozens characterizes as the most degraded-looking creatures he had ever seen. The women especially, he says, "were ugly, fat and dirty," and nowhere did he see any of the beautiful squaws described in the works of Cooper, the romancist of the Indians.

The hearty welcome given to the new-comers, however, compensated in a great degree for the absence of beauty in the inmates of the camp. Cozens was feasted on pemmican; a hut was set apart for him and Cochise; a concert—though of a somewhat ear-splitting character, the instruments consisting exclusively of drums and rattles—was given in his honor; and the next morning found the white stranger peacefully performing his ablutions in the stream, in the presence of an admiring crowd of women and children.

Later in the day, Cozens' sense of security was a little disturbed by the news of the approach of one Magnus Colorado, an Apache chief, noted for his hostility to the white men, and the number of their scalps he had at various times secured to himself as trophies.

"What," said Cozens to Cochise, in as careless a manner as he could assume, "will Magnus Colorado say to the presence in your camp of a white man?" "Oh," was the reply, "I sent him word as soon as I knew it was he; and you know, too, he is the white man's friend."

Not having hitherto had any proof of the latter assertion, unless scalping could be considered a token of friendship, Cozens withdrew to his hut; but

THE APACHES' HOME.

he was soon relieved from his anxiety by a visit he there received from Colorado, who extended his hand in a friendly manner, with the words, "Good day! give me bacca."

Cozens of course complied at once, adding to the usual chewing tobacco a small parcel for smoking, thereby winning the full confidence of his visitor, who proceeded to tell of his recent adventures, showing off as one of his best trophies a blood-stained baby's frock, the wearer of which he boasted he had himself sent home to the Great Spirit!

Disgusted with this and similar anecdotes, Cozens resolved to leave the home of the Apaches as soon as possible; but he found that he could not do so abruptly without risking his life, and, much against his will, he was compelled to be present at a scalp-dance given in honor of Colorado, and surpassing in weird horror any thing he had ever read or heard of.

A huge fire, over which hung a steaming kettle, formed the center-piece of the open-air stage on which the revolting ceremony was performed. Round this kettle danced a number of half-naked braves and squaws, each holding aloft a spear crowned by a scalp, while every now and then one of the women snatched a piece of meat from the caldron, and offered it in derision to the ghastly human relics.

Not until far on in the night was Cozens allowed to retire, and, when he did so, it was with a firm resolve never again to allow his curiosity to get the better of his judgment. A few days later he was on his way back to Mexico, whence, in spite of the resolution just quoted, he subsequently made two expeditions—one to the silver mines of Tucson, the other to the ruins in New Mexico.

The account given of the first trip is little more than a *résumé* of all that had been done by the early travelers whose work we have already recorded; but the second contains many a thrilling anecdote of intercourse with the Navajoes, who so long harassed the white settlers in the newly-annexed American territories.

Accompanied by a man named Jim Davis—"a small, wiry, hatchet-faced, red-haired Yankee, known as the Emigrant's Friend," on account of the welcome he gave to all new-comers to what he considered his own special domain—Cozens crossed the Rio Grande near its entrance into New Mexico, and, after visits to the pueblos or towns of Acoma and Laguna, commenced the ascent of the Sierra Madre, from the summit of which a magnificent view, stretching far away to the Pacific, was obtained.

Thus far all went well, and the descent of the western slope was all but accomplished, when it became necessary to encamp for the night. Cozens had fallen asleep, and was dreaming of the lovely scenes he was about to visit, when he was suddenly awakened by a hand laid on his shoulder. He started up, revolver ready, but no one except "Jimmy," the Irish servant, was near, who whispered, "She is calling me!" Thinking his servant had gone mad, or had woke up in terror from a nightmare, the master was about to order him off to bed again, when a low wail, like that of a child in trouble, fell upon his ear.

"Jimmy" was right. *She* was calling him, and *she* was one of the mules, at that moment in an agonized struggle with a panther, whose low, almost plaintive yell was one of triumph. Rushing forward, accompanied by two gentlemen of his party, Cozens came up just as the mule's sufferings were over, and shared with them the triumph of shooting the panther, who turned out to be one of the finest creatures of the kind ever brought down in the neighborhood.

On the following day a slight détour was made to visit the ruins of El Moro, one of the most stately of the old Spanish cities, bearing traces on its walls of the engraved names of many of the old heroes of the days when the power of the Roman Catholic Church was at its zenith. From El Moro a ride of a few hours brought the cavalcade to the Valley of Zuni, inhabited by a few survivors of a race of blue-eyed and fair-skinned Indians, who are said to have been descended from the Welsh miners who accompanied Prince Madoc on that visit to Cibola, concerning which so hot a war has been waged among archæologists.

Entering the town of Zuni, a ruin differing but little in general character from that of El Moro, the travelers were courteously received by the cacique, or chief—a fine-looking old man, with large, intelligent, dark-blue eyes—wearing a Spanish shawl and trowsers. He conducted them over his city, pointing out to them, among its special features, a sacred spring, from which neither man nor beast was ever allowed to drink, the genius of the place avenging any such desecration by instant death.

After a careful examination of the wonders of Zuni, the ascent of the mountain plateau on the west was commenced, and, after many a pause to examine the strange monuments of a departed race with which its sides and summit were strewn, the land of the blue-eyed Indians was left behind, and that of the fierce Navajoes entered.

Again, as in the Apache country, Cozens had encamped for the night with a sense of false security, when he awoke suddenly, a presentiment of danger, which he could not explain, causing him to start up and look around him. As he listened intently, the sharp crack of a rifle-shot struck upon his ear, succeeded by another and yet another. Springing to his feet, he saw a gentleman of the party advancing with stealthy steps, who laid his finger on his lips and whispered, "Hist! Navajoes."

Another moment and the Navajo war-whoop rang out, and about a dozen dusky forms, mounted on splendid horses, were seen advancing toward the camp. "We'd better go behind the wagon," suggested one of the white men. From behind the friendly shelter of the wagon, therefore, the heroes watched the approach of their enemies, who, however, to their great surprise, suddenly disappeared.

"It's the pits! the pits!" cried one of the party, rejoicing at the thought that the Indians had fallen into a hollow unperceived by them until it was too late to check their horses ; but again the wild war-whoop rang out, and as the white men fired, a shower of arrows cleft the air. Cozens received one of these missiles in his arm, but, drawing it out, he continued to fire at intervals, and by their judicious mode of aiming, the handful of white men managed to keep off nearly three times their number of savages, who finally rode off, leaving many of their warriors and horses dead upon the field of action.

A little later, Jimmy, who had been missing from the affray, came riding wildly into the camp with the news that he had, single-handed, worsted a large body of Navajoes, and that there had also been a struggle between some of these fierce savages and some Zunis, four of whom had been killed. The latter part of the story received confirmation, as the bodies of the Zunis were found on the ground, but of Jimmy's part in the tragedy no proof was ever obtained. It also transpired that seven hundred head of cattle had been stolen from the Zunis by the Navajoes, the attack on the white men's camp having merely formed part of a well-organized plundering expedition. The white men, who had experienced much hospitality from the Zunis, now resolved to return their courtesy by aiding in the recovery of their property. A consultation with the sufferers was held, and before many hours were over, a large body of horsemen were galloping across the lovely plains of the Navajo land to the pueblo where the cattle had been penned.

So prompt indeed were the measures taken, and so little did the Navajoes expect pursuit, that the whole of the cattle were recaptured, and on their way back to their old pasture-lands before the alarm was given. The same night found the white men and their escort once more in safety at Zuni ; and, taking the disturbed state of the country into account, Cozens resolved to attempt no further explorations among the Navajoes for the present.

In ascending the heights above the sacred spring of Zuni, however, an accident occurred which delayed for a considerable time the return of Cozens to Mexico. In following his guide along a narrow ledge of rock, our hero's foot slipped on a loose stone, and, before he could recover himself, he was flung over the bluff, and fell a distance of no less than three hundred feet into the abyss, clutching wildly at the rocks in a vain hope of saving himself. Presently, he tells us in his own account of the matter, the heel of his right boot hit the corner of a stone, he was thrown forward on his face, and as he flung up his arms to protect himself, one of his hands struck against something sharp. He grasped that something, and, clinging to it convulsively, lost consciousness.

When he came to himself, he was lying on blankets, surrounded by his companions, who had had themselves lowered down the abyss over which he

SACRED SPRING AT ZUNI.

had fallen, and, finding him still breathing, had given signals to the Zunis watching above to hoist the sufferer up. This was done with the aid of cords as tenderly as possible, and Cozens was then carried to camp on the shoulders of the faithful Indians.

A long and tedious illness, through which he was faithfully nursed by his own people and the Zunis, followed, and in the long weary hours of weakness the white man learned more perhaps of the ways of the people than he could have done in weeks of hurried traveling. While he was still at Zuni, there took place one the worst tragedies enacted by the Apaches in these the early days of the annexation of their territory to the United States.

A little party of emigrants, numbering some ten persons, under the guid ance of the head of the family, a Mr. Stewart, were crossing Arizona on their way to California, when they were one night surprised by a party of Apache warriors. Without warning or parley, the savages closed round the women and children, discharging showers of arrows upon them with deadly effect. All fell victims to the unexpected assault, except Mr. Stew art himself, who, seeing that he could do nothing, fled to warn two of his daughters, who, for some reason or another, had been separated from the main party, and were awaiting them a little distance off.

The daughters, alas, were not at the rendezvous, and after a long heart-rending search, during which he had again and again to dodge the Apaches hunting for him, poor Stewart returned to the scene of the massacre of his other dear ones. Arrived there, a horrible sight greeted him. A huge fire had been lighted, and on it, half consumed, were the naked bodies of his wife and six children. All night long he lay upon the ground in an agony of despair, and the next day commenced an aimless wandering to and fro, careless of what should happen to himself. He came presently, however, upon a little Moquis village, where he was kindly received, and whence two natives conducted him to Zuni. He lived but long enough to tell his terrible story. His heart was broken, and after a few days of suffering he passed peacefully away.

As soon as he was able to travel, Cozens left Zuni for the last time, re-turning, as he had come, to the Rio Grande, and thence to his old home in Mexico. Since his return, many a thrilling tale has been told of the wild doings of the Apaches and Navajoes ; but gradually they, like their more northerly brethren, are succumbing to the civilizing influence of the white man, and their final subjugation is but a question of time.

The completion of the Southern Pacific railroad, and the opening of the many supplementary transit lines of the Union, have at last united in indis-soluble bonds the States of the East and of the West. Fresh capital and fresh enterprise are ever flowing, like mighty arteries, throughout the once deserted wastes between the Mississippi and the Rocky Mountains; and the shrill whistle of the steam-engine replaces alike the war-whoop of the sava e and the wail of his victim.

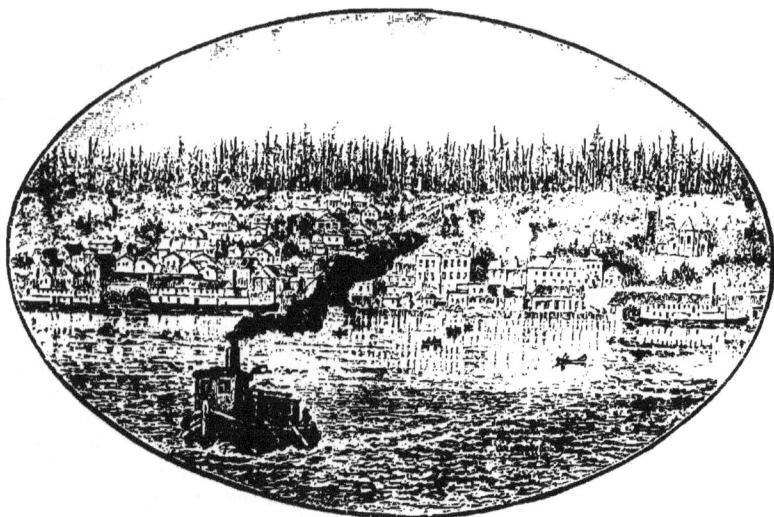

NEW WEST BRITISH COLUMBIA.

## CHAPTER XVII.

### CONCLUSION.

BEFORE closing our record of the advance of the white man westwards, we must glance once more at British America, which we left on the eve of the great political crisis at the end of the last century—a crisis which, after long years of absorbing struggles, resulted in the consolidation into a single colony of Canada, New Brunswick, Nova Scotia, British Columbia, and the vast territories long held by the Hudson's Bay and other North-west companies.

The banks of the Red River of the North, the shores of the Lake of the Woods, and the vast prairie lands beyond them, were by this time well dotted with French and English colonies. Lord Selkirk, a chief partner in the Hudson's Bay Company, had purchased land of the Indians far beyond the original limits of British territory, and the French fur-traders continued to push their outposts into the wilderness on every side ; while, as we know, the American colonies were ever spreading further and further to the north as well as to the west.

It was in the early part of this century that the Hudson's Bay Company, whose previous career we have already sketched, was in the zenith of its prosperity. Even so long ago as 1684, it had declared a dividend of 50 per cent.; while a little later, about the time of the Peace of Utrecht, we are told that, by a call of only 10 per cent. upon its shareholders, it was able to treble its income. But early in the present century—in 1827—a recent writer informs us, " the price of a flint-lock musket, valued in Fort Dunvegan at perhaps twenty shillings, was worth sables at three pounds a piece, piled up on either side of the weapon until they were level with its muzzle. A six-shilling blanket was bartered for beavers which would bring in London eighteen or twenty pounds ; and a black fox was obtained for a price at which the neediest Dog Rib or Locheaux would now laugh his loudest." The Hudson's Bay Company was indeed autocratic within the wide territories where it held sway, and it could make not its own prices merely, but also its own laws. As the century proceeded, however, a change came : first of all, the price of beaver decreased, from the growing use of silk in the manufacture of hats. Then came the rising tide of jealousy against monopolies and a consequent inclination to examine the Company's titles. Moreover, Canada itself was eager for "elbow-room ; " and still further, as we have seen, the United States were spreading northward, and so impinging upon its territory. Thus the story of the Hudson's Bay Company has gradually come to be one of decay, and the great triumphs won, with the wonderful bargains struck by the directors, are alike things of the past.

One can not but be struck with the lack of enterprise and enthusiasm which marked the relations of Great Britain to her American possessions during this period. The spread of United States settlements had necessitated the establishment of an international boundary line, and in 1818, the 49th degree of north latitude had been fixed by treaty as the limit between the Western States and British America, the St. Lawrence and its lakes remaining, as before, the boundary between Canada and the Eastern States of the Union. But another half-century elapsed before any attempt was made by the British Government to survey and mark this new boundary line. The outlying colonies struggled on, some of them almost entirely cut off from intercourse with the outer world, and many a noble life was lived and lost in the vain struggle for existence. Meantime, as we have seen, the United States were being intersected by railways, and their ocean boundaries were connected by iron bands. California—youngest state of the Union, and a few short years before but an unknown desert—had become the golden link between the East and the West. Yet the owners of a territory as vast, and perhaps as full of great possibilities as the mighty republic itself, still remained in ignorance of the true character of their possessions. Maps there were, but maps made up of sketches filled in on hearsay Indian evidence, and calculated only to mislead the unhappy explorer who should attempt to guide his course by their vague delineations. A change soon came, how-

SASKATCHEWAN STEAMER.

ever, and one as rapid as the course of events which led up to it had been slow. This change may be said to have been inaugurated in 1857, when Captain Palliser started on an expedition, which occupied three years, and resulted in the thorough and just assessment of the economic value of the districts, extending from the United States boundary in N. lat. 49° to the chief rivers flowing into the Arctic Ocean.

The admission of British Columbia to the newly-formed Dominion of Canada in 1871, the last act of the great political drama alluded to above, was clogged with the condition that a railway should be constructed within ten years "from the Pacific to a point of junction with the existing railway systems in the provinces of Ontario and Quebec." The English, if chary of undertaking new responsibilities, are prompt in acting on them, and the authorities of Canada, now fully alive to the fact that they had to do in a few years what had been done by their neighbors in a half-century, lost not a moment in sending out engineers to survey the ground, and ascertain as rapidly as possible the best route for the promised line of communication. In 1872 the preliminary reports were laid before the Canadian House of Commons, and the same year Sandford Fleming, the engineer-in-chief of the line to be laid down, made an extensive exploration of the districts to be traversed, which added greatly to the general knowledge of the course of the Saskatchewan, Athabasca, and other rivers west of the Great Lakes. This report has been followed by others not less important, and indeed the lengthened survey over which Mr. Fleming presides has become almost as valuable to the geographer as to the statesman and the colonist in its results.

In the month of February, 1875, the source of the Fraser River was found by Mr. E. W. Jarvis, "in a semi-circular basin, completely closed in by glaciers and high, bare peaks, at an elevation of 5,300 feet ;" and we can scarcely refuse this fearless traveler a place among our heroes, when we read of nine hundred miles traveled on snow-shoes, the thermometer often being "below the temperature of freezing mercury," or learn that he "lived the last three days on the anticipation of a meal at his journey's end." This same year, 1875, was still further signalized as being that in which the Saskatchewan was first navigated by steam, for in that year a ship of about 200 tons ascended from the Great Rapid to Edmonton, 700 miles higher, and now we learn that this great river is navigated from the neighborhood of Lake Winnipeg to the base of the Rocky Mountains.

In 1879, very great advances were made by Fleming and his staff in the exploration of the outlying portions of the Dominion ; and the Report presented in 1880, together with the Appendices contributed by the various members of the Survey, marks a new departure in North American geography. The extent of territory embraced in the particular expedition referred to extended from the longitude of Edmonton, east of the Rocky Mountains, to Port Simpson on the Pacific. The main object of this survey was to verify the reports of the navigability of Wark Inlet by ocean-sailing ships, and to ascertain how far the tract of country between it and the Skeena River, with the valley of the Skeena itself, were suitable for railway purposes. Its result was the indication of a choice of practicable routes in the districts examined ; but the Government, for reasons which, though not obvious, were no doubt well-grounded, decided in favor of the earlier route proposed, namely, that by the Yellow Head Pass and the Burrard Inlet. Thus the great expedition of 1879 was set aside, so far as its main purpose was concerned; but it accomplished much, and has perhaps really served a more practical end, in opening up immense regions barely known before, and providing the student of geography with maps urgently required. Sir J. H. Lefroy admirably expresses our indebtedness to the members who composed the expedition, in an address delivered before the geographical section of the British Association in 1880. He

FRASER RIVER.

says:—"The final decision of the Canadian Government to adopt Burrard's Inlet for the Pacific terminus of their railway, relegates to the domain of pure geography a great deal of knowledge acquired in exploring other lines; explorations in which Messrs.

Jarvis, Horetzky, Keeper, and others have displayed remarkable daring and endurance. They have forced their way from the interior to the sea-coast, or from the coast to the Peace River, Pine or Yellow Head Passes, through country previously unknown, to Port Simpson, to Burke Channel, to the mouth of the Skeena, and to the Bute Inlet, so that a region but recently almost a blank on our maps, which John Arrowsmith, our last great authority, but very imperfectly sketched, is now known in great detail." Thus it has happened once more, as we have so often noted in the course of our narrative, that the traveler, foiled in his main purpose, has opened for himself and for the world new scenes by the way ; and as we scan the pages of these Canadian reports, pictures rise before us of surpassing loveliness, while we dream of these vast territories as they will be when the glory of the gorge and the mountain pass is varied by the vision of plains covered with corn and dotted with smiling villages.

During the last ten years, another cause has also largely contributed to the opening up of the great West. A dispute between the United States and Canada, as to the exact interpretation of the Treaty of 1818, led to the sending out of a joint commission to settle the matter, and mark out the boundary line between the north-west corner of the Lake of the Woods to the summit of the Rocky Mountains. The Commissioners, most of them able men of science, embodied in their report much interesting geographical information of a supplementary character, the most noteworthy points established being the vast extent of the Great Plains, with their strange, bewildering succession of mirages, rendering surveying operations extremely difficult ; and the existence of a chain of salt lakes, with no outlet to the ocean, extending for fifteen miles in an east and west direction, near the very heart of the central watershed of the continent. Nine hundred miles were traversed in this successful trip, and the whole of the boundary line, now finally determined, was marked by stone cairns or earthen mounds, at intervals of three miles on the great plains, and by iron pillars one mile distant from each other for 135 miles through the southern prairie of Manitoba. These solitary landmarks, whether on the rich, fertile lands between the Lake of the Woods and the Pembina Mountains, the prairie steppe extending from the Pembina Mountains to the great Coteau of the Missouri, or the wild semi-desert stretching away from it to the Rocky Mountains, will soon, if we may so express it, be set in frameworks of colonization, for great and mighty are the changes which have taken place within the last few years. Emigration has more than kept pace with the advance of the Canadian Pacific Railway; the Red River settlers, no longer isolated from their kind, are at last enjoying the prosperity so long withheld; the number of settlers has increased rapidly since the opening of two outlets to the ocean for their produce; new settlements in the West are springing up as if by

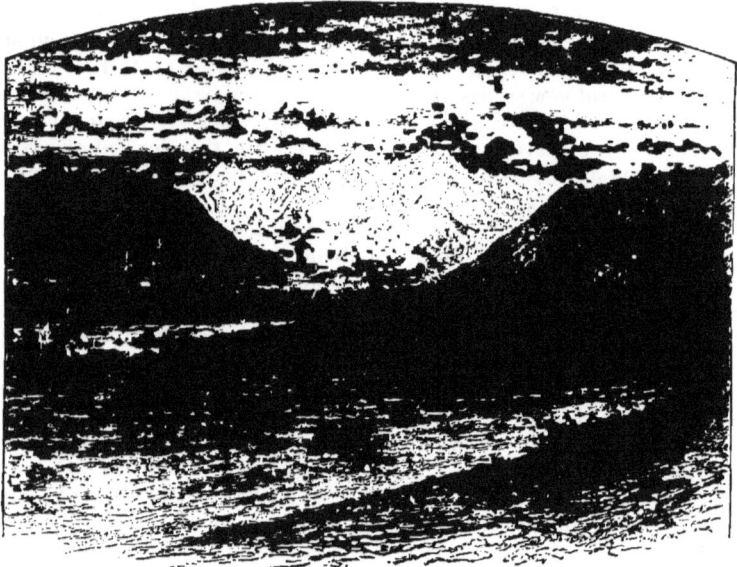

WINTER STATION FOR THE VESSELS OF THE ENGLISH PACIFIC SQUADRON. (*Esquimault.*)

magic; a line of telegraph is completed between the ports on the banks of the Saskatchewan and the chief towns of Canada; while the long inaccessible solitudes of the northern range of the Rocky Mountains echo to the many sounds of the ever-increasing traffic along the line which has at last brought about the long-desired connection between the northern shores of the Atlantic and Pacific.

# INDEX.

Acadia, 83, 118.
Alabama, 42, 173.
Alarchon, Fernando di, 144.
Alaska, 202.
Albany, 110, 124.
Alexander, Sir William, 88.
Algonquin Indians, 110, 112, 115-117, 130.
Alleghany Mountains, 168.
Allouez, Father, 128.
America known to the Ancients, 9.
Anastasia Island, 61.
Annapolis, 83.
Apache Indians, 149, 150, 184, 258, 260-264, 267-268.
Apalacha River, 37.
Arapaho Indians, 242.
Arctic Ocean, 216.
Argall, Captain, 79, 85.
Arizona, 142, 149, 150, 174, 258.
Arkansas River, 182, 235, 254.
Arkansea, village of, 132, 136.
Astor, John Jacob, 220.
Astoria, 220-232.
Athabasca, Lake, 214.
Atlantis, Island of, 7.
Ayllon, Lucas Vasquez de, 35, 37.

Bahama Islands, 31.
Balboa, Vasco Nuñez de, 31-33.
Baltimore, Lord, 80.
Bayaganda, Indian village, 164.
Barre, Nicholas, 58.
Bear River, 247, 248.
Bears, White and Brown, 188, 194.
Beaujeu, Admiral, 135.
Beer Springs, 247.
Behring, 200.
Biloxi Bay, 164.
Black Hills, 229, 242.
Blackbird, Indian chief, 226.
Blackfeet Indians, 228.
Block Island, 153, 154.
Bona Vista Bay, 52.
Boone, Daniel, 168-172.
Boonesborough, 171.
Boston, 99, 100, 162.
Boundary between United States and British America, 270, 274.
Brébeuf, Jesuit missionary, 110, 126.
British America, 174, 269, 271; French traders in, 212, 270.

Cabot, John, 26, 27.
Cabot, Sebastian, 27.
Cabrillo, Juan Rodriguez, 145.
California, 146, 150 to 152, 174, 256
California, Gulf of, 144.
Canada, First explorations, 51-57; Explorations and settlements, 112, 120; Captured by the English, 118; Ceded to the French, 118.
Canadian Pacific Railway, 271-275.
Cancello, Louis, 47.
Cannibalism, 55, 123, 124.
Cape Breton, 28, 37, 118.
Cape Cod, 9, 89, 92, 112.
Cape Fear, 157
Cape May, 109.
Cape Mendocino, 146.
Capuchin Friars, 107.
Carey, Apostle of the Indians, 237.
Carolina, 58, 157, 165.
Cartier, Jacques, 51-57.
Carver, John, 90-93.
Cass, Governor, 233, 234.
Cass Lake, 234, 239.
Catskill Mountains, 106.
Cevola, Indian village, 143, 259.
Champlain, Samuel, 83, 88, 112.
Champlain, Lake, 113-119.
Charlestown (Mass.), 99.
Charles River, 99.
Charlevoix, Father, 138, 139.
Chesapeake Bay, 68, 76.
Cherokee Indians, 159, 168-172.
Cheyenne Indians, 228, 242.
Chicago, 129, 133.
Chickasaw Indians, 43, 168.
Chippeway Indians, 122, 129, 179 to 181, 238.
Cibola, 143, 259.
Clarke, Captain, 184-198.
Cochise, Indian chief, 261-263.
Coligny, Admiral, 57.
Colony, the Lost, 69, 70.
Colorado River, 144, 245, 246.
Columbia River, 146, 188, 194-198, 246; Great Narrows, 198; Indians of the Columbia Family, 196-198.
Columbus, 7; Early life, 13, 14; At the convent, 15; At the Spanish court, 16-19; Sets sail, 19; Land discovered, 21; Landing of, 22; Desertion of Pinzon, 22; Return to Spain, 23; Second voyage, 23; Accusation and death, 25.

Comanche Indians, 136, 184.
Conant, Roger, 99.
Connecticut, 9, 87, 103, 104, 153-157.
Convict colonists, 82.
Cook, Captain James, 201.
Coppermine River, 214, 216.
Coronado, Vasquez de, 144, 145.
Cortereal, Gáspar, 28.
Cortereal, Miguel, 28.
Cortes, 140.
*Coureurs des bois*, 137, 206, 212.
Coxe, Dr., 165.
Cozens, Mr., 258-268.
Creek Indians, 158.
Crow Indians, 228, 229.
Cuba, 22.
Cumberland River, 170.

Dacotah Indians, 128, 177, 185.
Darien, Isthmus of, 32, 33.
Davenport, John, 156.
Davis, Jim, 274.
Delaware River, 109, 159.
De La Warre, Lord, 77, 78, 79.
Dermer, Captain, 87.
Des Moines River, 132.
Denys, John, 29.
D'Iberville, Lemoyne, 164-166.
Dorantes, Stefano, 142.
Dover founded, 88.
Drake, Sir Francis, 63, 68, 146.
Dreuillette, Jesuit missionary, 126-128.
Dutch settlements, 108-110.

Early Explorers, 7.
Eaton, Theophilus, 156.
Eliot, John, 158.
El Moro, ruins of, 265.
Emigration to California, 257.
Enciso, 31.
Endicott, John, 99, 154.
English Settlements, first, 64.
Eric the Red, 8.
Erie, Lake, 115, 133.
Esquimaux, 214.

Faroe Islands, 12.
First American Explorers, 7-12.
First steamer on inland waters, 234.
Flathead Indians, 198.
Fleming, Sandford, 272.
Florida, Discovery of, 33-35, 47; Early settle-
    ments in, 59, 63; Annexed to the United
    States, 173.
Fonte, Admiral de, 147.
*Fortune*, the, 96.
Fountain of Youth, search for, 33, 34, 35.

Fox, Luke, 206, 207.
Franklin, Captain, 216.
Fraser River, 272.
Fremont, John C., 241-254.
Fremont's Peak, 246.
French Settlements, 59, 116, 117, 164, 165, 209.
Freydis, Eric's daughter, 10, 11.
Frontenac, 133, 134.
Fuca, Juan de, 147.
Fundy, Bay of, 83.
Fur trade, 104, 109, 118, 127, 137, 173, 177, 212,
    220, 270.

Garay, Francis, 35.
Gates, Sir Thomas, 78.
Georgia, 158, 159, 173.
Gilbert, Sir Humphrey, 64, 65.
Gilham, Captain Zachariah, 208.
Gold, Search for, 37, 59, 141, 142, 149; Discov-
    ered, 256; Mica taken for gold, 76.
Golden Gate, the, 154.
Gorges, Sir Ferdinand, 87, 88; Robert, 88.
Gosnold, Bartholomew, 71.
Gourgues, Dominique de, 61, 62.
Gray, Captain, 188.
Grand Manan, Island of, 84, 85.
Great Bear Lake, 214.
Great Bend, Missouri River, 186, 226.
Great Plains, the, 274.
Great Slave Lake, 214, 247, 254.
Greenland, 8, 11.
Grenville, Sir Richard, 67, 68.
*Griffin*, the, 133.
Grijalva, Captain, 140.
Grosseliez, 207, 208.
Gunnbiorn, 8.

*Half Moon*, 105-107.
Harrisburg founded, 162.
Hartford, 104.
Hatteras, Cape, 65.
Hawkins, Sir John, 59.
Hearne, Mr., 210, 213-217.
Hennepin, 133, 134.
Hercules, Pillars of, 7.
Herjulfson, Bjarni, 8.
Hochelaga, 53, 54.
Holmes, William, 103.
Hontan, Baron La, 138, 247.
Hudson, Henry, 105-108.
Hudson River, 50, 106.
Hudson's Bay, 108, 137, 206-208, 210-213, 269,
    270.
Hudson's Bay Company, 138, 206, 208-217.
Hudson's Straits, 210.
Huguenot colonists, 57-62, 165.
Hunt, William, 225-232.

Huron, Lake, 115.
Huron Indians, 115, 126.

Illinois River, 132.
Independence, War of, 162.
Indians, conflicts with, 105, 110, 126, 153–156, 158, 167, 222, 226.
Indian princess, 42 ; King, 54 ; War challenge, 93 ; Ceremony in honor of the dead, 122 ; Concert, 263 ; Scalp dance, 264.
Indians :—174, 179, 214, 219, 229, 244.
  Algonquins, 110, 112, 115–117.
  Apache, 149, 150, 184, 258, 260–264, 267, 268.
  Arapaho, 242.
  Blackfeet, 228.
  Cherokees, 159, 168–172.
  Cheyennes, 228, 242.
  Chickasaw, 43, 168.
  Chippeway, 122, 129, 179–181, 238.
  Comanche, 136, 184.
  Creek, 158.
  Crow, 228, 229.
  Flathead, 98.
  Huron, 115, 116.
  Illinois, 130.
  Iroquois, 113, 116, 123, 124, 127, 134.
  Mohawk, 116, 123, 126, 127.
  Navajoe, 184, 264, 266, 268.
  Nez Percés, 197.
  Onquilaharas, 122.
  Osage, 181.
  Ottoe, 184.
  Pawnee, 181, 234.
  Pequod, 153–156.
  Root, 247.
  Seneca, 116, 127, 133.
  Shoshone, 187, 229, 247, 254, 256.
  Sioux, 128, 134, 177, 185, 225, 238.
  Snake, 195, 196.
  Zuni, 265.
Indians enslaved, 156, 158.
Indians, Penn's treaty with the, 160.
Indiana, 173.
Iroquois Indians, 113, 116, 123, 124, 127, 134.
Isabella of Castile, 19.
Itasca Lake, 239.

James, Captain, 207.
James, Captain, 234–236.
Jamestown, 73, 76, 78–81, 110.
Jarvis, E. W., 272.
Jesuit Missionaries, 84, 119, 120, 126, 148, 149, 167.
Jesuits, Loss of power, 150.
Jesuit, a heroic, 121.
Joques, Isaac, Jesuit Missionary, 123–125.
John II, of Portugal, 14.

Kansas, 241, 246.
Karselne, 10.
Kennebec River, 88.
Kentucky, 168–172.
Kino, Eusebius Francis, 148.
Kirk, Mr., 118.
Knight, John, 209, 210.

Lake of the Woods, 238.
Lane, Ralph, 68.
Latter-Day Saints, 255.
Laudonnière, René de, 58, 61.
Law, John, 166.
Laws, Mr., 258.
League of the Colonies, 157.
Le Gran Quivera, 259.
Leech Lake, 180, 233.
Leif the Lucky, 9.
Le Moyne, Father, 126.
Leon, Juan Ponce de, 33–35.
Lewis, Captain, 184–198.
Lion Caldron, 230.
La Paz, 146.
Long, Major, 234–238.
Long Island, 9.
Long Island Sound, 87, 109.
Louisiana, 135, 166, 167, 168 ; Ceded to United States, 173.
Louisville founded, 172.
Lost colony, the, 69, 70.
Luna, Don Tristan de, 47.

M'Dougal, Mr., 220–224.
Mackenzie, Alexander, 213, 217–219.
Mackenzie River, 214, 217.
Mackinaw, 225.
Mad River, 230.
Madoc, 11.
Magellan, 32, 49.
Magnus Colorado, Indian chief, 262.
Maine, 82, 85, 86.
Mandan Indians, 186, 227.
Manhattan Island, 106, 110.
Marco Polo, 12.
Marquette, James, 129–133.
Martha's Vineyard, 71.
Maryland founded, 80.
Mason, Captain John, 156.
Massachusetts, 71.
Massasoit, 95, 102.
Matagorda, Bay of, 135.
Maurepas Lake, 164.
Mavilla, Indian village, 42.
*Mayflower*, the, 93.
Meares, Captain John, 202–204.
Mendoza, 140, 145.
Menendez, Pedro, 60–63.

Merrimac River, 99.
Mesnard, René, 128.
Mexico, 140, 144.
Mexico, Gulf of, 30, 135.
Michigan, 236.
Michigan, Lake, 120, 133, 237.
Middleton, Captain, 210.
Minnesota River, 237.
Missionaries, 119, 120.
Missionary colonists, 115, 150–152.
Missionary settlements, 119, 120.
Mississippi River, 35, 43, 44, 129, 132, 138, 164–166, 170, 176, 178, 180, 233, 234, 239.
Mississippi Scheme, 166.
Missouri River, 131, 184–194.
    Great Bend, 186, 226.
    Source of, 194.
Mitchigamea, Indian village, 132.
Mobile Bay, 164.
Mohawk Indians, 116, 123, 126, 127.
Monterey Bay, 146.
Montreal, 53, 114, 120.
Monts, De, 83.
Moore, Captain, 210, 211.
Mormons, 255, 256.
Mount Desert, 84.

Narvaez, Pamphilo de, 37, 38.
Natchez founded, 165.
Navajoe Indians, 184, 264–266, 268.
Nebraska River, 234, 236, 241, 246.
New Amsterdam, 110.
New England, 92–104.
Newfoundland, 9, 52, 64.
New Hampshire, 86, 88.
New Haven, 157.
New Jersey, 109.
New Mexico, 136, 174, 258.
New Netherland, 109, 128.
New Orleans, 166.
Newport, Captain, 72, 76, 77.
New York, 110.
New York, Harbor of, 50, 106
Nez Percés, 197.
Niagara River, 122, 133.
Niagara Falls, 122.
Nipissing Lake, 115.
Nizza, Fra Marco da, 141–144.
Nootka Sound, 201.
Northmen, the, 11.
North-West Company, 212, 213, 217.
Nova Scotia, 9, 88, 269.
Nunez, Alvaro, 141.

Oglethorpe, General, 159.
Ohio River, 170 ; State, 171, 172.
Ohio Company, 167, 172.

Oldham, John, 89, 153.
Omaha, 226.
Ontario, Lake, 119, 127.
Ouquiaharas Indians, 122.
Opechancanough, Indian Chief, 73.
Ortiz, Juan, 40.
Oswego River, 127.
Osage Indians, 181.
Ottawa River, 114.
Ottoe Indians, 184.

Pacific Ocean, Balboa discovers the, 32.
Palliser, Captain, 271.
Parker, Dr., 259.
Pawnee Indians, 181, 234.
Pearl fisheries, 150.
Penn, William, 159–161.
Pennsylvania, 160.
Penobscot River, 82.
Pensacola Harbor, discovery of, 41.
Pensacola River, 164.
Peoria Lake, 134.
Pequod Indians, 153–156.
Perez, 16, 17, 18, 23.
Philadelphia, 161.
Pictured Rocks, 123.
Pigart, Claude, Jesuit missionary, 122, 123.
Pike, Major, 176–183.
Pike's Peak, 235, 242.
Pipe of Peace, 130, 131, 178, 227.
Pittsburg, 162.
Plymouth Company, 87, 88.
Pocahontas, 75, 79.
Pontchartrain, Lake, 164.
Port Royal, 58.
Portsmouth founded, 88.
Potomac River, 75.
Potawatomie Indians, 236.
Powhatan, 75, 77.
Providence founded, 102.
Puritans, the, 89–91 ; Embarkation of, 92 ; First landing, 93 ; Land at Plymouth, 94 ; Threatened by Indians, 95 ; Settlements by, 99, 105.

Quebec, 53, 112, 116.
Quakers, 161.

Railroads, 268, 271–275.
Raleigh, Sir Walter, 64, 65, 67, 70.
Red Cedar Lake, 180.
Red River, 166, 169, 182.
Red River of the North, 238.
Rhode Island, 9.
Ribault, John, 57–62.
Rio Bravo de Norte, 183.
Rio Grande River, 260.
Roanoake Colony, 67–69.

Rocky Mountains, 190, 193, 194, 231, 242-247, 256.
Root Indians, 247.
Rupert, Prince, 208.
Rose's Edward, conspiracy against Hunt, 228.
Russian Exploration, 200.

Sacramento, 256.
Sacramento River, 253.
Salle, Robert Cavalier de la, 133-136.
Salmon, 219.
Salt Lake, 236.
Salt Lake City, 248, 256.
San Diego, 146, 150.
San Domingo, 22.
San Francisco, 151, 240.
San Xavier del Bac, ruins of, 149.
Santa Fé, 184.
Saskatchewan River, 137, 272.
Savannah River, 158.
Saybrook, 104, 156.
Scalp dance, 264.
Schoolcraft, Mr., 238, 239.
Scotch colonists, 88.
Seneca Indians, 116, 127, 133.
Shawmut Point, 99.
Ship Island, 164.
Shoshone Indians, 187, 229, 247, 254, 256.
Sierra Nevada Mountains, 251.
Sioux Indians, 128, 134, 177, 185, 225, 238.
Skraellings, 9.
Slaves first landed at Jamestown, 79.
Slave Lake, 217.
Slave River, 217.
Smith, Captain John, 72-78, 85.
Smith, Captain, 210, 211.
Smith, Joe, 255.
Snake River, 230, 248.
Snake Indians, 195, 196.
Sothel, Seth, 158.
Soto, Hernando de, 39, 46.
South Pass, 245, 254.
Southern Pacific Railway, 268.
Spanish Explorations and Settlements, 30-48, 60-63, 140-146.
Spanish power in Mexico, Overthrow of, 152.
Standish, Captain Miles, 93, 97, 98.
Stansbury, Captain, 256.
Steck, Dr., 258.
Stewart family, Murder of, 268.
Stone, Captain, murder of, 152.
St. Anthony's Falls, 134.
St. Augustine, 62.
St. John's River, 57.

St. Lawrence, Gulf of, 29, 52.
St. Lawrence River, 52, 112-118, 178, 237, 238.
St. Louis, 131, 135, 225.
St. Mary's, 81.
Superior, Lake, 123.
Sutter's Fort, 240, 253.
Swedish colonists, 110.

Tampa Bay, 37.
Tennessee, 172.
Texas, 135, 136 ; ceded to the United States, 174.
Thinkleet Indians, 219.
Thorstein, 10.
Thorvald, 9.
Tonti, 165.
*Tonquin*, the, 220 ; loss of, 221, 224.

Ulloa, Francisco de, 141.
United States, Beginning of, 157 ; Extension of, 173 ; Northern boundary, 270.

Vaca, Cabeca de, 38, 39.
Vancouver, 204.
Verrazano of Florence, 37.
Verrazano, Giovanni, 49-51.
Vespucci, Amerigo, 25.
Vines, Richard, 87, 89.
Virginia, first settlement, 68.
Viscaino, Sebastian, 116, 188.
Voyage up the Missouri, Hunt's, 225-228.
Voyage down the Snake and Columbia, Hunt's, 230-232.

Walloons, 109.
Welsh, 12.
West India Company, 109.
White, John, 69.
White Mountains, 87.
Wilkes, Captain, 240.
Williams, Roger, 101-103, 155.
Wisconsin River, 130, 132, 138, 177.
Windsor, 104.
Winnipeg, Lake, 233, 238, 272.
Winthrop, John, 99, 101.

Yellowstone River, 187, 246.
Yellow Fever in Louisiana, 166.
Yerba Buena, 239, 251.
Young, Brigham, 255.

Zeni, the Brothers, 12.
Zuni, Ruins of, 265.
Zunis Indians, 265.

www.ingramcontent.com/pod-product-compliance
Lightning Source LLC
Chambersburg PA
CBHW020512270326

41926CB00008B/847